D1236911

PAPER PROPHETS

PAPER PROPHETS

A Social Critique of Accounting

by Tony Tinker

PRAEGER SPECIAL STUDIES • PRAEGER SCIENTIFIC

New York • Philadelphia • Eastbourne, UK
Toronto • Hong Kong • Tokyo • Sydney

Library of Congress Cataloging in Publication Data

Tinker, Tony.
    Paper prophets.

    Bibliography: p.
    Includes indexes.
    1.   Accounting—Social aspects.   I.   Title.
          HF5657.T5   1985   657   84-18305
ISBN 0-03-001657-6 (alk. paper)

Published and Distributed by the
Praeger Publishers Division
(ISBN Prefix 0-275)
of Greenwood Press, Inc.,
Westport, Connecticut

Published in 1985 by Praeger Publishers
CBS Educational and Professional Publishing,
a Division of CBS Inc.
521 Fifth Avenue, New York, NY 10175 USA

©1985 by Anthony Maxwell Tinker

56789 052 987654321

Printed in the United States of America
on acid-free paper

In Loving Memory of Dorothy Winifred Tinker

Acknowledgments

Relocating from the UK to the U.S., as I did in 1977, added enormous bewilderments and confusions to those that already afflicted my life as an average academic. At the root of my trauma was the culture shock induced by moving from a UK to a U.S.-based academic position. In 1977, British universities still ferociously defended a notion of academic independence: research and scholarship were regulated by rather introverted academic values and norms, vested social interests—such as recruiters from large companies and accounting firms—were usually barred from the premises, many universities still paid lip-service, at least, to producing well-rounded citizens, and, with regard to social controversies, the curriculum aspired to rise above partisanship by masquerading as a lofty spectator on the world of affairs. Through such pretenses, the university was declared a kind of socially neutral "no man's land."

I have no wish to idealize the kind of academic independence that prevailed in UK universities at the time of my departure. In many ways, this brand of academia is as sectarian as anything found in North America. The penchant for tradition and scholasticism indicates, not neutrality and independence, but a system of social allegiances built on precapitalist social mores that capitalism has been none-too-successful in extinguishing, even in the last decade.

Compared with the UK system, the "cash value of ideas" is frequently cited as the dominant ethic of U.S. universities. Certainly, this thesis is rejected by some as a vulgarization of what actually happens; it does, however, draw attention to the extent to which knowledge, research, and education have become commodities in the United States, with the corollary that they have become increasingly rationalized, standardized, and "useful." Accordingly, U.S. academics tend to evaluate teaching and research against highly functionalist and instrumentalist criteria, without once suffering a glimmer of the discomfort that this would create for their UK counterparts. U.S. universities share few of the European pretensions of an academic priesthood; instead they brandish their practical involvements in the "world of affairs" with a relish and innocence that is sometimes disconcerting to Europeans such as myself.

This comparison of the UK and U.S. academic contexts is offered by way of an introduction to the dilemmas that faced me on arriving in the United States, and the very special role friends and colleagues played in orienting me to the new situation. It was not enough that I was facing a

major intellectual challenge of finding a social grounding for an obses-
sively technical subject like accounting; I was also facing a major "communication" problem in dealing with U.S. audiences. The solution to these
difficulties involved developing two kinds of facility: first, that of trans-
versing and integrating results from a range of disciplines; second, that of
being able to show the practical relevance of "high theory" to understanding the scandals and controversies that bedevil contemporary corporate accounting in the United States.

During my two years at the University of California at Los Angeles
(1978–80), I undertook the first major forage into empirical issues, initially
with Bill Bretchell, and subsequently with Annie Poon. Annie laid the
groundwork for a system of information files on companies and incidents
that subsequently formed the empirical basis for the whole study. Annie always proceeded critically, sometimes skeptically, and she taught me early
on to have good reasons for my decisions.

The New York area has provided me with a wealth of good colleagues
and friends. The accounting department of New York University (NYU)
assumed, in 1980, the aspect of a rather staid University of Chicago look-a-
like. Soon after my arrival, I befriended several misfits and heretics who refused to knuckle down to the party line that was then in office. Barbara
Merino (now at North Texas State) and Marilyn Neimark (now Baruch Col-
lege-City University of New York) were my earliest intellectual affiliates at
NYU; our early joint researches provided me with invaluable lessons in relating my ideas to the intellectual and accounting history of the United
States. The influence of these two colleagues is evident in the sections of
the book dealing with marginalism and accounting.

Marilyn Neimark has been an outstanding contributor to this project;
she has a faculty in social criticism that is unsurpassed by others working in
her various fields of interest, and she applied these epistemological skills
with ruthless consistency to improve early drafts of the book. Marilyn not
only contributed an enormous amount of time and energy to this project
but, in the face of a fair amount of right-wing hostility at NYU, she has
acted as the very best kind of intellectual colleague. Indeed, if I had to name
my main coworker on this book, it would be Marilyn.

Later, during my tenure at NYU, I met Cheryl Lehman. In one respect
(and probably only one respect) Cheryl is uniquely un-American. When
Cheryl examines problems, she does so with exceptional patience, and a tolerance of ambiguity. Friends and colleagues are often placed "on wait" as
she stalks every problematic. Whereas some scholars foreclose problems
prematurely, Cheryl's talents lie in respecting complexity, and assimilat-
ing that complexity into her analysis. She possesses an extraanalytic sen-

sitivity to the subtleties, ambiguities, and conflicts inherent in social situations. As Marxists will recognize, these are the qualities of a good dialectician.

I could not have hoped for a dearer friend and more supportive colleague than Donna Montanino. She has accepted my arcane enthusiasms at face value, and typed, retyped, and copied numerous early drafts of this book. Age is a characteristic of people of which I am rarely conscious; in Donna's case however, I cannot help but be struck by how consistently she exhibits a level of maturity and professionalism that is way beyond her years.

This book took nearly five years to complete, and while I was occupied by the task, I underwent a great many changes in my personal life. Diane Darby was my dearest friend during this period: she helped me navigate through a range of problems, reawakened sensibilities that had been dormant since childhood, and taught me many things for which I will always be grateful.

Paul Johnston, with some very indirect help from Barbara Johnston, created an outstanding title for this work. In the end, I decided not to use Paul's suggestion and to proceed instead with *Paper Prophets*. By not disclosing Paul's invention, yet acknowledging my gratitude to Paul in this volume, I hope this earns me the right to use Paul's suggestion in my next book.

Bertell Ollman has been a major source of support and inspiration. His reinterpretation of Marx's writings represents a major theoretical breakthrough, and this book has drawn liberally from this perspective. Bertell has been unstintingly generous in his encouragement and support, to a degree that has made him truly exceptional among the scholars that I have met at NYU.

It was Bertell who first suggested that I contact Praeger Publishers. This led to a very enjoyable association with Barbara Leffel and Rachel Burd at Praeger. Their openness to different viewpoints and perspectives restored my rather idealistic hopes about a positive, political-activist role for publishing. I discovered from talking to Barbara and Rachel that even the corporate publishing giants are not one-dimensional monistic entities; rather, they are quite capable of initiating humane and radical changes (just like accounting firms!).

The efforts of those who have contributed towards my long-haul intellectual development are also reflected in this work. Tony Lowe had an early and profound influence on my intellectual development; he showed me the enormous vision and ambition of economics, when that subject is properly regarded. Working with Ankie Hoogvelt taught me how to

critique and radicalize my views on conservative and ideologically en-
trenched subjects, such as accounting. The inclusion of a synopsis of the
Delco study speaks to the importance that I attach to this early work.

My association with Anthony Hopwood reaches back to the early
1970s, and I have little hesitation in describing it as one of the most complex, turbulent, fascinating, and ultimately rewarding friendships that I
have had. Anthony has not only helped improve my research through extensive comments and criticisms, but perhaps more than any other person,
he has brought about institutional changes in accounting that have made it
habitable for people like myself. Finally, David Cooper, who over the
years has become a kind of intellectual soul-mate (and is irreplaceable in
that regard) has, through our numerous correspondences and interchanges,
shared with me in developing the theoretical underpinnings of this enterprise. I do hope that he approves (with reservations of course).

If there are any errors or mistakes in this work, the reader should really
blame those people listed above. Unfortunately, practicalities do not allow
me to assign responsibility in this fashion, thus reluctantly, and unrealisti-
cally, I accept the entire burden.

Contents

List of Tables

List of Figures and Exhibits

Introduction

Would you like to pursue a socially meaningful career, but are tempted to sell out for a CPA meal ticket? Are you baffled by the contrast between the exhilarating world of business and the accountant's boring language of business? Are you one of those accountants who does good deeds on the weekends to make up for your misgivings about your daily work? As an economist, are you fascinated by the awesome presence of public accounting in business affairs, a presence that has little meaning in orthodox economic theory? Subscribe to the questions? If so, read on.

This book is about some of the most complex, intractable, and vexing problems of our times, and about the part that accounting has played in creating and exacerbating them. In the following pages, we will examine cases of multinational exploitation, stock price collapses, the dumping of toxic waste, price gouging by public utilities, and the frailties of the world banking system. While accountants are not exclusively responsible for this list of social evils, I will argue that the full measure of the accountant's responsibility has been, and continues to be, systematically understated. Members of the public do not appreciate the impact of accounting practices, politicians and public policy analysts underestimate the power of accounting, and most frequently, accounting professors, students, and even practitioners fail to realize the import of what they are (and are not) doing.

The systematic understatement of accounting's significance is reflected in the images of accountants in popular culture: as the technician, the innocuous bookkeeper, the "ink-stained wretch," the recordkeeper whose lack of creativity and imagination makes him trustworthy. The profession has done little to repudiate these false images, perhaps because they help to mask the full impact of the profession, thereby diminishing the amount of responsibility for social crises and disasters that accountants are asked to shoulder. This work attempts to disclose the power of accounting practice; we will sweep away the mystifications and the false images of bookkeepers and technicians and show how accounting policy and practice affects the quality of life of millions of people.

In order to reveal the true social and economic significance of accounting, I have enlisted the support of some of history's most distinguished authorities. The greatest contribution of Marx, Aquinas, Smith, Ricardo, Sartre, and many others was to show that things are not as they seem; this lesson is especially true when applied to accounting. These great social philosophers will help us see accountants in a different light: not as

xv

harmless bookkeepers, but as arbiters in social conflict, as architects of unequal exchanges, as instruments of alienation, and as accomplices in the expropriation of the life experiences of others. More than this though, these voices from the past teach us that this dismal picture of accounting need not be so. There is no absolute necessity that accounting be rapacious or exploitative. Indeed, as we review some of the historical case material, we will see that a constructive, emancipatory role for accounting is quite possible.

But this discussion is running ahead of itself, especially for those readers who are still puzzled about what accounting is, and what the fuss is all about. We will deal with the origins and nature of accounting on a preliminary basis, and return for a more comprehensive analysis later.

The origins of accounting have been traced back to antiquity. The palace of Nestor in ancient Greece maintained not only accounting records, but income tax computations and detailed inventory records of grain, sheep, and other assets (Stevens, 1982, p. 2). However, the profession of public accounting as we presently know it is much more recent. It came into being in Great Britain in the 1850s with the introduction of the companies acts and the bankruptcy acts, legislation designed to protect shareholders and promote capital accumulation during the early stages of the industrial revolution. In the decades following the U.S. Civil War, British chartered accountants came to the United States to monitor the capital investment of the Old World in the New World.

By protecting shareholders and maintaining investor confidence, accountants performed the primary service of stimulating capital accumulation in the United States in the early twentieth century. The firm of Marwick Mitchell helped J.P. Morgan avert a bank collapse and restore investor confidence in the Knickerbocker Trust Co., thereby ending the panic of 1907. The state's ratification of an income tax constitutional amendment in 1913 led to a substantially increased demand for professional accounting services, as did the call for official accounting standards and guidelines by the Federal Trade Commission and the Federal Reserve Board. But it was the stock market crash of 1929 and the Securities Acts of 1933 and 1934 that produced the largest growth in demand for the services of accountants. Peat, Marwick, Mitchell's experience provides some indication of the magnitude of this growth. In 1947, the firm's revenues stood at less than $10 million; by 1981 revenues had reached $979 million (*Public Accounting Report,* April 1982, p. 5). British accounting experienced a comparable growth as a result of the 1948 Companies Act; Britain today (with some 100,000 chartered and certified accountants) has more accountants per head of population than any other advanced capitalist country.

In the United States, the profession is dominated by eight large professional firms (known as the Big Eight). On a world scale, the Big Eight are joined by one other to form the Big Nine. These firms are large multinational partnerships whose aggregate sales revenue for 1981 exceeded $7.8 billion. They are Coopers and Lybrand; Peat, Marwick, Mitchell; Arthur Andersen; Arthur Young; Klynveld Main Goerdeler; Price Waterhouse; Ernst and Whinney; Deloitte, Haskins and Sells; and Touche Ross (*Public Accounting Report,* April 1982). Each of the Big Nine is large enough to appear in the Fortune 500 (if they were industrials and were not private partnerships). Established as accounting firms and auditors and still widely regarded as such, the Big Nine nevertheless offer a sweeping array of business services to their clients. They act as auditors, accountants, actuaries, attorneys, tax specialists, consultants, executive headhunters, takeover and merger specialists, estate planning specialists, expert witnesses, financial planners, and lobbyists.

Despite the proliferation of services that the Big Nine offer their clients, approximately 60 percent of their revenues still come from auditing services (*Public Accounting Report,* June 1978). Auditing consists of an independent review of the books of account and financial statements published by large corporations. These financial statements are intended to meet the needs of a variety of users (e.g., creditors, shareholders, tax authorities, employees, regulatory bodies). The preparation of financial statements (accounting) and auditing both the statements and the accounts from which they are prepared are means of achieving accountability in society. Accounting systems and the information that they present are used to control a diverse range of institutional activities, including payment of income tax obligations, rate fixing by public utilities, price fixing and cost control in government contracts, and in the regulation of banks and insurance companies.

The demand for the services of independent auditors arose from the potential conflict of interest inherent in the relationship between corporate management and the stockholders whom the management represents in a fiduciary capacity. Financial statements are one way of evaluating how well corporate management has discharged its stewardship responsibility to the owners. It is the auditor's responsibility to ensure that the financial statements are free from bias and distortion and that they accurately reflect the financial condition of the enterprise.

The Big Nine accounting firms represent an enormous concentration of power and influence. In 1981 they audited 493 of the Fortune 500, employed over 170,000 people in more than 100 countries, and operated out of 2,000 offices. In the United States alone, they annually interview

160,000 students from colleges and universities, hire 11,000 students, and create more than 1,000 new partners (*Public Accounting Report,* October 1981; Stevens, 1982, p. 8). The Big Nine have over 15,000 partners. In 1981 the annual salary of a senior partner was estimated to be as high as $390,000 (*Source Finance,* 1982). The top eight of the Big Nine dominate the auditing of New York Stock Exchange members. A study performed by the Congressional Research Service found that clients of the Big Eight account for 94 percent of sales and profits of 90 percent of income taxes paid by, and 94 percent of all people employed and assets owned by, New York Stock Exchange members.

Big Nine firms far exceed the size of their counterparts in other professions. The annual revenues of the largest law firms are less than $100 million, a mere 10 percent of the revenues of the largest accounting firms. Legal services, which account for less than 10 percent of the revenues of a typical Big Nine firm, employ enough attorneys to place Big Nine members on par with some of the largest law firms in the world (*Public Accounting Report,* June 1978, Stevens, 1982, p. 9). Management advisory services, which typically earn the Big Nine around 20 percent of their revenues, are large enough to place the Big Nine accounting firms (plus two others) on a list of the 100 leading consulting firms in the United States (*Public Accounting Report,* November 1981, p. 1). Even among accounting firms, the Big Nine dwarf others. Touche Ross employs 1,400 persons full-time on its audit of General Motors. This contingent of staff alone is larger than 99 percent of the world's accounting firm staffs (Stevens, 1982, p. 8).

It would be a mistake however, to assume that the influence of the accounting profession is limited to the activities of the Big Nine. In 1981 it was estimated that there were 275,000 certified public accountants in the United States, of which 173,900 were registered as members of the American Institute of Certified Public Accountants (AICPA) (*Source Finance,* 1981; 1980–81 Annual Report of the AICPA). Of the total AICPA membership, only 43,680 (30 percent) belonged to the 25 largest public accounting firms (including CPAs with the Big Nine). This leaves more than 120,000 AICPA members and nonmembers (who nevertheless are CPAs) who do not belong to large accounting firms. If all CPAs are distributed across occupations in the same way as the AICPA membership, then an estimated 33,000 CPAs work for the Big Nine, approximately 112,000 are employed in public practice with firms other than the Big Nine; 111,650 work in business, government, and commerce; 7,700 are employed in education; and 9,075 are government employees.

It is clear, then, that while the Big Nine may exercise a disproportionate amount of influence, they are still a minority in the profession at large. In industrial accounting for example, CPAs occupy some of the most powerful positions in U.S. business, earning salaries in the hundreds of thousands of dollars. In a typical industrial corporation, a vice-president is in charge of all financial operations including controllership, treasury, and sometimes internal audit functions. The controllership function normally includes responsibility for complete financial accounting and reporting; the treasury function includes responsibility for all matters relating to cash, securities, and capital, and the internal audit function seeks to ensure that all management decisions and practices conform to properly authorized policies and control procedures.

A profile of a typical CPA reveals a profession dominated by white males who earn in excess of $40,000 per year and have a college degree. Minorities and women have not fared well as employees in public accounting. A survey of 72 large firms (employing at least 25 AICPA members) disclosed in the AICPA's Minority Recruitment and Equal Opportunity Committee 1980 report that black employment had remained steady at 1.8 percent of the total professional work force of these large firms since 1976, while employment of all other minorities had increased from 2.1 percent in 1976 to 2.6 percent in 1980. The percentage of black new hires actually dropped from 3.8 percent in 1979 to 2.8 percent in 1980.

Female employment in public accounting more than doubled over a five-year period, from 5,800 (10.3 percent of all professionals) in 1976 to over 13,000 (19.8 percent of all professionals) in 1980. Nearly one third of all hires were women, a significant increase from the previous year, but only a small proportion of females and minorities were promoted to the level of partner. Partners comprise some 10 percent of all professional staff in large accounting firms. There were only 12 black partners (1 percent of all black professionals) among the 72 firms in the survey, and 54 female partners (0.4 percent of the 13,000 women professionals). Minorities other than blacks fared somewhat better: 80 partners out of almost 1,800 total professionals (4.5 percent).

The preceding is only a preliminary review of who accountants are and what accountants do; a more systematic and comprehensive account is the prime objective of this book. In what follows we will move beneath the mythology of the accountant as an impartial messenger of economic facts and examine the manner in which the profession shapes our economic and social reality through the partisan set of accounting rules that governs the reporting and disclosure of information about corporations.

   Rule-making is always an ambitious project, and the making of rules
to govern the reporting of information about corporations is especially ambitious. Accounting rules supply one of the most fundamental ingredients
of economic and social choices: the valuation of alternatives. Unions, hos-
pitals, banks, taxpayers, investors, Bowery bums, federal authorities,
churches, managers, consumers, employees, socialists, presidents, and
junkies all share one thing in common: the problem of deciding, of
economizing, of discovering needs and ways to fulfill them. The valuation
component of decisions is the object of accounting rules. Orchestrated
throughout the economy, accounting rules may distribute widespread benefit and damage between different members of the community. Alternative rules may, for the individual citizen, mean the difference between employment and unemployment, reliable products and dangerous ones, enriching experiences and oppressive ones, stimulating work environments
and dehumanizing ones, care and compassion for the old and sick versus in-
tolerance and resentment.

   Members of a society are interconnected through their economic and
social interdependencies: employees to investors to consumers to taxpayers
to mothers to welfare recipients to students to insomniacs. Accounting information is not merely a manifestation of this myriad of interdependencies; it is a social scheme for adjudicating these relationships. We are all
costs and revenues to each other; everyone is potentially a benefactor and a
victim in the accounting nexus of social decisions.

   How should we decide on the rules that adjudicate and galvanize our
social relationships? What kind of understanding do accountants need for
inventing our history in this way? Contemplation, reflection, criticism, and
debate about the nature of society and its potentialities would seem to be in-
dispensable for achieving constructive social change.

   Unfortunately, intellectual expeditions of this kind are rare in the accounting literature. Today's students and tomorrow's practitioners are
saturated with a litany of rules and procedures that are supported by little
other than expedient reasoning, ad-hoc explanations, and piecemeal
rationalizations. Professional accounting education is certainly not a talk-
shop for exploring the meaning of social existence: rather it resembles a
rote learning process in which students are inculcated with the profession's
party line by pendantic and legalistic methods. The role of accounting in
major social controversies is never articulated in accounting education because the intellectual apparatus necessary for conducting a comprehensive
appraisal is withheld. Instead, every year some 50,000 new U.S. students
are overwhelmed with a welter of technical and legalistic material that has
no apparent connection to the conflicts and complexities of social exis-

tence. The ultimate trivialization and degradation of accounting is the near obsession with rules and bookkeeping procedures. Today's students are trained to become greyhounds in bookkeeping and ignoramuses in social analysis.

Many Americans have found that an appreciation of their ethnic and social lineage is important in understanding their own identity. So it is also the case with professions: an appreciation of their unique historical past may give insights into contemporary problems and concerns. Just as the real history of certain ethnic groups has been neglected, distorted, and mystified, so has the true role and history of many of our institutions. The law, medicine, psychology, education, economics, the caring professions (and even motorcycle maintenance) have undergone major reappraisals of their social roles in recent years. The results have often been dramatic: radical criticism has stimulated fundamental redefinitions of the social missions of various professions. Demystifying the real functions and purposes of social institutions must be a continuous struggle if it is to serve as a prelude to radical change. Accounting is one of the few bastions of the establishment that still lingers in the twilight of social comprehension: it is immature in terms of the state of its social consciousness, fairy tales pass for its history, and narrow technical obsessions still obliterate social awareness.

Successful social rule-making requires a political mechanism for translating ideas into action. In a very modest way, this book is intended as a political device. Equally suitable titles would have been *The Political Economy of Accounting, The Alternative Accountant's Handbook,* or *The Role of Accounting in the Development of Capitalism.* The book has been written in such a way as to serve readers from inside and outside the profession. Appealing to a readership beyond the profession may help to provoke a measure of change. The first task is to debunk the subject's camouflage of "objective," "technical" expertise and expose the discipline's social, human, and moral malaise.

The book consists of four main parts. Part I recounts a series of controversies involving large corporations. Some of these controversies are well known: a great deal has already been written about the tragedy of Love Canal, the Slater Walker scandal in the United Kingdom, and the National Student Marketing affair. Less well known and less understood are the common themes that connect these incidents and their special pertinence to accounting. No attempt is made in this first part to "solve" the problems. Indeed solutions, in the usual sense, are not the aim here. All I ask of the reader is an acknowledgment of the seriousness and ubiquity of such problems and of the possibility (however remote) of an accounting culpability in such affairs.

Professions other than accounting have made significant progress in recent years in reconstructing their understanding of their social and historical roles. This process of self-reflection shows how professions are molded by social conditions and are actors in social conflict. The long view of history reveals the importance of specific social and historical conditions in shaping current professional policies and behaviors.

Parts II and III outline a social history of accounting thought that is comparable to that found in other professions. In Part II, the social origins of conflict underlying institutional and professional life are described. This discussion is given a special accounting flavor by introducing the theory of value and its historical evolution. Here we will explore the meaning of terms such as "exploitation," "unequal exchange," and "social conflict." By explicating the conflicts and tensions that are characteristic of most social systems, Part II sets the stage for subsequent discussion. Part III shows how these tensions and struggles manifest themselves in the intellectual area: specifically in the form of different theories of value. Contributions by Aquinas, Smith, Ricardo, Marx, Jevons, Böhm-Bawerk, Wieser, Clark, Sraffa, and Sartre are explored, together with the exponents of the marginalist theory of value, which supplies the intellectual foundations for much of accounting. This history of ideas reveals the conditions under which particular value theories emerged, flourished, and eventually declined, and the social interests who benefitted and suffered under different intellectual regimes.

Part IV returns to modern controversies facing accounting, including those introduced at the outset, and reviews this material in the light of the previously discussed socio-history of value theory and accounting. The controversies are shown to illustrate different types of social conflict, oppression, and alienation. The analysis shows that it is possible to devise accountability systems capable of detecting these different types of domination and alienation. Insofar as modern accounting systems fail to uncover forms of social domination and alienation, we can view these systems as ideologies that conceal important aspects of social reality. I argue that as it is presently practiced, accounting is incapable of recognizing even the most blatant forms of alienation, and that as long as this persists, public criticism of, and dissatisfaction with, the profession's conduct will continue.

Part I
Controversies Over
Corporate Accountability

1

Love Canal

Introduction

In recent years, there has been increasing evidence that waste disposal practices in the United States are inflicting severe damage upon both the environment and its inhabitants. In 1979, the Environmental Protection Agency (EPA) estimated that in the United States there were as many as 51,000 sites containing potentially hazardous waste. The number of sites with "significant problems" was anywhere between 1,200 and 34,000. Of the 35 million tons of hazardous waste produced in the United States each year, approximately 90 percent is disposed of illegally. The EPA noted, "Industry has shown a laxity, not infrequently to the point of criminal neglect, in soiling the land and adulterating the waters with toxins" (*Time*, September 22, 1980, p. 58). The story of Love Canal is but one example of the consequences of inadequate waste disposal practices. Although usually portrayed as a failure of public policy and/or as a regulation or pollution problem, Love Canal was also an accounting problem.

On July 2, 1980, the Securities and Exchange Commission (SEC) charged the Occidental Petroleum Corporation with failing to disclose to its shareholders hundreds of millions of dollars of potential liabilities arising from the firm's environmental practices. Among the largest contingent liabilities were those stemming from the activities of the Hooker Chemical and Plastics Corporation, an Occidental Petroleum subsidiary in Niagara Falls, New York. Hooker Chemical was heavily implicated in the Love Canal disaster in which the dumping of toxic chemicals caused hundreds of families to abandon their homes. By July 1980 there were 90 pending or contemplated legal proceedings outstanding against Hooker Chemical.

Responsibility for the emergency relief program for Love Canal residents fell largely on the State of New York and on federal authorities.

These two bodies filed legal claims against Hooker Chemical and Occidental Petroleum totaling an estimated $750 million. To these claims must be added the $2.65 billion in private lawsuits on behalf of residents in the area.

In settling the case with the SEC, Occidental Petroleum, an oil, gas, and chemical enterprise with $9 billion in sales in 1979, neither admitted nor denied the SEC's accusations. The outcome of the case established an important precedent in reporting practices as it required corporations to report not only the actual costs of complying with environmental regulations (a principle established in an SEC filing against United States Steel Corporation in September 1979) but also the potential costs of compliance. The SEC noted: "The total cost of compliance with environmental regulations includes not only those costs of bringing facilities into full compliance with environmental regulations, but also costs associated with past non-compliance with environmental regulations" (the *New York Times*, July 3, 1980, p. D6). Occidental Petroleum also agreed to establish a comprehensive, government-sponsored environmental monitoring system. To this end, the company was to appoint three persons (an independent consultant, an environmental executive, and a board member) to be approved by the SEC, to oversee the firm's activities and to report systematically on potential liabilities and disclosure vis-à-vis the environment.

The Love Canal Story

In the late nineteenth century, William T. Love began building a canal that was to extend seven miles from the upper Niagara in order to provide cheap power for an as yet uncreated city. Love's canal only got one mile before his money ran out, leaving a trench 20 yards wide and from 10 to 40 feet deep. The trench was eventually acquired by Hooker Chemical.

Hooker Chemical has been a major employer in Niagara Falls. In the 1940s the company provided employment for approximately 3,000 blue-collar workers in the economically depressed area. Furthermore they were planning to build a $17 million headquarters in downtown Niagara Falls. The city was so anxious for this new commitment that it gave Hooker Chemical generous loan and tax incentives and made available to the firm a prime parcel of real estate previously occupied by a hotel.

Between 1930 and 1953, Hooker Chemical used the canal as a chemical dump. The bottom and sides of the trench were lined with clay to prevent leakage into the water table and water supplies. There were some complaints about odors from the trench during this period, but the company reportedly assured the city that "the wastes were only a hazard if physically touched or swallowed" (Brown, 1980, p. 80). Hooker Chemical eventually covered the trench and its contents with loose dirt and in 1953 the Board of Education of Niagara Falls purchased the canal from Hooker Chemical for $1. The company warned that use of the land should be restricted.

The Board of Education began building a school and a playground at the midsection of the canal. When excavations hit a drainage trench that gave off a strong chemical odor, the authorities moved the school 80 feet away. Land peripheral to the canal was sold by the city for residential developments, and some 80 young families settled alongside the dump. The authorities reportedly allowed some of the dirt and clay that Hooker Chemical had covered the site with to be removed for landfill elsewhere.

Over the years there were rumors in the area that the residents of Love Canal seemed to have more than the usual share of afflictions. Children were born with birth defects including clubfeet, mental retardation, and deafness. (One baby girl, born in 1968, had an irregular heartbeat, a hole in the heart, bone blockages in the nose, partial deafness, deformed ears, an enlarged liver, a second bottow row of teeth, and was mentally retarded. Another baby was born so badly malformed that its sex was indeterminate.) Minor maladies were also commonplace: allergies, sinus trouble, rashes, throbbing headaches, fatigue, weight loss, dizziness, nosebleeds, bone marrow damage, respiratory problems, and hair loss. Pets that were left tied up in backyards lost their fur and developed skin lesions and internal tumors. Even gardens seemed afflicted. Properties that years before had won horticultural prizes for beauty and attractiveness had become wastelands where trees and plants died and nothing would grow, and the ground was marred with a thick oozing sludge. As the rumors spread, property values plummeted. Residents with mortgages were unable to sell without suffering losses they simply could not afford.

Evidence of serious pollution dangers was made available to Hooker Chemical by the city authorities in 1976. The New York State Department of Environmental Conservation revealed that it had discovered extremely dangerous halogeneted hydrocarbons, including PCBs, in the area. Very serious environmental problems can result even from one part PCB to a million parts normal water. A much higher ratio was present in Love Canal. Hexachlorocyclopentadene (C-56) was also found: a highly toxic pesticide capable of damaging every organ in the human body. Only 18 months after the first reports, the Environmental Protection Agency (EPA) discovered heavy doses of C-56 in the basements of residences. This was during a period of heavy rain, when the canal overflowed. Residents complained of abnormally heavy fumes, throbbing headaches, skin ailments, respiratory discomforts, and hair loss. In May 1978, the City of Niagara Falls installed two 15 dollar window fans in those basements where the odors were strongest and a fragile wooden fence was erected around part of the canal.

In mid-1978 the EPA discovered the presence of benzene, a chemical capable of producing many of the symptoms that residents complained of and, in addition, bone marrow deterioration and cancer. The announcement that benzene had been found was delayed because officials were reportedly in disagreement as to how to disclose the information without causing panic.

In May 1978, partly in response to the inaction of local authorities, the State of New York announced it was going to survey families in the area and conduct blood tests to determine if enzymes that cause liver destruction were present. Meanwhile, residents were shocked by disclosures from other investigations. In addition to benzene, 80 other compounds that could affect the brain and nervous system were found, including two (carbon tetrachloride and chlorobenzene) that could cause narcotic and anesthetic results. There was still no evacuation.

The State of New York published the results of its study in July 1978. The rate of miscarriages was abnormally high (1:250) as was the level of birth defects. On August 1, the state was advised by an epidemiologist that residents were suffering liver damage.

The next day, the state's Health Officer declared Love Canal an official emergency that was "a great and imminent peril to the health of the general public." Pregnant women and children under the age of two were urged to leave. The emergency was still unofficial however: there was no government-sponsored evacuation. The public warning was only a recommendation, and people who abandoned their homes at this stage risked losing everything. In the following weeks, the Board of Education announced the closure of the school; an application for federal help was made, and residents formed the Love Canal Homeowners Association.

President Carter declared the Hooker Chemical dump a national emergency on August 7, 1978, and by September many people had taken advantage of state and federal offers to purchase their houses. By the following spring, 237 families had vacated houses adjacent to the canal (97th Street and 99th Street). A green chain link fence, eight feet high, stood around a six-block area of the canal. During that period, 75 buses were on permanent standby in the area to provide an emergency evacuation in the event of an explosion. The state initiated a cleanup operation that comprised building a drainage system and a trench and then topping the canal with clay and trees.

Five hundred families remained stranded around this desolate setting. Their apprehensions increased when the state announced that it would not buy any more homes. New evidence that contamination had reached beyond the streets that straddled the canal was made public as early as August 1978. A state memorandum confirmed this on September 24, 1978, when it acknowledged that significant infiltration had taken place outside the canal zone to 93rd and 103rd streets. In the following month a young boy who lived in a far-off northern residence died from kidney trouble. The child played in a creek connected to the canal. The boy's parents (a chemist and a medical research assistant) believe that their child died from chemical poisoning from the creek. Medical studies of the 245 families who lived outside the evacuation zone revealed 34 miscarriages, 18 birth defects, 19 nervous breakdowns, and 10 cases of epilepsy.

In response to the new evidence, the state offered a temporary evacuation scheme to families outside the original evacuation zone. The offer only extended to families with a pregnant mother or at least one child below the age of two years. Once these measures expired, the families were required to return to their residences. The state also reaffirmed its earlier decision not to purchase any more houses. Twenty-three families took up the state's offer and seven more left their homes at their own expense, a considerable financial burden.

Toward the end of 1978, evidence began to emerge that one of the most potent toxins synthesized by man was present in Love Canal: tetradioxin. Tetradioxin was used in the manufacture of Agent Orange, the defoliant employed in Vietnam until its withdrawal in 1971. The U.S. government was recently being sued by veteran's organizations for compensation for the injuries this toxin inflicted on U.S. military personnel operating in Vietnam. It is estimated that one million people could be killed by just three ounces of tetradioxin. Skin contact with dioxin causes disfigurations, lesions, and cysts and can lead to calamitous internal changes. It is suspected of causing cancer and other malignancies. In 1976 in Seveso, Italy, between 2 and 11 pounds of dioxin were dispersed in an explosion at a chemical plant. The bodies of wildlife and pets littered the streets; a 300-acre residential area was abandoned and the topsoil was removed. In Amsterdam, a factory was found to be contaminated by the toxin; the building was dismantled brick by brick and dumped in the Azores. From the records of Hooker Chemical, it is estimated that 130 pounds of tetradioxin had been buried at Love Canal.

People remaining at Love Canal became desperate. They seized two state officials as hostages and released them only when the FBI threatened to storm the residence where they were held. They burned an effigy of the state commissioner, traveled to the state capital with a mock coffin for a child, marched on Hooker Chemical (who had not expressed any regret), and arranged the lights on a holiday Christmas tree to spell Dioxin. In October 1979, Governor Carey relented and announced that an additional 240 homes would be purchased for $5 million.

Some Accounting Issues Suggested by Love Canal

The settlement between Occidental Petroleum and the SEC focuses on a relatively narrow accounting issue—the problem of calculating and reporting periodic profits. When examined fully, however, this issue has broad implications for the role and responsibilities of the accounting profession. To the extent that Hooker Chemical failed to report the potential costs of its waste disposal practices, the company overstated its periodic income. There is a rule in accounting that costs should be matched against the revenues generated in a period in determining profits. But what additional costs should Hooker Chemical have reported, and when?

Retrospectively, the costs associated with Love Canal began to accumulate when the company poured toxic waste into the canal in the 1930s, and hence should have been matched against the revenues for that period. That payment by Hooker Chemical, in the form of legal damages, may not have occurred until the 1980s is, in principle, no different from the accepted practice of recording the utilization of goods or services as costs in periods prior to payment for them. The prodigious feat of prognostication required to anticipate such costs in the 1930s is no different, in principle, from estimations and reports of the current depreciation expense of long-lived fixed assets. Excluding such costs requires as great a subjective prediction about what will happen in the future as does including them. Certainly by the 1970s one could argue that Hooker Chemical had some substantial clues regarding the environmental and human impact of its waste disposal practices.

The SEC settlement focused on the failure of Hooker Chemical to report potential legal liabilities. It is an open question, however, as to whether these liabilities, even if correctly reported, would have represented the real cost. Current accounting practice usually underrates long-term costs and certainly excludes costs that will not be paid directly by the company. The overall effect is to exaggerate current profits, a result likely to have contributed to the tragedy at Love Canal.

Even if all the costs (borne by the company and by others) had been properly estimated, it is still not clear that a focus on monetary values responds adequately to contemporary standards of morality, ethics, and humanitarianism. After all, what is the cost of a miscarriage or a premature death?

What lessons should the accounting profession have learned? Do they have any applicability to other situations in which corporations affect the quality of the environment (for instance, in the building and operation of nuclear power plants, the use of toxins in pest control in agriculture, and the practice of dumping wastes into city sewage systems that let out into the sea)?

Accounting academics and practitioners are strangely quiet about such questions. Yet increasingly, various social groups are challenging the social costs of corporate behavior, and the judgment of professional accounting spokesmen who mystify questions of efficiency with spurious claims of objectivity and independence.

While the responsibility of accounting in questions of environmental pollution is a relatively recent concern, financial controversies involving the impact of accounting on different fractions of the shareholder group is a well-established concern. The next case, involving the Slater Walker Co., is an example of a financial scandal on a grand scale. The issues here, however, are basically the same as those considered previously: accounting bears a responsibility in the way it helps resolve the distribution of income, whether between corporate polluters and local communities, or between inside and outside shareholders.

2

Slater Walker Company

Introduction: The Silent Collapse

The collapse of Slater Walker Company* must have been one of the quietest conglomerate failures in history. Jim Slater, the company's managing director and cofounder, resigned in July 1975 to "spend more time with his family." On September 14, 1976, the Bank of England disclosed that it had made available to Slater Walker a special £70 million line of credit (of which £45.2 million had been used prior to the company's liquidation and was not recovered). In addition, the Old Lady of Threadneedle Street (the Bank of England) had indemnified creditors against default on loans made to Slater Walker's banking subsidiary up to £40 million. The total loss to the public purse (excluding the investing public) has so far exceeded £50 million.

In its last full year of operations (1975) Slater Walker lost £44.4 million, consisting of a £28 million write-down in the value of the investment portfolio (including £5.8 million for a satellite company formed for David Frost), a £4.3 million loss in the normal course of business, £3.9 million owed to financial advisors and accountants, and £2.4 million in taxes. These poor operating results were accompanied by dramatic losses to investors: the share price fell from around £2.45 in April 1973 to £0.08 in September 1976.

---

*The major source of references for this case is Charles Raw, *A Financial Phenomenon: An Investigation of the Rise and Fall of The Slater Walker Empire* (Harper & Row, London, 1977).

11

The reasons for the Bank of England's massive but silent rescue with British taxpayers' money are not hard to find. Slater Walker had been very successful in capturing the hearts and wallets of small investors in several countries. Jim Slater and his cofounder Peter Walker were viewed as financial folk heroes. News of the firm's operations and undertakings was followed by the grass-roots investing public with the enthusiasm of football fans. The failure of Slater Walker was the finale of a long line of incidents that were to leave the investing public disillusioned by (and poorer as a result of) its flirtations with the stock market. Small wonder that the Bank of England let the truth out gently.

Slater Walker was not just any corporation: it had become a symbol of the aspirations of both Labour and Tory factions in British political life. The new Labour government of 1964 sought to infuse Britain with the "white-hot technological revolution." The revolution was to be achieved by a major restructuring of British industry into economic units large enough to challenge the high-technology giants from Japan, America, and Europe. The government set up the Industrial Reorganization Corporation as a trigger and pump-primer for this industrial renaissance and Slater Walker was seen by many as the private sector equivalent in this process of economic change.

The Conservative government of 1970 was often referred to as the Slater Walker government. Peter Walker, the firm's cofounder and deputy chairman, was one of the most influential members of Edward Heath's cabinet. As minister for trade and industry, Walker had special responsibilities for reforming the laws that governed the accountability of large corporations and their directors. Peter Walker was widely touted as a future prime minister.

The Tory government's mission in 1970 was to counteract the effects of a socialist welfare state that had eroded individual assertiveness and personal responsibility. As Edward Du Cann, a senior member of the Tory party described it, "We must seek to reverse this trend, to give people the opportunity to accept responsibility and to participate in the management and organization of British industry. This is the social necessity for encouraging a wider spread of share ownership. To spread wealth: to spread responsibility; to spread power; that is the aim" (Row, 1977, p. 29).

Described as the Mr. Efficiencies, the new Tory government in 1970 was considered unsentimental, hardworking, self-made, and competitive. Its vision was to turn Britain into a property-owning democracy. Slater Walker exemplified the new Tory dream of personal success achieved by hard work, personal initiative, and self-help. The press added to the fantasizing by portraying Jim Slater and Peter Walker as lower middle class heroes who, by making their millions "within the system," were positive proof that the system worked. Their firm was described by Raw as the "unprecedented nexus between the political and business ethics which the country has still barely comprehended."

The new Tories planned to reinvigorate free enterprise; the state bureaucracy was to be streamlined by the new technocrats and "meritocrats"; business would be exposed to the stringent standards of survival of the fittest; "lame ducks" and ailing industries would no longer be bailed out. The social interest was to be pursued by unleashing the aggressive self-interests of management; money was to become the dominant measure of success. "We are money makers not thing makers" was Jim Slater's response to Harold Wilson (the Labour party leader) when the latter contended that "what's wrong with our society is that those who make the money are more regarded than those who earn the money" (Raw, 1977, p. 9). Little did Slater realize that he was participating in a major economic controversy, one that has troubled economists for over a century: Does money have a value in its own right? Or is it merely a veil through which we can describe "real" assets, with no independent status of its own? Slater Walker has been variously described as "a seething pyramid of escalating paper" and "a mammoth paper chain around the world." In 1971 it was about to discover whether it was possible to make money without making things.

The Midas Touch

The rise and fall of Slater Walker is an extremely complex financial history that, even today, is neither fully documented nor fully understood. It involved a vast network of international subsidiaries and associate companies that were quoted on the stock exchanges of the United Kingdom, the United States, South Africa, Australia, Canada, Hong Kong, and Singapore. These enterprises were industrial, commercial, and financial in nature. The latter group consisted of a battalion of investment vehicles including unit trusts (mutual funds), investment companies, dealing companies (security dealers and brokers), and life insurance companies. As we will see, the financial arm of Slater Walker, consisting of funds held on behalf of the investing publics of several countries, was a key element in the growth strategy of the Slater Walker empire.

The case material discussed here is confined to a few select examples from Slater Walker's history; it highlights some of the central dilemmas in corporate accountability. Slater Walker is an illustration of the social conflicts inherent in corporate growth. Like many other "go-go" stocks, Slater Walker expanded by conglomerate growth and merger. New companies were secured not for cash but for issues of shares to their owners. Consequently, a firm could acquire other companies, on very favorable terms, if it could inflate its own share price.

Share prices do not reflect historical asset values but rather the earnings that those assets are expected to generate. A share with underlying assets of say $1 might be quoted at $3, $6, or even $20, if investors are convinced that management is capable of superhuman feats of efficiency in using those assets. It is to management's advantage therefore, to extol its extraordinary abilities through news releases, public relations, promotional and advertising schemes, and (of course) accounting reports. The latter details historical earnings, perhaps the most significant "track record" from which investors can estimate future earnings performance. Amplify those earnings, and the amount investors are prepared to pay for the shares will also increase, thereby increasing their market price.

The disparity between the historical asset value and the market value of a firm's shares can lead to a paradoxical situation. Since share prices are based on expectations, not current (let alone historical) asset values, company takeover situations can arise in which "the mouse can devour the elephant." In these cases, known as reverse takeovers, a smaller firm is able to take over a larger firm (in terms of the relative value of their underlying assets) by using its higher share price (as when Leyland Motors purchased the British Motor Corporation).

Conglomerates are composed of a heterogeneous amalgam of subsidiaries that sometimes have no obvious comparative advantage from, or business rationale for, being part of the same combination. The synergy in such cases is supposed to be reflected not in immediate physical input savings or increases in physical output, but rather in financial and managerial benefits.

If a merger, even of heterogeneous firms, results in a better overall management, this should be reflected in higher future earnings, a higher current share price, a lower cost of raising new capital for expansion (in terms of current earnings per share), and therefore greater long-term efficiency in terms of the ratio of physical inputs to outputs. Jim Slater's dictum "We make money, not things" was intended to starkly underscore this long-term relationship: greater moneymaking is a prerequisite for greater "thing-making" in a market economy. Opportunities for making superprofits represent a state of market disequilibrium: a signal to producers and investors that resources are currently allocated inefficiently and could be redeployed in a more economical and productive fashion. (So goes the rationale of neoclassical economics and the authentication of conglomerates as instruments of social efficiency.)

But what if the current market price of a share is an abberation rather than a reliable indicator of the long-term earnings potential of managers and assets? What if a share price is a myth, embodying all the lies, deceits, half-truths, misinformation, speculations, and corporate daydreams inflicted by management on innocent buyers and sellers of shares? In such circumstances, the correlation between moneymaking and thingmaking must break down: share prices no longer portend future worth and earnings; they are distortions and perversions of future reality.

What distinguished Slater Walker from virtually all other growth-oriented conglomerates were the range and sophistication of its myth making tactics. Creative accounting practices were but one of a number of strategies the company used to promulgate fictions and fantasies for massaging its share prices. Slater Walker accomplished its share price management through a variety of schemes, only a few of which will be described here. These schemes involved creating an international chain of satellite companies and investment vehicles through which Slater Walker proceeded to churn the accounts of investment clients and employ warehousing practices and asset-stripping techniques.

Slater Walker's manipulations demonstrated an understanding of the determinants of share price behavior far more imaginative and perceptive than anything appearing in the scholarly literature of accounting, finance, and economics. In just ten years, from 1963 to 1973, Slater Walker grew from nothing into an international maze of holdings with a peak market value of £250 million. Jim Slater's personal fortune grew to an estimated £8 million over the same period.

Were there any recurring patterns in the practices that produced the phenomenal growth record of Slater Walker? What do these patterns suggest about the behavior of the system by which society allocates its economic resources among investment alternatives? What do they suggest about the roles of accounting and accountants in such a system? To investigate these and other questions, we need to consider the origins of Slater Walker, particularly the early career of Jim Slater and his attempts to control the laws of supply and demand.

Jim Slater began his career as a share tipster for a newspaper. Ironically, one of the secrets of becoming a successful share tipster is to never take one's own advice. Indeed, some share tipsters have made substantial personal fortunes by doing exactly the opposite of what they advised their clients to do. The share prices of many small companies are determined from relatively few transactions; such stocks are said to be thinly traded.

The recommendations of investment brokers, security analysts, and financial columnists with national newspapers may dramatically affect the price of such shares. An unscrupulous security analyst can make a considerable amount of money in such circumstances. If an analyst bought 1,000 one-dollar shares in a small firm and then recommended the investment to thousands of clients, this would drive the share price up and create a handsome gain for the expert upon selling the holdings. Selling short is the reverse of this procedure, except that the expert does not even need to own any shares. The expert instructs a broker to sell, for example, 1,000 shares at the prevailing market price of $1.20 each and then advises investment clients to dispose of their holdings. These sales reduce the market price to, let's say, $1, at which point the expert instructs the broker to purchase 1,000 shares to cover the previous sale.

In 1962, Jim Slater wrote to Nigel Lawson, Conservative member of Parliament and the city editor of the *Sunday Telegraph,* suggesting that Slater write a monthly investment advice column. Lawson was initially cautious since a columnist for another newspaper had only recently been dismissed for dealing in his own tips. However, after making further inquiries and receiving Slater's assurance that the column would not be used for personal gain, Lawson agreed to allow Slater to write the column under the pseudonym Capitalist.

The *Sunday Telegraph* had a circulation of 2.5 million copies: quite sufficient to affect the quoted price of any share recommended by its financial columnists. For example, in one of the companies favored by Capitalist, the number of shareholders grew from 900 to 2,000 after it was touted in the pages of the *Sunday Telegraph.*

Jim Slater's personal profits from trading on Capitalist's recommendations were modest. Charles Raw, financial correspondent for the *Sunday Times,* estimated them at a minimum of £20,000 (Raw, 1977, pp. 75–98). There were numerous small transactions that Slater profited from as a result of his special position as Capitalist. As examples, Charles Raw cites Slater's dealings in the shares of Wardle Company, UK Opticals, and Clear Hooters. Slater purchased 15,000 shares in Wardle Company in 1962 and an additional 4,000 shares just before Capitalist touted them on April 23, 1963. These personal acquisitions cost Slater £4,758. In late June 1963, Slater sold his total holding for £9,737.

Slater's personal profits on dealings in shares of UK Opticals were between £1,800 and £1,900. By the time Capitalist recommended UK Optical in the *Sunday Telegraph* on October 31, 1963, Slater had accumulated 13,000 shares on his own behalf, at a total cost of £6,207. Within weeks of the recommendation, he disposed of his holding in two blocks of 6,000 and 7,000 shares respectively, yielding a profit of between £1,800 and £1,900. Slater acquired Clear Hooters shares in two lots, one in 1962 and the second in 1963. The total cost was £1,203. Capitalist recommended the shares on March 3, 1963. Slater told 750 shares on March 26, 1963, and the remainder of his holding shortly thereafter. His profit on these transactions was estimated at £887.

Slater did not always take advantage of his advance knowledge of Capitalist's recommendations. Nor did he always profit from deals that he did undertake. On other occasions he could have made an even larger profit than he actually did. For example, he sold Wardle Company at £0.53 per share when he could have gotten £1.05 per share had he waited. Nevertheless, Slater's personal dealings while he was writing for the *Sunday Telegraph* did provide some of the starting capital necessary for launching his more ambitious ventures.

The early lessons Slater learned as a financial columnist were to later stand him in good stead in his meteoric rise to fame and fortune. The most important lessons was that no man in his right mind enters into the free market to do unarmed combat with the laws of supply and demand. There was no need to: both the supply and the demand for a security could be managed and so, therefore, could its price. We find this basic lesson working repeatedly to Slater's benefit later in his career, albeit on a larger scale and in a more complex form.

The Early Partnership of Jim Slater and Peter Walker

Peter Walker and Jim Slater joined forces to form Slater Walker on July 24, 1964. At about this time, Slater became interested in an electronics firm called Astaron-Bird and invested heavily in the firm's shares, both personally and on behalf of the Mount Street Investment Trusts. Additional purchases were made by Peter Walker, investment clients, friends, and other associates, and within two months Astaron-Bird's share price had doubled. Walker disposed of his 2,000 shares on August 27 and 28, 1964, and Slater sold 1,500 shares on April 22, 1965. Walker's profit was around £400 and Slater cleared slightly less than £6,000. In both cases the shares were sold to investment clients in Slater Walker. Included among these clients was Donald Stokes, Slater's old employer and the managing direc- tor of British Leyland. The clients were not told that their own investment advisors—Slater Walker—were the sellers of the shares they were buying. (Slater and Walker have both denied that they knew such transactions had taken place.)

An ambitious variant on this supply-side share price management was introduced in January 1972, when Slater Walker launched a mutual fund called Dual Trust. This was at a time when Slater's personal stature was at its highest. Dual Trust offered half its investors the income, and the other half the capital gains, accruing from its investments in young, aggressive, financially oriented companies. It was no coincidence that Slater Walker happened to own a ready-made portfolio of young aggressives that it was proposing to sell to Dual Trust at 2 percent below their average market price for the period between January 7 and January 26, 1972. This bargain bun- dle was composed of shares in the investment banking clients of Slater Walker. Dual Trust was to pay £17.7 million for the securities; Slater Walker's potential gain was £4,650,000. In addition to an underwriting fee on the issue, Slater Walker was to collect a management fee of £150,000 a year for running the trust.

Dual Trust's issued share capital was to be 30 million £1 units. Slater Walker was to receive £14.9 million of Dual Trust shares and £2.8 million in cash as payment for the £17.7 million portfolio of securities it was trans- ferring to the trust. The remainder of Dual Trust's shares was to be issued to Slater Walker's investment clients, who were invited to subscribe for £10.5 million.

The financial press's reaction to Dual Trust was less than enthusiastic. The *Investors Chronicle* dismissed Dual Trust as "an exercise in pyramid- ing." In the City (London's Wall Street), the trust came to be known as "the Dustbin." *The Economist* noted with regret how "massaging" had become a euphemism for share rigging. The *Sunday Times* described Dual Trust as one of the most sophisticated ways of selling off large blocks of shares that the market had seen for some time. Many people in the City were uneasy about the lack of regulations on the London market, which was permitting giant operators such as Slater Walker to massage the market with these shares. The *Sunday Times* expressed concern that profits were being created out of paper by bypassing the market: Slater Walker was selling a portfolio to Dual Trust and its new subscribers at a price (and therefore at a profit) that it could not have obtained by selling into the open market. Slater Walker's profit was fictitious because it was based on a transaction that was not at arms length between independent and equal parties.

The public did not rush to buy shares in Dual Trust. Dual Trust shares were heavily undersubscribed, and in consequence the shares were soon quoted at a substantial discount on the issue price. Slater Walker and an associated company, Euroglen, halted the slide in Dual Trust's share price by buying up 4.9 million shares on the open market. By the end of 1972, the Slater Walker unit trusts (mutual funds) also held £800,000 worth of Dual Trust shares.

The skepticism about the real value of Dual Trust and its new share portfolio, as expressed in the near collapse of Dual Trust's own price, hardly penetrated the accounting fantasy land of Slater Walker. In its 1972 accounts, Slater Walker recognized a total gain of £4.6 million on the flotation of Dual Trust. Overall, Slater Walker made a profit of £5,385,000 in 1972, which included a profit on share trading of £2.7 million on sales of the initial portfolios to Dual Trust and another new trust.

The Internationalization of Slater Walker

The discipline of the market place, as represented by the laws of supply and demand, was successfully suspended in another Slater Walker adventure, which was unfolding at about the same time as the Dual Trust debacle. This was Slater Walker's now-famous series of exploits on the Hong Kong stock exchange. It began with the acquisition of Haw Par Brothers. In June 1971, Haw Par had two subsidiaries: a banking firm and a newspaper. Slater Walker was not interested in developing these lines of business, and the subsidiaries were immediately sold off, together with Haw Par's remaining operations. All that remained were Haw Par's listings on the Hong Kong and Singapore stock exchanges. The stripping of Haw Par down to its quotations did cause some resentment among local Hong Kong business establishments, as did similar asset-stripping in Australia and Canada when Slater Walker expanded in those parts of the world.

Armed with Haw Par's stock exchange quotations, Slater Walker proceeded on its now familiar path of buying up local companies. The first was an insurance group called Motor and General Underwriters, which was quoted in Hong Kong and on the Singapore exchange. In March 1972, Haw Par announced that it had acquired 80 percent of the shares of a pharmaceutical company called Kwan Loong and 65 percent of King Fung, a listed property firm. At the same time, it was announced that King Fung— by now a "shell company"—was purchasing the assets of a Fijian holiday resort from a Slater Walker associate: Southern Pacific Properties. These assets were acquired in exchange for 70 million newly issued King Fung shares. The Fijian assets were somewhat intangible in that the resort development had yet to be completed. This was a mere detail however, for a market poised to leap into the biggest boom in its history. The heady atmosphere, together with the Hong Kong public's knowledge that Slater Walker magic was behind the deal, ensured that the prices of King Fung shares "took off into the blue azure," in the words of one local commentator. Nor were Southern Pacific Properties securities to lag far behind. Valued at £13.7 million for the purposes of the transfer, Southern Pacific Properties's market value soared to £21 million as soon as the market heard of the deal.

The next twist in Slater Walker's far eastern fling was the creation of a unit trust (mutual fund) called Slater Walker Overseas Investments Limited (SWOIL). The Hong Kong public was asked to subscribe £3.2 million to the new trust; Slater Walker was to donate a portfolio of securities valued at £2.6 million. The portfolio was sold to SWOIL at a 10 percent discount from its market value, and Slater Walker was paid with 45 percent of the share capital of SWOIL. The portfolio was made up of shares in Slater Walker subsidiaries and associates in Australia, South Africa, and Canada, as well as in Haw Par and Slater Walker itself. On the first day of dealing in SWOIL shares, their price rose from $HK5 to $HK6.5.

In the following months, stock prices on the Hong Kong exchange rose fivefold. Back home in London, Slater laid plans that would enable British investors to share in these treasures of the East. Slater Walker Far Eastern Investment Trust (SWFEIT) was invented for this purpose. Approximately £6 million was solicited from investors in a prospectus filed on June 7, 1972. Slater Walker absorbed the entire £6 million by selling to SWFEIT a portfolio of securities already owned by Slater Walker companies. On July 3, 1972, shares in six associated companies of Haw Par were sold to SWFEIT at a profit of £1.4 million. Slater Walker (U.K.) and Slater Walker (Australia) also made substantial profits on sales to SWFEIT, including sales of their own shares in Haw Par. All sales were made at the ruling market prices, even though it is unlikely that these prices could have been obtained for such large blocks of shares on the open market.

Slater Walker's activities in the Far East were significant in many ways. First, the downfall of the Slater Walker empire in 1976 was initiated by the Hong Kong authorities when they started extradition proceedings in London against Jim Slater and Richard Taring, a member of Slater Walker's board of directors and chairman of Haw Par. Taring was eventually extradited, convicted on several counts, fined, and jailed for four months in Hong Kong. Second, Slater Walker's Far East exploits formed part of an international empire of satellite companies. Much has been written about the internationalization of capital and its destabilizing affects on both world and national economies. For instance, Kindleburger (1956) has argued that the freedom allowed in the movement of international capital has rendered the nation state obsolete. At the level of world economy, the disastrous consequences of the cycles of slumps and booms that typify modern industrial economies were at one time ameliorated by nation states being at different stages of the cycle. For an individual nation state, this meant that the effects of stagnation at home could be offset by increasing exports to countries that were in an expansionary phase. Not so today: the liberation of capital has synchronized the cycles of booms and slumps of individual states. Countries can no longer relieve stagnation at home through an export-led boom.

While much has been written in general and abstract terms about the internationalization of capital, there have been few micro-level studies of the mechanisms at work in individual firms. Slater Walker's international empire of satellite companies gives a concrete example of the factors that mobilize capital on an international scale. The complicity of accounting standards and practices in authorizing, directing, and sanctifying these international money flows is also revealed by the Slater Walker affair. In its ten short years of existence, Slater Walker opened up satellite companies in Hong Kong, South Africa, the United States, Continental Europe, Australia, and Canada. The pattern was similar in each case: Slater Walker would buy out a locally quoted company and would install Slater Walker personnel. From then on, the satellites were free to imitate the same techniques of acquisitive growth pioneered by their illustrious parent. Not all the satellites were successful; the much heralded American venture ended in an ignominious loss. In all cases however, Slater remained faithful to his dictum of making money not things. This was reflected in the amount of managerial energy devoted to financial restructuring, making new acquisitions, and shuffling the ownership of assets between associated companies.

Institutionalizing Self-Interest: Tokengate

Seizing control of the forces of supply and demand for shares would be a meaningless exercise without also developing the means to profit from the situation. Slater's column with the *Sunday Telegraph* provided relatively minor opportunities for personal profit when compared with the opportunities afforded by Slater Walker. Slater Walker grew so rapidly, and into so many diverse schemes, that a full-time security-dealing company was required to promote the interests of Slater and other executive directors. Tokengate Investment Trust was acquired in 1960 for this purpose, as was a smaller, Hong Kong–based firm called Spydar Securities.

Slater and the majority of his executive directors owned between 40 and 50 percent of Tokengate's shares. Most of the remaining shares were retained by Slater Walker for allocation among favored clients and executives. When asked about the purpose of Tokengate, Slater was reported to have said that it helped executives within the company who might otherwise leave to set up businesses on their own. On other occasions, Slater suggested that Tokengate served to "incentivize" executives and to obviate the need for them to deal on their own behalf. By all accounts, Tokengate was astonishingly profitable for Slater Walker executives. Tokengate's shares rose 576 percent by the end of 1969, 340 percent in 1971, and peaked at £2.08 in the summer of 1972: a 245 percent increase on the adjusted starting price of £0.08 per share that Slater Walker paid for the firm. On September 18, 1970, Jim Slater sold his Tokengate holding at a profit of £50,381. After making additional acquisitions of Tokengate stock, he made a further profit of £184,217 on a sale in November 1973. Another executive director, Anthony Buckley, sold his Tokengate holding in 1971 at an estimated profit of £215,000. At that time, it was estimated that the gain to all directors was approximately £1.15 million.

Peter Walker was deputy managing director of Slater Walker, but he was not regarded as an executive director of the firm. In consequence, he was not allocated any Tokengate shares. He did however, have fairly well-developed views on the kind of insider dealing perpetrated by Slater and his colleagues. In July 1973, while he was secretary of state of trade and industry in the Heath government, he published a white paper detailing plans for company law reform. It stated:

> The Government's view is that dealing in a company's securities by any-
> one who, by reason of his relationship with the company or with its of-

ficers, has information which he knows to be price-sensitive, should be a criminal offense unless he can show that his primary intention in dealing at that particular time was not to make a profit or avoid a loss.

If Peter Walker's high-sounding words had been translated into legislation, it would have led to criminal proceedings against his fellow directors at Slater Walker.

We can examine the Tokengate magic through its role in two Slater Walker acquisitions: Oriental Carpet Manufacturers (OCM) and a Canadian firm called Stanley Brock. Both cases exemplify the way the Slater Walker group transferred substantial profits and assets to Tokengate, the company in which Slater and other directors had substantial personal interests. The real cost of such transactions was born by the outside shareholders of Slater Walker and its subsidiaries and the clients of the investment trusts. In May 1969, Slater Walker acquired a majority holding in OCM for £458,214. At about the same time, Tokengate also bought a stake of £114,588.

In August 1969, the capitalized market value of OCM was approximately £2.5 million. Slater Walker had big plans for the firm: it was to be "injected" with another Slater Walker company (Ralli Brothers Trading), and the new group was then to be refloated as Ralli International. The situation was obfuscated by some fancy financial footwork: each OCM share was split into ten new shares and each new share was to earn one bonus share. Overall, the old share in OCM was replaced with 20 new shares. None of these maneuvers should have significantly affected the total value of a shareholder's investment, only the number of shares held should have been affected.

Somewhere in this series of stock splits, bonuses, and pirouettes, however, the value of OCM did increase. For the merger, Slater Walker had valued OCM at £3.75 million, a 150 percent increase on the market value of the firm a few months before. After adjusting for the share split and the bonus, the merger value of each OCM share was £0.75, compared with the £0.0248 price paid for OCM shares by Slater Walker. The overall gain to Slater Walker on the reflotation of OCM shares was £926,676.

Tokengate's profit on the merger of OCM and Ralli Brothers Trading was not confined to the gain on its original purchase of £114,588 worth of old OCM shares. Tokengate also profited from purchasing additional OCM shares directly from Slater Walker at £0.34 per share just prior to the merger. This was a generous discount indeed as Slater Walker was about to revalue OCM shares at £0.75 in its reflotation as Ralli International. Tokengate purchased between £108,480 and £158,812 worth of OCM shares at this time. (The exact amount is uncertain because nominee accounts were used.) Tokengate's net gain was £187,688 as a result of Slater Walker's generosity, or at least its generosity with the funds of its outside shareholders. Within four months of the reflotation, the total market value of Tokengate's stake in OCM was valued at £1,262,405, compared with its original cost of £329,000.

Tokengate was not the only benefactor of the pre-reflotation clearance sale of OCM shares by Slater Walker. A total of 49,000 old OCM shares was sold at pre-reflotation prices. Nine-hundred shares were purchased on behalf of Edward Heath, the then leader of Her Majesty's opposition and one of Slater's clients. Twenty-five thousand shares went to Ivan Investment Trust. Ivan Investment Trust was run by Slater Walker and was experiencing high redemptions by clients after press criticisms by a periodical called *Planned Savings*. The company was much in need of a profit boost and this was provided by injecting 25,000 OCM shares obtained from Slater Walker at a 15 percent discount on the prevailing market price.

Slater Walker's outside shareholders also came to the rescue of Tokengate in May 1970. Tokengate's main investments, Ralli International and Barclay's Securities (both Slater Walker companies) were hit badly by the market crash in 1970. Ralli International's share price fluctuated erratically between £0.60 and £0.775 over the summer in its attempt to take over a property company. Tokengate sold its entire shareholding in Ralli International, the transaction being recorded in the share register on August 26, 1970. The estimated profit to Tokengate on the sale was £330,000; Slater Walker, and therefore its outside shareholders appear to have helped Tokengate dispose of this large holding. On May 18, 1970, Slater Walker announced that it had sold exactly the same number of shares in Ralli International that Tokengate had sold in August. After a number of intervening transactions, Slater Walker repurchased almost the same number of shares on July 29 and July 30.

The rationale underlying this series of transactions is not clear. One possible interpretation is that the dates of the various share transfers were decided after the fact, to obscure the real chain of events; Slater Walker probably acted on Tokengate's behalf in selling Tokengate's holding in Ralli International (perhaps to a Slater Walker client or a buyer on the outside market). If this were the true version of what happened, then the real losers were Slater Walker's outside shareholders, who lost their share of the £300,000 profit on the transaction, and any investment clients of Slater Walker whose funds were used to acquire the Ralli International shares.

Tokengate was invited to share in the booty that arose from Slater Walker's expedition into the Canadian stock markets. Slater Walker's game plan was essentially the same one it had used in Australia in 1967 when the company's ruthless financial practices had provoked much public criticism. In April 1971, Slater Walker acquired 53,000 shares in Stanley Brock, a company with a quotation on the Toronto and Montreal stock exchanges. The acquisition cost $803,000, or $15 per share.* The name Stanley Brock was changed to Slater Walker of Canada on July 31, 1979, and every old Stanley Brock share was replaced with three shares in the new company. Rumors about Slater Walker's plans sent the new share price up from $15 to $20.

Slater Walker then announced a rights issue in the new company: shareholders were entitled to buy two new shares at $5 each for each share held. As the prerights market value of the company's share was $20, and $10 was required to exercise the rights, the postrights value per share was ($20 + $10) ÷ 3 = $10. So Slater Walker's original purchase of 53,500 shares was split, two-for-one, into 106,500 shares, and these entitled Slater Walker to subscribe for 213,000 additional shares. After exercising the rights, the market value of Slater Walker's holdings in the Canadian satellite was around $10 per share. It was a selfless and generous act for Slater Walker to then sell 166,969 of these new shares at $5 each, $5 below their adjusted market value, to three investment "clients." The total profit to the clients (at the expense of outside shareholders) was of the order of $835,000. Tokengate netted $281,000 by buying 56,268 shares; Flag Investment Trust purchased 43,200 shares at a gain of $216,000, and the International Fund (an Investors Overseas Services unit) secured 67,500 shares for $337,000 profit.

The Canadian satellite was now in place to launch into a takeover binge by emulating the growth techniques pioneered by its parent. Slater Walker of Canada began by buying a large holding in a Canadian department store and then proposed a merger with a quoted investment company called Unas. Slater Walker (U.K.) already owned 22 percent of Unas, held on behalf of investment clients and itself. The merger produced an immediate gain of $200,000 and an underwriting fee of $265,000.

Unas and Slater Walker of Canada merged in June 1972; each share in the latter company was exchanged for two shares in the new company. In the ensuing months the share price of the merged company nearly doubled, so that Tokengate had 112,000 shares valued at $1.12 million that had originally cost $281,000.

Transferring assets from Slater Walker to Tokengate at giveaway prices was one thing, but the directors of Slater Walker still had to get their winnings out of Tokengate. Once again, the Slater Walker group—with the aid of monies from outside shareholders—proved to be more than accommodating. Slater disposed of 100,000 shares in Tokengate on September 18, 1970, and despite a major drop in Tokengate's share price, he made a personal profit of £50,000. It is unlikely that such a large sale could have been made on a single day. Moreover, the share register of Tokengate suggests that the shares were not sold on the open market. Was it a coincidence that, at about the same time, Jaydean Securities—a company that, for technical reasons, escaped classification as a Slater Walker subsidiary but was, in reality, controlled by Slater Walker directors—sold 249,000 shares in Tokengate? Or that Flag Investment Trust (another Slater Walker operation) purchased a lot of shares of about the same size? Tokengate's quoted price then rose, and Flag sold out, making a comfortable profit. In May 1971, Slater bought, on his own behalf, a further lot of Tokengate shares for £321,083 and sold them in November 1973 at a profit of £184,214.

And so the merry-go-round continued, the Slater Walker group providing both the supply and the demand for shares. These incestuous relations and the Disneyland valuations that were used were totally divorced from the world outside Slater Walker. A fairyland of accounting profits and asset values was spun which the auditors failed to halt with the touchstone of reality.

There were occasions when the outside world rudely interrupted these accounting contrivances. One such interruption came from Investors Overseas Services (IOS), a Geneva-based offshore investment operation whose $1 billion collapse in April 1970, shook stock markets throughout the world. Investors Overseas Services was a major client of Slater Walker; Slater Walker managed a £16 to £17 million portfolio for it. Perhaps as a token of esteem for its financial advisor, IOS invested heavily in Slater Walker shares. By the end of 1969, IOS owned 580,000 Slater Walker shares at a cost of £1,055,000 and a market value of £1,365,000. Apparently IOS had a commensurate degree of confidence in the subsidiaries of Slater Walker: £350,000 had been spent on shares in the South African and Australian satellites, and these investments had appreciated to £553,000. The investments in Slater Walker companies were made on behalf of two IOS funds based in the United Kingdom: the Sterling Fund of Funds and the International Life Assurance Company. Through its Geneva-based International Investment Trust, IOS bought an additional 440,000 Slater Walker shares for £1.2 million. The largest single investment by IOS in

Slater Walker companies was a purchase of 1.4 million shares in Slater Walker (Australia) for £2.6 million on behalf of International Telephone and Telegraph.

The collapse of IOS took place between March and May of 1970. During that time IOS dismissed Slater Walker as its advisor and dumped over 600,000 Slater Walker shares on the market. Those months were a period of acute uncertainty for stock markets throughout the world. Slater Walker's share price fell from £3 to £1.875. During May 1970, Slater and his family disposed of 450,000 shares in Slater Walker for £962,000. A very substantial profit was earned on this sale.

The final word on Tokengate and other insider dealing operations is left to Peter Walker. Peter Walker became minister for trade and industry in November 1972. In January 1973, he lectured at the London Graduate School of Business on the "unacceptable face of capitalism" and the indispensible role of state intervention in preserving the integrity of the system:

> It is the task of government to see that the impetus of capitalism is harnessed to the interests of all the people. Capitalism should not be regarded as the means for a few to get rich without regard to the needs and hopes of the majority of people. The government must see that commercial activities are fair, open and just. The framework of company law must be correct. Practices which give an unfair advantage to a few to the detriment of many, such as the practice of insider dealing must be stopped. If major sections of the economy are to merge or the efficient firm is to take over the inefficient, it should be done on the basis of full information about the likely advantages and disadvantages for the interests directly concerned and the community as a whole. I cannot overemphasize the importance for the working of capitalism that it should be open, free and based on integrity.

Implications

Many of the issues and problems we are concerned with here are graphically illustrated by the Slater Walker affair. A fairly straightforward methodological issue raised by Slater Walker's activities concerns the value placed on assets transferred between interrelated companies. How should we value intracompany transfers of securities or indeed, place a value on any thinly traded security? The difficulties such questions raise are compounded when we realize that information concerning asset values and profits calculated by accountants feeds into a societal investment process in which decisions are based on gossip, rumor, ritual, faith, and speculation, that is, the real simple economics of wealth maximization. Keynes referred to the "animal spirits of businessmen" to describe these unstable, unpredictable, and irrational aspects of society's investment decision making. But where, really, is the irrationality? Is it in the stock exchanges of the world? Or is it in the theories of accounting and finance that purport to describe stock market behavior? Many of these theories take for granted that the appropriate objective for a firm is the maximization of its stock market price. Is this criterion for business behavior still appropriate if the stock market price can be rigged and massaged by creative accounting and a slick public relations campaign?

Accounting education cannot escape unscathed from this discussion. Slater and many of his compatriots were chartered accountants. Their respect for moneymaking and their contempt for "thing-making" did not arise out of thin air; it is, in part, a product of the accounting education system. This system elevates monetary values as ends in themselves; the surrogate role of money as a mere token expression of human and social needs is ignored. Marx distinguished between the surface appearances of market phenomenon and the underlying social structure that generates the appearances. For Marx, it was a cardinal sin to mistake market appearances for the underlying social reality: market exchange does not, in and of itself, reveal the volatile social struggles and conflicts that may seethe in a society's underlying class structure. Indeed, those antagonisms in the underlying social structure determine market behavior, not the other way around.

Accounting education appears to have outstripped Marx's worst fears in this regard: students are not merely taught to conflate appearance with reality; they learn to reify deceitful appearances and ignore the structure of social reality. Such ignorance was manifest in the Slater's "money makers not thing makers" comment; it was in evidence again when Slater celebrated the income manipulation talents of "Taring's school of accountancy" (Taring, a fellow director, was also a chartered accountant). Ignorance of this kind multiplies when an accounting education system elevates profit and wealth as ends in themselves and fails to articulate the social purpose of profit and its tenuous connections to social welfare.

A glimpse into the part accounting plays in the world economy is provided by the Slater Walker affair. After the oil companies, the Big Eight accounting firms provide one of the best examples of the growth of multinational business in recent years. The Big Eight have simply taken on the character of their clients: as their clients have become multinational, so have the accounting firms.

Slater Walker was not just a British phenomenon. The firm's satellite system provided an international network for moving speculative capital to different parts of the globe. Through this network, Slater Walker joined the Australian boom in the mid-sixties, rode the British bull market in the late sixties, and arrived in time to partake in far eastern bonanza in the early seventies. With international financial institutions like Slater Walker, investment capital is free to roam the globe, seeking the most lucrative employment. Whether the most lucrative is also the most socially necessary is open to doubt. Charles Raw's meticulous assessment of Slater Walker's contribution to the productive efficiency of the British economy very strongly suggests that the operation had little social worth. Indeed, all too often it appeared that what was to Slater Walker's profit was at society's expense.

Where was that international team of watchdogs and bloodhounds known as the Big Eight while Slater Walker was soaking the investing publics of the world? They were solemnly certifying the extravagant asset values and inflated profit claims of Slater Walker companies. Worse, they were advising investors that these accounting figures represented a true and fair view of the firm's operations and were claiming that the accounts were prepared according to general accepted accounting principles. So we find that the mediocrity of accounting practice has been internationalized; it now serves to certify and authenticate such buccaneering exploits as the Slater Walker affair. When neoclassical economists note, with some apprehension, that the booms and slumps of national economies are now synchronized and that the "animal spirits" of businessmen the world over now erupt in lockstep, they can thank the international accounting community for the small part it played in creating the situation.

Responsibility for the Slater Walker debacle also lies in part with the media and the financial columnists. With few exceptions (as with Dual Trust, for instance) the company's activities enjoyed an uncritical and undiscriminating press. Many financial journalists abandoned the investigative duties of the Fourth Estate and joined in the ideological euphoria of the property-owning democracy and the high-technology society. Slogans substituted for factual analysis and asset strippers and speculators were promoted as folk heroes. An outstanding exception to these lamentable standards was the reporting of Charles Raw and the *Sunday Times* Insight Team. Charles Raw challenged the popular mythology about Slater Walker from the earliest days of the company. His definitive book on the Slater

Walker empire was the most important source of material for this account. Regrettably, Raw's prognostications came true with the collapse of the company in 1976 and the Bank of England's £50 million bail-out with public money.

A postscript is warranted in view of Jim Slater's recent comeback on the financial scene. Once again, profit and money are in favor with the British establishment, and Jim Slater has staged his return to coincide with this hospitable climate. "After five years of lying low, postwar Britain's most famous failed financier is gingerly returning to public view," announced *Forbes Magazine* in September 1980.

Slater's current net worth is estimated to be around £3 million. His modus operandi is familiar; he has invested heavily in thinly traded companies. According to one stockbroker who is close to Slater, "All that Jim Slater has to do to make money is to tell his good friend Patrick Sargeant [(sic) city editor of London's *Daily Mail*] what he's buying, and the herd thunders after the shares" (Minard, 1980, p. 122).

"Has Jim Slater learned from his past mistakes?" asks *Forbes Magazine*. The question would be more appropriately directed at the British investing public and its watchdog, the accounting profession. Jim Slater's "second coming" suggests that he has indeed profited from past mistakes—the mistakes of others.

3

Accounting for Multinationals: The Sierra Leone Development Corporation

Introduction

The Scottish-owned iron ore company Delco operated in Sierra Leone its 46 years, beginning in the early colonial period and remaining through the late colonial period, until its collapse in 1976 under a newly independent postcolonial state. The case of Delco is reported in detail in Hoogvelt and Tinker (1977, 1977A, 1978) and Tinker (1980). It is of interest to accountants because it allows the examination of, on one hand, traditional indicators of economic efficiency and performance (accounting profit estimates of changes in economic wealth) and, on the other hand, measures of domination and exploitation of various participants in the venture (e.g., shareholders, suppliers, customers, and particularly Sierra Leone labor, tribal groups, state bureaucracy and indigenous elites). These divergent aspects of the firm's history may all be viewed using the same evidence: the firm's accounting history.

Conventional Financial Appraisal of the Multinational

The 46-year social and financial history of Delco was pieced together using a financial simulation model. Data were collected from the firm's annual accounts, internal records, public documentary material, and interviews held in the United Kingdom and in Sierra Leone. From this data,

receipt and cash expenditure patterns of the company were reconstructed
for each of the 46 years of the company's operation. These monetary flows
were then adjusted by an inflation index in an attempt to present all monetary amounts in units of the same purchasing power (thus all calculations
are expressed in 1976 pound sterling equivalents).

These inflation-adjusted amounts were then used to estimate the division of the firm's total income, as shown in Table 3.1. Profitability indexes
for assessing the value of the firm to its owners were also devised: For
Delco's shareholders, the project produced an annual average profit rate of
13 percent (inflation-adjusted) or 16 percent before inflation.

Table 3.1.   Delco's Distribution of Income: 1930–75

	£m	%
Sales Revenue	424.14	100
U.K. Constituencies		
Shippers	169.66	40.02
Suppliers	104.11	25.56
Delco owners	42.70	10.07
White directors, management, and employees	31.40	7.41
Government	2.51	0.59
Leaseholders	0.62	0.15
	351.00	82.80
Sierra Leone Constituencies		
Local government	39.87	9.41
Black manual staff	26.84	6.33
Tribal authorities	6.16	1.45
	72.87	17.19
Total revenue	£423.87	100.00

Source: Hoogvelt and Tinker, 1978.

Table 3.1 shows how the total 46-year (inflation-adjusted) sales proceeds were distributed among various parties. The bulk of the proceeds from the sale of ore (40 percent) went to pay shippers and insurance agents. As Delco's parent firm owned an insurance broker that frequently acted on behalf of Delco, the £169.66 million paid to shippers and insurance agents includes a return to the parent company's investors. It was not possible to determine the exact amounts involved here, however several estimates suggest that they were not material to the overall results. The next largest benefactors from the venture were United Kingdom suppliers (25 percent), who mainly provided mining equipment. Delco's investors obtained 10 percent, white employees 7.4 percent, and the United Kingdom government secured 0.5 percent in taxes and 0.2 percent in land and mine leases. The overall share of proceeds taken by United Kingdom–based parties averages out to 82.7 percent over the 46-year period. The remainder (17.3 percent) accrued to Sierra Leone participants, the lion's share (9.4 percent) going to the local government in the form of taxes and the black labor force securing 6.3 percent as wages.

Table 3.1 evidences the adequacy of the project from the shareholder's viewpoint. For an outlay of £500,000 in 1930 (approximately £3 million in 1976 pounds sterling), the project generated an increase in wealth for the owners (a net present value) of £18.9 million at a 3 percent discount rate—after allowing for inflation.

In October 1975, Delco, Sierra Leone's second–largest export earning industry, went into voluntary liquidation and with it went several thousand jobs. We are not concerned with whether "excess profits" were made from the venture, and no great significance is attached to the absolute shares in proceeds taken by each group. What is of interest are the struggles and conflicts that ensued in establishing and changing those shares. From an accounting viewpoint, it is important to ask to what extent accounting information engenders distributional instabilities and, thereby, participates in conflict and exploitation. In this latter regard, it is the political instability that can result from acute inequality in the distribution of income that is of interest.

Alternative Appraisal of the Multinational:
A Periodization Analysis

A new way of interpreting accounting data is offered here. Table 3.2 shows a breakdown of the 46-year summary provided previously, in the form of a series of periodic income statements (a periodization analysis). These income statements are prepared on a cash basis rather than an accrual basis, which is more common in conventional accounting. As each statement extends over a number of years, however, the distinction between the two bases is not significant for the purposes intended here. The period covered by each of these distribution-of-income statements represents a particular institutional regime (early colonial, late colonial, and post-colonial). Each regime had its own unique configuration of social and political institutions. The finer breakdown of periods in Table 3.2 into four eras corresponds to successive mining agreements. As these agreements revise the entitlements of the various parties to the venture they also signify major changes in the social relations of production.

Table 3.2 shows a distribution of income statement for each institutional regime. Over the first two periods, from the early colonial to the late colonial, we see that the percentage share of proceeds collected by the British constituents declined slightly (from 84 percent to 79 percent), and that this was accompanied by increasing allocations (mainly through taxation) to the colonial state, whose share of the proceeds peaked in the beginning of the postcolonial period (from 7 percent to 14.9 percent).

These figures, together with other evidence from the period, indicate that with the passage from early to late colonialism, the British colonial system, which made mineral extraction possible in the form of military, ideological, and other support, gradually devolved its authority to an increasingly bureaucratic elite in Freetown (Hoogvelt and Tinker, 1977a). This devolution of "law and order" responsibilities was accompanied by a decentralization of responsibilities for funding these activities (as the figures suggest). The important thing to note is that the basic relations of production characteristic of capitalist enterprises, that is, the relationships between the factors of production—capital versus land and labor—remain unaltered.

Despite major changes in the way the social order was conducted and funded over the 46 years, the returns to the tribal authorities (representing the original owners of the land) and to black wage labor remained stagnant. Moreover, other evidence indicates that none of the new and swelling government revenues ever benefited the native workers or the people and local

Table 3.2. Periodization Table: Distribution of Income by Periods

	Early Colonial 1930–47		Late Colonial 1948–56		Postcolonial			
					1957–67		1968–75	
	£m	%	£m	%	£m	%	£m	%
Sales Revenue	55.08	100	94.50	100	171.81	100	102.81	100
U.K.-based constituencies								
Shippers	22.03	40.00	37.80	40.00	68.71	40.00	41.12	40.00
Suppliers	12.86	23.35	27.50	29.11	26.58	15.47	37.26	36.15
Owners and investors	5.67	10.30	7.79	8.24	23.37	13.60	5.87	5.71
White directors, management, and employees	4.91	8.91	3.88	4.11	15.79	9.19	6.82	6.62
Government	0.88	1.60	0.02	0.02	1.44	0.84	0.17	0.16
Leaseholders	0.07	0.12	0.20	0.21	0.27	0.15	0.11	0.11
	46.42	84.28	77.19	81.69	136.16	79.25	91.35	88.75
Sierra Leone constituencies								
Government	0.96	1.74	12.21	12.92	25.67	14.94	1.08	1.05
Black labor:								
Manual	7.61	13.82	5.06	5.35	8.14	4.74	6.01	5.95
Salaried	—*	—	—	—	1.77	1.03	4.30	4.18
Tribal authorities	0.09	0.16	0.04	0.04	0.07	0.04	0.07	0.07
	8.66	15.72	17.31	18.31	35.65	20.75	11.46	11.25

*Data not available.
Source: Hoogvelt and Tinker, 1978.

authorities of the iron-producing province. The revenues did, however, secure the continued service of the local state in serving the interests of the multinational.

In the 1960s and early 1970s, a new factor began to progressively frustrate the financial position of the company. This concerned the appearance and the rise of a new participant: a contingent of black salaried staff. In response to pressures for indigenization after independence, Delco began to recruit black managerial, clerical, and technical supervisory staff, most of whom were not "productive" in the usual sense. The mining agreements of 1967 and 1972 formulated this indigenization program in increasingly stringent terms: By the time of its closure, Delco employed some 218 supervisory salaried staff, of whom 164 were Sierra Leoneans earning an average annual salary of £3,041. While the total of the 164 black supervisory employees' salaries was substantially below that of the 54 white supervisory employees (who received on average £12,000 in 1975) it had grown substantially in the previous decade. In 1974, this black salaried contingent received a total income of £422,320, not much below the £513,215 paid as wages to black manual laborers, who numbered 2,317 (giving an average black wage of £221, compared with an average black salary of £3,041).

This indigenization program was difficult to justify on the usual commercial terms of efficiency and productivity. As the figures in the table suggest, we should interpret the bonanza in black salaried staff as an attempt by the company to retain the approval and support of influential groups in Sierra Leone. These tactics only delayed the company's ultimate shutdown, and by the mid-1960s, expanding indigenous pressure, coupled with the prospect of diminishing returns from the mine, induced the company to leave. In doing so, it was simply following a strategy for survival in a market context.

What is revealing about Delco's history are the numerous instances of conflict and coercion that manifest themselves in the firm's income statements. For example, in the early colonial period, British troops were deployed on the company's behalf to defuse a strike by black employees. Earlier, in the same period, black males were induced to leave agricultural employment to work in the mine to earn cash to pay marriage and head taxes imposed by tribal chiefs. These tribal chiefs derived their authority and power from the colonial administration. Prior to colonization, they had little power and could easily be "destooled" by tribal members. By bolstering the chiefs' power, the colonial administration increased its ability to administer and control the local population. Finally, in the weeks prior to the firm's shutdown, there were widespread press reports that a £2 million loan, made to the company by the Sierra Leone government, had been secured by bribing senior government officials.

These instances underscore the conflict and exploitation surrounding the distribution of Delco's income. The representation of Delco's financial history in terms of three institutional regimes highlights different states in the struggle over Delco's income and the specific forms that struggle took. What remains open is the question of how successfully the Delco venture was carried out. Is it sufficient to look to the shareholders' profits in appraising such activities, or should the effects on all parties be scrutinized? If the latter then what criteria should be used; particularly in assessing the distribution of income for multinationals such as Delco?

What the Delco incident neglects is the spurious accuracy underlying income distribution numbers that accountants provide. This arbitrariness, while frequently played down by accountants, is often an important factor in the frauds and deceits inflicted on the investing public by unscrupulous management. The next examples—Ponzi schemes and California pyramids—examine a range of frauds that show what happens when greedy investors and unscrupulous promoters meet under conditions of high uncertainty and arbitrariness.

4

Ponzi Schemes and California Pyramids

Ponzi Schemes and Home-Stake

Introduction

Many miles below the sea's surface, there are deep fissures in the ocean floor. These fissures are openings that lead to the molten core of the earth. The ocean floor surrounding the fissures is extremely rich in mineral deposits; plant and animal life are warmed by the hot water that flows through the openings.

The fissures are important field-laboratories for scientists. Not only are they thought to be vital in the processes by which the sea rejuvenates itself, but their unique climatic conditions and the presence of certain mineral deposits create a chemical environment similar to that under which life itself may have begun. Thus they provide a live laboratory of unusual and extreme conditions under which some very important questions may be investigated.

Ponzi and pyramid schemes are to accounting what ocean floor fissures are to biochemistry and oceanography. They represent extreme and unusual circumstances atypical of the mundanities of everyday investing. They are in the same league as the most audacious and extravagant confidence tricks, such as selling the Eiffel Tower, the Brooklyn Bridge, or Buckingham Palace.

From another point of view, however, buying into a California pyramid scheme or a Ponzi scheme is no different from investing in General Motors or Dupont. First, they all involve an outlay followed by an uncertain return (they differ not in principle, but rather only in the degree of uncertainty of their returns). Second, they all attract soothsayers and financial medicine men who can conjure up scenarios that portray risky prospects as sure bets. Finally, the accountant's job is the same in all cases: to decide, at various intermediate stages prior to completion of the venture, how much profit has been earned and what the investment is worth. These commonalities make Ponzi and pyramid schemes especially instructive for accountants. As with the ocean-bed fissures of oceanography, many of the complexities are stripped away; what is left exposed are the elements that disrupt the accountant's fine calculations.

Ponzi schemes are named after Charles Ponzi, a confidence trickster who operated in Boston in 1919–20. Ponzi offered investors a return of $1.40 for every $1 they invested over a 90-day period. Some investors were indeed given such a return, but only in order to elicit a further contribution from them. But these dividends were not paid out of profits earned from trading; they were, in effect, paid out of the capital contributions of subsequent investors. In British terminology, this is none other than the infamous practice of "teeming and lading." On either side of the Atlantic, the accountant's puzzle is the same: Were such dividends paid out of capital or out of profits? In Charles Ponzi's case, the courts decided that the payments were made out of capital and sentenced him to five years for larceny and fraud. In the meantime, Ponzi had collected $10 million from investors.

We will examine three cases: two recent Ponzi schemes (Home-Stake Production Company and S-J Mineral Associates) and California pyramid schemes. All three are haunted by one of the most fearsome ghosts ever sent to plague accounting methodologists: the Isit-income, Isit-capital ghost.

Mediums and Messages: The Packaging of Financial Data

Home-Stake was a Tulsa-based company started by Robert S. Trippet in 1955. Its primary form of business was managing oil and gas drilling projects. Home-Stake's appeal to investors was as an income shield for tax purposes. Every year the company announced its drilling plans and invited subscriptions from investors. A separate company was then set up to manage the activity. Home-Stake usually retained a reversionary interest in the subsidiary that was to be satisfied only after satisfaction of the claims of investors.

The schemes operated as a tax shelter for investors; their entire contribution was allocated to intangible drilling costs. As with all such oil-drilling funds in the United States, this meant that the entire investment could be written off immediately against taxable income. If an investor were in the highest tax bracket, 70 percent, then 70¢ out of every dollar of otherwise taxable income would be saved. In the worst of all possible situations, in which no oil was found, the net loss of the investor was 30¢ on every dollar invested.

The investors' tax write-off could be increased by borrowing part of the initial outlay, as the entire investment was deductible, not just the investor's own contribution. For instance, an investor could contribute a total of $100,000: $20,000 out of pocket and $80,000 borrowed from a bank. At the 70 percent tax bracket, the tax savings would be $70,000 even though only $20,000 was contributed from personal funds.

Of course, Home-Stake was never promoted as a mere tax-saving scheme; it was portrayed as an extremely lucrative investment opportunity. Because Home-Stake units were sold directly to the public rather than through brokers, the company avoided much of the expert scrutiny that is part of the SEC's system for monitoring the selling activities of brokers. For example, if Home-Stake had been sold through brokers, investors would have automatically received a prospectus: a document describing various matters concerning the investment, regulated with regard to content, veracity, and mode of presentation. Investors in Home-Stake received a prospectus only if they requested one. Instead, investors and their advisors were sent a copy of the "black book," a promotional document that emphasized the profit opportunities and tax benefits of the venture. The black book was extremely simple and naive, and it is surprising that so many investors accepted its content without question. A sample form from the black book is provided (p. 42): it details the annual profits (before and after taxes) that an investor could expect on a total investment of $20,000. The black book claims that such an investment would yield a before-tax percentage return on investment of 302 percent and an after-tax return on investment of 764 percent.

A successful Ponzi scheme relies on much more than unwarranted financial optimism: the key to its success lies in understanding the dynamics of investor expectations and how those expectations may be manipulated over time. For Home-Stake, the first step in this process was to establish a "medium," steeped in respectability and reliability, through which to deliver its sales pitch and financial message. Through his own contacts and those

Table 4.1.   Home-Stake's Return on a $20,000 Investment

Year	Disregarding Taxes	Considering Taxes (Assume 58% Bracket)
1970	$ 250	$ 190
1971	2,520	2,086
1972	4,300	3,559
1973	5,480	4,536
1974	6,460	5,347
1975	7,150	5,919
1976	7,260	6,010
1977	7,600	6,291
1978	7,350	6,084
1979	6,920	5,728
1980	5,810	4,809
1981	4,810	3,982
1982	3,990	3,303
1983	2,765	2,289
1984	2,140	1,771
1985	1,620	1,341
1986	1,280	1,060
1987	1,625	1,345
	$ 79,330	$ 65,650
Add: Salvage	1,055	1,035
	$ 80,385	$ 66,685
Less: Budget cost	20,000	7,715
Participants' total net profit	$ 60,345	$ 58,970
Total percentage profit	302%	764%

Source: Data compiled by author.

of an early colleague, William E. Murray, a well-known tax and estate lawyer, Trippet met key figures in the General Electric hierarchy. Eventually, over 20 current and former officials of General Electric contributed over $3.7 million to Home-Stake's oil-drilling programs. The First National Bank of New York (Citibank) was a similar target for Trippet. With senior executives from Citibank and General Electric ranking among Home-Stake investors, Trippet and his salesmen were able to claim a respectable, high-quality clientele. Hoyt Ammidon, Chairman of New York's U.S. Trust Company, became involved in this way, and he, in turn, was used to bait investors from J. Walter Thompson and other corporations.

Two other key figures were Kent Kilneman, a tax lawyer, and Martin Bregman, who ran a talent agency and managed the careers and monies of famous entertainers. Clients of both men, including Alan Alda, Candice Bergen, and Barbara Walters, made substantial investments in Home-Stake. Investors eventually brought class action suits against Kilneman and Bregman, accusing them of fraud, conspiracy, and failure to disclose their financial interests in Home-Stake (loans and commission). Both men vigorously denied the charges.

Siegel and Golburt, a firm of certified public accountants, was accused by the IRS of receiving $42,000 in illegal commissions from Home-Stake for promoting its investments. Siegel and Golburt enjoyed a fiduciary relationship with its clients and was therefore especially well positioned to promote Home-Stake. The firm has denied that the payments were commissions but has not said what the payments were for.

In addition to New York, Los Angeles was the other major center selling Home-Stake's programs. The late Oscar A. Trippet, Robert Trippet's cousin, was a lawyer, a notable civic leader, and president of the Los Angeles Chamber of Commerce and the Hollywood Bowl Association. Harry Fitzgerald, a senior Home-Stake salesman, visited Oscar Trippet in 1964. Through Trippet, Fitzgerald met Donald McKee, an investment banker, stockbroker, and consultant, and Marvin B. Meyer, a partner in the prestigious Beverly Hills law firm of Rosenfeld, Meyer and Susman. The firm's clients included Jack Benny, Andy Williams, and Bobbie Gentry, all of whom invested in Home-Stake. The firm of Rosenfeld, Meyer and Susman did not accept any commissions because, as they later testified, it would have been unethical.

Home-Stake's greatest coup in enhancing its respectability involved Harry Heller, former deputy chief of the SEC's division of corporation finance, long-time personal friend of Manuel F. Cohen (chairman of the SEC, 1964–69), and partner of one of Wall Street's biggest and most prestigious old law firms: Simpson, Thatcher and Bartlett. In each of the years from 1964 to 1971, Heller passed upon the legality of, and thus, according to investor suits against him, lent his reputation to the veracity of, Home-Stake's promotion literature. There was no evidence to suggest that Heller acted fraudulently or that any of the other partners of Simpson, Thatcher and Bartlett were in any way involved.

Home-Stake's sales force numbered 24 at one stage and was made up of wealthy former stockbrokers and corporate executives. They were all well connected and held positions as vice-presidents. One was a well-spoken Englishman who had taught economics at Oxford and Harvard. The sales force dealt with the less wealthy and less prominent clients of Home-Stake. It operated on extravagant expense accounts, entertaining potential clients at places like the 21 Club and the Brussels Restaurant in New York City.

There is more to a Ponzi scheme than assembling a formidable selling team, however. More important is the way that team plays the game. Effective game playing requires an understanding of the psychological and social dynamics of investor expectations and of how those expectations can be manipulated. The secret of Trippet's success lay in his appreciation of the importance of these aspects and of serendipity in financial analysis: the importance of pleasant surprises in eliciting additional investment contributions. To this end, investors were not merely promised a handsome return on their initial investment, but frequently received larger and more prompt returns than had been originally promised. For example, a group of New Yorkers committed $200,000 in 1966 and $365,750 in 1967. When their returns exceeded what they had been led to expect, they increased their investments by an additional $2.2 million in 1968 and $1.3 million in 1969. They curtailed their involvement when returns began to fall dramatically below the projected return of 700 percent.

There was an additional twist to Home-Stake's relationship with its investors: not everyone was paid the same percentage rate of dividends on investments. For example, the former treasurer of General Electric invested $50,000 in 1970 and obtained a return of $2,418 or 4.8 percent. A Western Union executive invested $60,000 at about the same time and was paid a dividend of $6,220 or 10.4 percent. The intention of this individualized dividend policy was clear: dividends were ways of making investors happy so they would make further donations. People differ in their happiness thresholds, so dividend payouts were attuned to individual cases.

A surprising number of investors kept silent when their returns diminished or ceased. A few larger investors were given partial refunds and some participants were offered common stock in Home-Stake in exchange for their oil-drilling units. In other cases investors were advised to donate their holdings to a charity and then take a further tax write-off based on an exorbitant valuation of the units by Home-Stake. The valuation was contained in an "evaluation report," a document that investors could present to the IRS if they were challenged. As soon as units were donated to a charity, dividends on those units were either curtailed or stopped. Charities that benefited from these donations included the American Cancer Society, the American Red Cross, Harvard University, the Salvation Army, the Boy Scouts, and (a favorite in parts of Beverly Hills) Actors and Others for Animals. Needless to say, the IRS is challenging all tax deductions relating to Home-Stake.

The Public Watchdogs: The SEC, the IRS, and Independent Auditors

A great deal of evidence was available to the SEC that suggested that all was not well at Home-Stake. Investors brought suits against the company in 1966, 1968, 1971, and 1972. All alleged violations of the securities laws. Unfortunately, all were settled out of court and none was disclosed in SEC filings until 1971.

The local office of the SEC in Fort Wayne, Indiana was advised of the disparities in the dividend payments to investors. However, the lawyers in Fort Wayne had little experience; the office was understaffed and was struggling to stay abreast of several other major cases in the area. The enforcement division of the SEC did not act on Home-Stake until 1973. The reason for the delay was the division's backlog of 13,000 written complaints about securities violations, together with the additional daily toll of telephone complaints. Because of this work load, the SEC was unable to investigate reports promptly enough to prevent the frauds; instead it relied on the prospectus to give full disclosure to investors.

The IRS began auditing Home-Stake in the late 1960s. The audits were directed at determining whether the company was paying sufficient tax on its oil-drilling business. They did not set out to establish whether funds that were collected were invested in oil drilling. The IRS passed $100 million in deductions taken by investors, and many of them took this to signify that the company had been scrutinized by the IRS. In reality, the IRS usually does little more than check the addition on the tax returns in such cases.

Home-Stake's activities might have been discovered much earlier if the authorities had noticed a number of irregularities concerning the audited statements. Home-Stake changed auditors three times between 1965 and 1968. The 1967 statements were qualified. Three of the auditors were small Tulsa firms. Although Home-Stake itself was audited, the partnerships through which contributors' monies were supposedly invested annually were never audited. Consequently, there was never any independent verification that the money of contributors had actually been invested.

The Collapse of Home-Stake

In mid-September 1973, the SEC filed a suit against Home-Stake; within three weeks the company was declared bankrupt and was being reorganized. A summary of receipts, expenditures, and assets of Home-Stake for its entire period of operation (from the early 1960s through 1972) was estimated in mid-1974 as follows:

Table 4.2. Estimates of Home-Stake's Receipts and Payments from the Early 1960s through 1972 and Assets Held at September 1974

			$M
Revenues			
From the sale of investment units in oil			130
Issues of common stock			3
Total revenue to be accounted for			133
Expenses and repayments to investors			
Oil drilling expenses	21		
Returned to investors	30		
		51	
Assets found by Coopers and Lybrand			
Noncash	18		
Cash	4		
		22	
Assets allegedly misappropriated by Robert S. Trippet	6		
Assets accounted for			79
Assets not accounted for (September 1974)			54

As the financial statement shows, Ponzi's $10 million was small change compared with the $133 million that Home-Stake raised during the years it was soliciting money from the public. Some of these funds were accounted for in terms of oil-drilling expenses ($21 million), funds returned to investors ($30 million), and assets on hand ($22 million); however, a thumping $54 million was unaccounted for and a further $6 million was allegedly misappropriated by Robert Trippet.

Did Home-Stake invest any funds in productive assets? If we were to rank Home-Stake's investment opportunities by their wealth-creating capacities, what would such a productive opportunity schedule look like? The trouble with undertaking such an isoquant analysis is that it neglects the crucial fact that the entire formulation is mediated by perceptions, and those perceptions may be formed by concrete experience, insight, creativity, daydreaming, fantasy, fictions, and figments of the imagination. All of these elements are expressed when a productive opportunity schedule is drawn. Indeed, some would argue that the more subjective, speculative, deviant, and crazy an entrepreneur's productive opportunity schedule, the better, because it is likely to reflect originality, enterprise, and technological innovation. But in such cases, how do we distinguish hallucination from insight, fact from fiction?

With the advantages of hindsight, we are able to say that there were more fantasies than facts in Home-Stake's productive opportunity schedule. The company supposedly spent $21 million on oil drilling; however, it was difficult to locate the assets acquired with these funds. Some investors did visit a site in the late 1960s in order to verify that Home-Stake was indeed in the oil business. The site was on a vegetable farm near Santa Clara in central California. Five wells had been drilled on the site. In order to make things look official, permission had been obtained from the vegetable farmer to paint some of his gray concrete irrigation pipes oil-field orange and code them with oil field markings. Unfortunately, no wells had been drilled near these pipes. Of the five wells that had been drilled, one was a legitimate 3,500-foot well, and at least three were shallow 500-foot wells. The company knew that there was no oil at 500 feet, but they showed the wells as assets on the books.

In the Home-Stake fraud, some of the richest, most famous, and most financially astute names in U.S. public life were persuaded to part with $133 million. Moreover, the entire operation was carried out right under the noses of public watchdogs: the Securities and Exchange Commission, the Internal Revenue Service, and (last but not least) the firm of independent auditors who had certified Home-Stake's accounts. What does the affair say about the performance of these regulatory bodies, especially the accounting and auditing profession?

Home-Stake's "accomplishment" may be attributed to two factors: the medium and the message. The message consisted of the financial details of the investment, which tempted so many of the best and the brightest with tax write-offs and prospective profits and returns. The medium was the manner in which the message was presented, or "packaged." While many accountants pay lip service to McLuhan's dictate that the medium is the message, few appreciate its profound applicability to the conditions in which accountants and decision-makers typically operate: conditions of ignorance and uncertainty. In the real world, it is the medicine man, the zealot, the demagogue, or the wizard who is king, not a mythical sophisticated investor. To ignore the overwhelming presence of such actors, by trying to develop narrow, technical accounting standards, is likely to prove disastrous. As Ralph A. Hart, former chairman of Heublein said of Trippet, "he was such a good salesman, I just kept on buying." He bought over $322,000 of investments between 1961 and 1971.

Implications for Sophisticated Investors and Superstars

One of the principal assumptions underlying much of the theorizing and policy making in financial accounting is the sophisticated investor hypothesis (Dyckman, Downes, and Magee, 1975, pp. 3–4). This hypothesis (which is not really a hypothesis but more an article of faith because those who use it show little interest in testing its veracity) asserts that there exists in the stock market a cadre of sophisticated investors who know the "real" price of any share and are able to make money whenever the actual market price gets out of line with this "real" equilibrium price. And, so the argument goes, even if the bulk of investors are village idiots and sophisticates are rather thin on the ground, these conditions are quite sufficient to ensure that market prices will equilibrate and that therefore, overall, the market is efficient.

The extremes to which some are prepared to go in order to assert that the free market will give us an equilibrium have come under severe criticism by some eminent members of the economics profession. (Kornai, 1971; Kregel, 1975, 1976). Many criticisms center around the likeness between equilibrium theories and fairy tales—that everything will come out all right in the end. But even if we assume that the sophisticated investor is something more than a mythical fairy godmother, we still need to know what she looks like in order to verify her regular appearances at our stock markets. Now fortunately, a large number of very sophisticated people invested in Home-Stake Production Company. If we are to allow the veracity of the sophisticated investor hypothesis to ride on the fortunes of any one group, who better than those who invested in Home-Stake?

A list of the names of those who invested in Home-Stake reads like the cast of a movie starring the best of Wall Street, Hollywood, Main Street, and the legal profession. Estimates of the number of investors range between 2,400 and 3,000. That number includes some of the leading names in entertainment, business, legal circles, and politics. Here is a sample: Bob Dylan, $78,000; Jack Benny, $300,000; Senator Jacob Javits, Republican, New York, $28,500; R. McFall, President and Chairman of Western Union, $394,000; H.D. Brundage, Executive Vice-President of Finance, J. Walter Thompson Company, New York, $38,000; Alan Alda, $145,000; Dean P. Fite, Vice-President and Group Executive, Procter and Gamble Company, $162,000; David Begelman, President, Columbia Pictures, $25,000; Lewis W. Foy, President, Bethlehem Steel Corporation, $18,000; Ralph A. Hart, Director and former Chairman, Heublein, $322,000; Tony Curtis; Thomas S. Gates, former Defense Secretary and Director and former Chairman, Morgan Guaranty Trust Company of New York, $133,000; Mia Farrow; Walter Matthau, $200,000; Liza Minnelli, $231,000; Paul Miller, President, First Boston Corporation; G. Moore, former Chairman, First National City Bank of New York (Citibank—the nation's second largest) $407,903; W. Morton, President, American Express Corporation, $57,000; Senator E.F. Hollings, $19,000; Ted Westfall, Executive Vice-President, International Telephone and Telegraph Corporation, $466,000; David Cassidy, $300,000; Bobbie Gentry, $98,000; V.B. Day, former Vice-President of General Electric and former member of the Pay Board under the Economic Stabilization Program, $63,000; and F.J. Borch, former Chairman of General Electric, $440,920.

General Implications

With such a sophisticated investor group, the Home-Stake enterprise case affords an excellent opportunity to study the validity of those finance and economic theories premised on the so-called sophisticated investor hypothesis. These theories support a spectrum of political and public policy positions concerning the desirability of public regulation of auditing, accounting practice, and the stock market. The most "extreme" public policy viewpoint supported by these ideas is that state regulation to protect investors is unnecessary because a cadre of sophisticated investors exists, who can see through inflated stock prices and will express this judgment by selling the stock (causing a dramatic decline in its price). A corollary of this argument is that "private" watchdogs, such as the American Institute of Certified Public Accountants, are also unnecessary.

Since the sophisticated investors in Home-Stake faired rather badly, the sophisticated investor hypothesis is put into question together with the assembly of public policy proposals that depend on it. True, Home-Stake was found out in the end, and therefore, it might be argued, the market equilibrated correctly in the long run. What this argument forgets, however, is that while the market might be considered efficient in the aggregate and in the long run, this is little comfort to those investors impoverished in the process. Dynamic considerations are also ignored by those who subscribe to the self-correcting powers of the market. Investors who lose money are less likely to participate in savings and investment decisions in the future. This is an important social "cost externality" to ventures such as Home-Stake, in which the cost of misdemeanors—such as those perpetrated by Home-Stake—are not born by those immediately responsible but by other enterprises who, in the future, will have to pay a premium to induce now wary investors to part with their cash.

The Home-Stake experience provides little comfort for public watchdogs. When a manager pays a dividend, is that payment made out of genuine earnings or profits, or is it a return of the shareholders' capital? Ambiguity about this issue allowed management to represent Home-Stake as though it were earning substantial profits, an appearance that was convincing enough to entice investors to part with more cash. In other cases, this ambiguity about true profit performance has enabled managers to cover up gross inefficiencies and to misappropriate shareholders' assets. What is capital? and What is income? are important questions in ascertaining how well managers and directors have discharged their fiduciary responsibilities to owners. Accountants do not have adequate answers to these questions: the futuristic element in profit and earnings makes it very difficult for accountants to distinguish, with any certainty, between fact, wishful thinking, fantasy, and fraud. These circumstances expose a large number of small investors to predatory practices that, in many cases, the auditor is powerless to prevent.

S-J Minerals Associates

The Hour of Need

There is nothing quite like an external threat from a foreign power to rekindle a nation's spirit of unity and purpose. There are several rare and precious examples in our history: London during the darkest days of the blitz, or the United States at the height of the Iranian hostage crisis. During such times, internal differences are set aside and replaced with a unified effort for the common good. Old antagonisms and assumptions are put on the shelf; we discover new qualities in our fellow citizens, taste ever-so-briefly the awesome experience of comaraderie in working side by side with others, and forge lifelong memories and friendships.

The era of the oil crisis (and the energy crisis that succeeded it) could also be said to be such a period in U.S. history. The oil embargo and the subsequent demands of OPEC caused the U.S. government to unleash private enterprise from the fetters of regulation in order to increase energy supplies. Tax incentives, decontrol of oil and gas prices, and a multibillion dollar federal investment program were used to mobilize the private enterprise system to deal with the national emergency. It was a classic opportunity for private interest to work hand in hand with the public good.

S-J Minerals Associates exemplified the speed and flexibility with which private enterprise can react to a national need. The company was set up to exploit coal-mining opportunities. So fast did it respond to the nation's energy emergency that it began collecting money from investors long before it had any land to mine. In fact, because word had gotten around that the company's investments offered one-year-only tax advantages, subscriptions began pouring in before any prospectus had been prepared for potential investors. All this would have been unimportant if the company had eventually boosted the nation's energy stock. Unfortunately, it never mined one bucket of coal.

The Financial Medium and Message

One SEC official described S-J Minerals as the "Home-Stake of coal." There were many similarities between the two, including the presence of a large number of seemingly sophisticated investors and their advisors. Athletes, politicians, entertainers, and others were persuaded to part with huge amounts of money in return for promises of exorbitant profits and substantial tax deductions. Elvis Presley alone put in $505,000. Other subscribers included the former Maryland attorney general Francis Burch, the basketball star Spencer Haywood, and actress-model Margaux Hemingway.

S-J Minerals starred four supersalesmen: two members of a Boston law firm and two partners in a firm that, apart from selling tax shelters, sponsored Broadway musicals. (Their one and only hit was *Annie*.) Investors were offered tax shelter on $150,000 units. The trick was that they only had to find $30,000 in cash; the remaining $120,000 was contributed by writing a promissory note that the investors could repay out of their shares of the coal-mining profits. Thus investors who contributed $100,000 of their own funds and wrote a promissory note for $400,000, making a total contribution of $500,000, would receive a $250,000 tax reduction, assuming they were in the 50 percent marginal tax bracket. A total of 720 investors contributed $20 million in cash and $92 million in promissory notes in 60 hectic days. The stock was heavily oversubscribed: instead of floating one partnership, the sponsors were forced to create four in order to keep pace with the level of demand. In the rush to meet tax deadlines, many investors subscribed before knowing which of the four partnerships their money had been committed to. (Each partnership was a separate venture.) Moreover, very few of the investors displayed the degree of financial acumen one might expect of "sophisticated investors." One group of Denver residents formed an investment association called U.S. Exploration Associates and donated $100,000 on the strength of an offering memo. They did not run a credit check on any of the sponsors because, according to one of their number, "It was our understanding he [one of the sponsors] was from a well-to-do good family" (the *Wall Street Journal*, February 5, 1979). When the sponsors did get around to producing a prospectus, they used one that had been written for another tax shelter scheme and attached a legal opinion as to the tax benefits that was written for a different coal mine in a different state. Overall, the projected return on investment was 43 percent; this would have required mining 2.6 million tons of coal a year and selling it for $10.50 a ton. At the time they made these forecasts, S-J Minerals had not purchased any land and the market price of a ton of coal was only $7.50.

The "Real" Assets

S-J Minerals's process of acquiring land was something of a fiasco. Two of the investors were shown to a tract near a huge mining area in Wyoming. The geologist who took them proceeded to sell them a geological survey for $30,000. This was a copy of a government survey that could be purchased for $3. Finally, the geologist accepted a down payment of $50,000 for the land, neglecting to mention that he didn't actually own it.

Undeterred, the two lawyers from S-J Minerals eventually unearthed the real owner of the land and, because of its "obvious" potential, paid him $300,000 to lease 11,000 acres for one year. Then setbacks began to materialize. First, the IRS ruled that all schemes starting after a certain date did not qualify for tax deductions. The SEC has since claimed that S-J Minerals back-dated its lease in order to qualify. Second, it was discovered that the lease only referred to surface rights: all coal below the surface belonged to the federal government (barring 400 acres). With few exceptions, the federal government had not sold a coal lease for several years and was not likely to sell one for several more. Even if S-J Minerals had the authority to mine in the area, a survey by a mechanical engineering firm indicated that $20 million would be required for a plant and equipment to mine the amount of coal they wanted to produce. When, after several years, an investor who had put in $30,000 asked why mining had not begun, he was told that a herd of elk was grazing on the land tract and was holding up production.

The SEC estimated that of the $20 million collected by S-J Minerals, $3.6 million was taken by its two lawyer-owners; $6.5 million went into companies they owned or controlled; they spent $400,000 on a jet, and $1.9 million was used to buy out another partnership. The two owners who managed the theatrical agency obtained $1.4 million; other salesmen took $2.6 million, and the law firm that supplied the tax opinion (in which one of S-J Minerals's owners used to be a partner) received $370,000 as compensation. These outlays virtually exhausted the $20 million of cash receipts.

Soon after the SEC began its investigations, the four original sponsors of S-J Minerals transferred their interests in the assets and liabilities to a newly formed company, Java Mining, and appointed a president for it, James T. Melillo. Neither the new company nor its president had had any previous mining experience. The original sponsors then moved into a new tax shelter: diamond mining in South-West Africa (Namibia). S-J Minerals investors were then invited to subscribe for shares in the new venture, a company called Imperial Finance N.V.

In September 1978, the SEC filed a civil complaint in a federal court in Boston accusing twenty men and seventeen companies of violations of security laws. Many have since signed consent decrees in which they have neither admitted nor denied guilt but have agreed to be enjoined from violating securities laws.

The challenge to accounting in the S-J Minerals case is much the same as in the Home-Stake case. If, as a society, we wish to improve the efficiency with which we select projects for investment, then the accountant must begin to assess the realism of financial predictions pertaining to these investments.

What can we learn from the antics of those running operations such as Home-Stake? What kinds of accounting, auditing, and other controls should be installed to improve the integrity of investment processes?

A way of investigating these issues is to take the most extreme case of investment uncertainty: the pyramid party. This is essentially a lottery where a successful outcome is pure luck. In such cases, where there is no relevant information about the future, we can study the dynamics of situations without the interference and pretensions of accounting "insights" about the future.

Income Determination at a Pyramid Party

Pyramid schemes started in Oregon in 1979 and subsequently flourished in California. At the height of their popularity, dozens of meetings involving thousands of people were being held every night. Hundreds of people were arrested and fined for contributing to an "endless chain." Banks experienced a 50 percent increase in demand for large-size dollar bills and faced a run on safety deposit boxes requested by winners who wanted to protect their winnings from the IRS. As the police intensified their campaigns against pyramid parties, the sponsors responded with weekend meetings and concerts attended by thousands of people, who celebrated the pyramid phenomenon and reaffirmed their belief in the constitutional rights of citizens to spend their money as they pleased. A prestigious Los Angeles law firm announced that it would champion these rights in the courts by challenging the constitutionality of the position taken by the authorities.

A pyramid scheme works as follows: imagine a pyramid of people with one person at the top level, two at the second, four at the third, eight at the fourth, and so on until we reach the bottom (sixth) level, where there are 32 people. This last level is made up of the latest recruits. They contribute $1,000 each to the pyramid; $500 goes to the person at the top, and the remaining $500 is divided among the people immediately above the new recruits. As soon as 32 newcomers have been recruited (this may take hours, days, or weeks), the person at the top of the pyramid is fully paid off with $16,000 and leaves. The pyramid then splits into two new pyramids with one person at the top and sixteen at the bottom. Each new pyramid then embarks on a search for 32 more new recruits.

The goal of members of a pyramid is to climb to the top for the $16,000 prize. This is in addition to the refund of their original $1,000, which is provided by the 32 new recruits. There is an incentive, therefore, for every member of the pyramid to attract new recruits in order to move up the hierarchy.

Elaborate rituals evolved at the parties at which the transfer of money (ostensibly nontaxable gifts) takes place. The proceedings are usually initiated by "leaders" or "shakers" (often salespersons in working life) who bear witness to the profits that can be made and the importance, in times of inflation, of "helping one another." New recruits are then invited to come forward and their "gifts" are divided according to the rules and entitlements of the particular party. Some parties collect as much as $60,000 a night.

With pyramid party membership growing exponentially, it wasn't long before the reservoir of potential recruits began to dry up. Pyramids found it increasingly difficult to fill each successive level; members became anxious that they might not recoup their outlay; arguments, fights, and, in some cases, shootings began to occur. The police received hundreds of complaints every day (especially from concerned spouses), and in desperation, members of existing pyramids applied increasing pressure on neighbors, friends, relatives, sons, wives, fathers and lovers to join.

How does someone decide whether to stake $1,000 at a particular pyramid party? What is the maximum amount someone should pay to buy out a position on an existing pyramid? Having already invested $1,000 in a pyramid, how much can a person reasonably expect to earn at various intervals of progress up the pyramid? (People who answer "nothing" must be prepared to sell for a zero amount any position they might hold on the pyramid ladder.) The problem of determining the amount of profit that has been earned during a period is a generic problem that applies to "real" investments as well as to pyramids. Is accountants' advice to investors on forming realistic expectations about "real" investments any better than their advice on gambling and pyramid schemes? There seems to be strong grounds for believing that, from an accounting viewpoint, there is little difference between capital markets and pyramid parties.

5

National Student
Marketing Corporation

How many corporate executives are capable of taking charge of a firm with a share price of $6 and, in little over a year, achieving a price of $140? Cortes W. Randell did just that. In his heyday, his personal holdings grew by $100,000 per week until they reached an estimated $3 million. He enjoyed a mansion on the Potomac, a 55-foot yacht, and a $700,000 jet named Snoopy. By early 1970, only two years after joining the company (and well before his thirty-fifth birthday) Randell had acquired 1.3 million of the 11.8 million outstanding shares of the National Student Marketing Corporation (NSM).

In December 1974, Federal Judge Harold R. Tyler sentenced "Cort" Randell to 18 months in prison and fined him $40,000. In addition, Judge Tyler imposed fines and prison sentences on two certified public accountants: members of the largest firm of accountants in the United States: Peat, Marwick, Mitchell and Co. It was estimated that investors lost well over $100 million as a result of NSM's collapse. And the hoodwinked investors were not of the naive little old lady variety. Very few of NSM's shares were publically traded. The company's major shareholders were institutions that purchased shares in blocks subject to restrictions on their resale. Numbered among the financial sophisticates that invested heavily in NSM were Morgan Guaranty Trust Company, First National City Bank (Citibank), Harvard University Endowment Fund, and the securities firm Donaldson, Lufkin and Jenrette.

Aftershocks from the NSM debacle were still being felt in the 1980s. In what was described as a landmark case, the SEC charged two prestigious law firms of violating federal laws by failing to disclose unfavorable information about the company to shareholders. Both firms were accused of failing to disclose information they had learned about NSM in connection with a 1969 merger plan. The SEC charged that the firms knew that the company's auditors had recommended that significant changes be made in NSM's financial statements, and that the shareholders had approved the merger without knowledge of the changes. The case centered around the controversial question of when lawyers must blow the whistle on the wrongdoings of corporate clients, if such information has come to them by virtue of their special relationship of trust and confidence. With the exception of Lord, Bissell and Brooks, a Chicago law firm, most of the principal defendants, including White and Case, a New York law firm, and the company itself, had settled the suit by 1978 without admitting or denying any of the charges. In January 1980, the respected firm of Lord, Bissell and Brooks and two of its partners agreed to a settlement with the SEC in which they would pay $1.3 million into a fund for shareholders. The judge noted in his findings that in circumstances such as those of NSM, lawyers have a responsibility to disclose any wrongdoings to the authorities, even if information about such wrongdoings is obtained through a privileged relationship.

What of NSM's auditors, Peat, Marwick, Mitchell and Co.? A jury convicted the partners in the firm in November 1974 of making false statements in NSM's 1969 proxy statement. This was the first time public accountants from a major auditing firm had been sentenced to jail for fraud. The partner in charge was given the maximum fine of $10,000 and a one-year term, with all but 60 days suspended. The second partner was fined $2,500 and given a one-year term with all but ten days suspended. At the time of sentencing, Judge Tyler told the two defendants that he did not want to single them out for "an opprobrium which is really shared by many people in your profession and indeed in many professions including my own—some sort of myopia as to what is really the public responsibility of someone who performs services as a public accountant." The judge noted, "I seriously doubt that you are any worse than many in your profession. And, indeed, I suspect you are much better. . . . As individuals, I am most sure you are." The judge identified the main issues of the case as whether the defendant was "guilty of blinding himself to facts that he should have inquired about" and whether he was "so recklessly indifferent to what was going on [as] to be culpable" (the *Wall Street Journal*, December 30, 1974). The jury concluded that both men were guilty. What the jury, the judge, and many commentators, then and since, failed to realize was that the ringleader and principal culprit had escaped scot-free and to this day has never been brought to justice. The name of this villain is Generally Accepted Accounting Principles.

To understand what happened to NSM, it is necessary to have a sense of the spirit and climate of the times, especially the electrifying climate of Wall Street at the time. In NSM's case, this climate was made up of two intoxicating ingredients: the youth movement and the earnings per share craze. In combination, these made NSM the kind of growth stock that promised investors untold overnight riches.

National Student Marketing had sold Wall Street on the "baby boom" business: that campuses throughout the country represented a vast reservoir of virtually untapped purchasing power just waiting for the arrival of the first entrepreneur. It had created a marketing organization that was designed for tapping this potential. Campus marketing schemes were devised for brand-name clients such as Eastern Airlines, American Airlines, General Motors's Pontiac Division, Clairol, Fabergé, and Chicken Delight. Headed by the then 28-year-old Cort Randell and Andrew Tobias, the brilliant 21-year-old vice-president, NSM was offering to lead American business to the new campus El Dorado.

The second ingredient in the breathtaking rise in NSM's share price was Wall Street's obsession with earnings per share as the formula for valuing a company's stock. Indeed, Wall Street's belief in this one measure transcended rationality. Earnings per share took on an almost mystical quality. It solved the problems that all myths solve; it made known the unknowable, replaced ignorance with meaning and provided a rationale for actions and decisions in situations in which decision-makers would otherwise be impotent. There are many similarities between religious and stock market belief systems. Both systems are dependent on faith—in the stock market it is faith in earnings per share as an indication of the intrinsic, long-term, real value of a share. The logic is extremely simple: the real, underlying value of a share (not necessarily its present market value) depends on the profits or earnings that will be earned for shareholders in the future. Thus, if we begin with known facts (the earnings of the most recent year of operations that have been audited and certified as correct by highly respected and handsomely remunerated certified public accountants) and qualify these historical and verified amounts with subjective estimates by managers and other experts as to their future growth rate, then we have a way of establishing the present value for the stock. For example, IBM's shares might be selling for 20 times every dollar of historical (1979) profits earned per share; a railroad stock may be selling for only five times its 1979 earnings. The difference is due to the belief that IBM's earnings will grow tremendously, while the earnings per share of the railroad stock may well decline. Thus, we begin with "objective," historical earnings, and temper them with subjective estimates as to their growth prospects, to create a basis for estimating the real, underlying value of the share.

One way an investor can become wealthy is to estimate the real, underlying value of a share more accurately and more quickly than the rest of the market. If the market values a share at, say, ten times its 1979 earnings of $2 per share, but you have private information that suggests that the earnings will grow much faster than is generally expected, then you can make a killing. If you value each share at 15 times the historical earnings ($30 per share) and buy up to 100,000 shares at the current market price of $20 each; then when the market eventually comes around to your way of seeing things (driving the price up to $30) you will have just made $1 million.

So where are the weaknesses in this seemingly infallible chain of logic? How was it that some of the most sophisticated investors and prestigious custodians of society's savings lost over $100 million in NSM? We can begin by examining the historically "objective" facts that made up the 1969 profit figures that Peat, Marwick, Mitchell and Co. certified.

The total reported profit for NSM for the year ending August 31, 1969, was $3,865,080. This figure was arrived at by starting with the sales revenue earned during the year and then deducting the expenses incurred in producing those sales. Our problems begin when we attempt to determine what the costs of generating the revenue were for the 1969 fiscal year. For instance, one expense item, described in a footnote as "deferred new product development and start-up costs," amounted to $533,000 and was actually incurred in 1969, but it was not charged as an expense in that period. Clearly it was felt that the sales of future periods would benefit from these expenditures, and it was therefore those future periods, not 1969, that should suffer the cost of the items.

A similar item was noted as the "unamortized cost of prepaid sales programs," in the amount of $1,048,000. This amount was spent in 1969 but was not included in figuring the profits for that period. Instead, $486,000 spent in 1968 was offset against the revenue earned in 1969, and the $1,048,000 was carried forward to be set against revenues for future periods. If this latter item and the $533,000 on deferred new product development had been expensed in 1969, profits would have been slashed by approximately $1.5 million. Assuming that the stock market maintained the same expectations about historical earnings and share price—the price-earnings ratio—then this fall in earnings would have translated into a 40 percent reduction in the value of NSM's shares: from $140 down to around $85. This demonstrates the extreme sensitivity of share prices to historical earnings and, therefore, the overriding importance of getting the profit figure right.

Did the "unamortized cost of prepaid sales programs" and the "deferred new product development and start-up costs" belong in the 1969 profit calculations? Accountants are supposed to appeal to the "matching principle" to resolve such problems. Accordingly, they should allocate or match such expenditures to those periods that derive the benefit from them. Thus, if 1970, 1971, and 1972 sales benefited from carefully laid plans and programs set up in 1969, then the expense of setting up those plans may be properly carried over (capitalized) from 1969 and offset against the sales of 1970, 1971, and 1972. But who is to say, in September 1969, whether the sales of 1970, 1971, and 1972 will benefit from expenses incurred in 1969? Moreover, it is not sufficient simply to know whether the future periods will benefit: we need to know the degree of relative benefit so that we have a way of apportioning the costs among those periods.

The discerning reader will have observed that the above problem presupposes a degree of foresight and ingenuity not normally associated with accountants or their principles. How are we to distinguish expenditures of the catastrophic type from daring, enterprising, creative, inventive, and above all, profitable investments?

We may now return to the NSM's accounts with a less sanguine eye. In 1968, the assets included $1,763,000 in "unbilled receivables," and the profits for 1968 were enhanced by this amount. When we look at the 1969 accounts, which include the 1968 figures for comparative purposes, the 1968 "unbilled receivables" are shown as $945,000. A sum of $818,000 seems to have "disappeared." Presumably the 1968 profit was overstated because some of these receivables turned out to be uncollectible. No mention is made of this retroactive correction in the 1969 accounts.

Difficulties in pinpointing the expenses for 1969 are surpassed only by difficulties in pinpointing the sales revenues for 1969. According to the realization principle, accountants should only include sales revenue items in calculating the profit for a period if the revenue has been "substantially earned." A degree of tautology may be detected here between our matching principles and our realization principles. Matching requires that we associate costs against revenue, while realization requires that we include sales only when the productive work has been substantially completed. But how do we know if work has been substantially completed except with reference to the costs? What we include in the cost for a period depends on the revenue for that period! The argument is circular: each principle cites the other as its authority.

Included in NSM's 1969 earnings was a $369,000 profit on the sale of various Canadian subsidiaries. Erstwhile vice-president Andrew Tobias notes in his book, *The Funny Money Game,* that these sale agreements were signed some 90 days after the end of the 1969 accounting period. Did this profit properly belong to 1969? Who knows! No doubt it could be argued that most of the painstaking negotiations had taken place before the accounting year-end, and therefore, the costs of management's time were already included in the 1969 accounts. It would be only right, then, that the benefits be shown there also. These arguments lose some of their impact when we learn that no cash had actually been paid to NSM by the buyers of the subsidiaries. Nor was it their intention to do so in the near future. The managers of NSM's Canadian subsidiary (who happened to be the buyers of CompuJob) "paid" NSM with one-year and five-year personal promissory notes.

Cash in hand is not a prerequisite for recording the profit on a sale: credit sales contribute to current profits as long as it can be established that the "accounts receivable" represent a genuine asset that will eventually mature into cash. In the case of promissory notes, additional security is often provided, an additional asset that the creditor can resort to if the promissory note is dishonored when it falls due. It is not surprising to learn, then, that the promissory notes were secured by 3850 shares, owned by the NSM's Canadian managers and other buyers. What is surprising is that they were shares in NSM. At the time the sales contracts were completed, the posted security was estimated to be worth about $400,000. Within one year, it had fallen to approximately $13,500.

An even more dubious item is represented by what Tobias describes as "the Killer Footnote": an item of $3,754,103, which about equaled the entire profit for 1968. The footnote stated that if you eliminated from the 1969 figures the $3,754,103 in the earnings of companies that were legally acquired by NSM after the year-end, then 1969 earnings would be only $110,977. This would drop the earnings per share from $1.35 to 4¢. In order to lend authority to this application of accounting principles, the chairman of Peat, Marwick, Mitchell and Co.'s ethics committee appeared at NSM's annual meeting and read those parts of generally accepted accounting principles that require that acquisitions made shortly after the end of a firm's financial year be included in the financial statements of that period.

If the 1969 profit figure is purged of all the dubious items discussed above, a reported profit of $3,865,080 is transformed into a $2,657,023 loss. This is not to say that this was the "real" result, whether viewed from 1969 standpoint (*ex-ante*) or with the advantages of hindsight (*ex-post*). All we can conclude is that the "real" result probably lies somewhere between these two figures (assuming we have dealt with all the major uncertainties).

On reading the auditor's report however, one might be forgiven for concluding that much greater weight could be attached to the accounting statements than the previous analysis would suggest:

> In our opinion, based upon our examination and the aforementioned reports of other independent public accountants, the accompanying consolidated balance sheet and statements of earnings, retained earnings and additional paid-in capital present fairly the consolidated financial position of National Student Marketing Corporation and subsidiaries at August 31, 1969, and the results of their operations for the year then ended, in conformity with generally accepted accounting principles applied on a basis consistent with that of the proceeding year in all material respects.

The blemishes on the books were by no means limited to 1969 figures. In entering a plea of guilty at his trial, Cortes Randell admitted that 1968 earnings were "more of an expectation or a hope than a firm assurance of income" (the *Wall Street Journal,* September 9, 1974). For example, $695,600 of NSM's 1968 pretax profits came from "unbilled receivables": earnings that the company hoped to eventually receive from marketing programs currently under development. Randell conceded that in the past such programs were carried forward on the books as assets long after it became clear that they had little or no value. He also admitted to boosting NSM's earnings by falsifying or altering letters from clients to show commitments to buy NSM's marketing services. One such letter showed a commitment to a $1.2 million program by General Motors's Pontiac Division. Others falsely showed American Airlines as committed to $534,000 and Eastern Airlines to $820,000.

It is the dynamics of "go-go" stocks that reveals their true nature. Such stocks may begin with an accounting fiction about the level of profits, but it is the nature of fictions that they quickly convert into facts. Indeed, the whole purpose of the NSM enterprise was to create a reality out of fictions. Exaggerated earnings figures, together with unfounded optimism about the future, produced a grossly overstated stock market price. That price was then "cashed in" by an exchange of shares through an acquisition or a merger. Thus, the profit fiction becomes a reality when used to acquire the "real" assets of other companies and, most importantly, provides additional material for creating even larger fictions in the future. It is this dynamic snowballing of fictions that underscores the part played by accounting data: accounting does not merely describe history passively, it helps create it.

In early 1970 NSM was poised on another era of acquisitions when the discrepancies finally started to emerge. At that time, NSM was ready to acquire three huge firms: National Tape ($60 million sales), Josten's ($70 million sales), and Champion Products ($50 million sales). Lawyers advised NSM to make a public announcement about the discrepancies, and in February 1970, the company announced a loss of $1.2 million on sales of $18 million for the three months ending November 30, 1969. Two days later, this was corrected to a loss of $1.5 million on sales of $14 million. (The discrepancy was attributed to an error in transcribing figures from one set of books to another.) The fortunes of NSM (and those of its investors) went downhill from then on. By August 1970, the shares stood at $3.50, a 98 percent drop from its high of $143 the previous December.

National Student Marketing has provided us with one further invaluable contribution to the theory of finance: evidence and insights into the psychological postures and mental dispositions of the various actors. Andrew Tobias's *The Funny Money Game* presents some excellent firsthand material in this regard. Tobias became vice-president of NSM at the age of 21. He resigned his position at age 23, soon after the collapse. During his brief reign, he watched the value of his stock options peak at $400,000 and then decline to around $5,000. He was not with the company long enough for the options to become exercisable.

How did Andrew Tobias justify remaining with such a precarious (albeit lucrative) venture? In his book, Tobias relates several rationalizations that lept into the breach when the need arose. There was always room for disbelieving the severity of the situation: would internationally prestigious accounting and law firms really risk their reputations by overlooking such questionable practices? There was also evidence that such practices were fairly commonplace. After all, where should one draw the line between the information supplied in accounting statements and that contained in public relations and advertising material? Indeed, is there any fundamental distinction between the two? Even when the last shred of doubt about the precise nature of the venture had left Tobias's mind, there was always the option of resigning, as soon as his stock options became exercisable.

There is something that can be easily lost in a review such as this: NSM was not run by particularly disreputable persons; they were a mixed bag with their fair share of idealism, morality, sincerity, and integrity. The original mission of bringing the fruits of business to the campus, to give youth its rightful stake in the consumer society, had been widely welcomed. And while it may not have the meaning it once had, the fact that Cortes Randell was a church deacon and was regarded by many as a deeply religious man should warn against an overly simplistic analysis of the situation. It is easy to forget that Cortes Randell once commanded the respect of Wall Street. As he told *Fortune* magazine: "Their confidence in me to succeed is what brought them here. Why do people like Morgan Guaranty buy the stock? Because they have talked to Cort Randell and they have confidence in what we are trying to accomplish" (Tobias, 1972, p. 244).

6

The Role of Accounting in Public Utility Pricing

The Role of Accounting in Resource Allocation and Income Distribution

Approximately one third of new capital raised on U.S. stock exchanges in the 1970s went into industries regulated not by market forces, but by accounting standards and practices. These are the utility industries: they include the familiar electricity, gas, and telephone giants of American Telephone and Telegraph, Con Edison Company, and General Telephone and Electronics Corporation, as well as numerous other power and telephone companies located throughout the U.S.

City and state authorities determine the rates at which utility services are charged to customers. Applications for rate increases are submitted by utilities to local public utilities commissions (PUCs) that are mandated to protect consumers from excessive price rises and to ensure that utilities do not abuse their quasi-monopolistic power as sole providers of services to the local community. Disputes between the PUCs and the utilities are usually resolved through the courts.

How are the rates or prices a utility is allowed to charge for its services determined? A utility's rates are determined on a cost-plus-profit basis. The amount of profit allowed is determined by applying a regulated profit percentage to the value of the company's investment plant, equipment, and other assets needed to produce the services. This investment is called the rate base.

The regulated profit percentage is usually set at a level that will give the company a return on its investment that is commensurate with what could be obtained on an alternative investment having an equivalent risk level. There are widespread differences between states both in how they define the rate base, and in what is allowed as an expense for rate determination purposes. The general procedure described in the following example shows how the rate-per-unit of service is arrived at in most cases.

Figure 6.1. The Determination of Utility Rate Charges

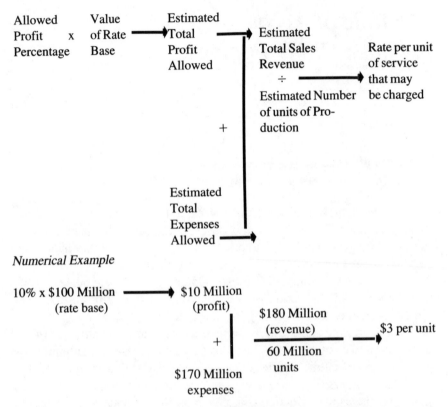

Numerical Example

In the example, the utility is allowed to charge its customers $3 per unit. This rate is arrived at as follows: On an investment of $100 million, the Public Utilities Commission allows the utility to earn $10 million (the regulated rate of return being 10 percent). To this profit allowance must be added the allowable expenses (assumed to be $170 million in this example) in order to arrive at the total allowable revenue of $180 million. With an estimated level of unit sales of 60 million, the final allowable price is set at $3 per unit. It is important to note that the final result depends entirely on the figures assumed at the outset, notably the values of the rate base and the total expenses. If the value of these parameters can be inflated, then the rate that is charged will also be increased.

These accounting calculations have rather important implications for the U.S. economy. The services produced by most utilities are priced by procedures analogous to that exemplified above. The prices that result affect consumers directly and indirectly because they are transmitted through the economy as costs of production of enterprises that consume utility services. In this way, utility services become embodied in virtually all goods and services produced by an economy. A customer in Detroit is affected by rate-fixing for utilities in California; export customers in Japan, Korea, and Ireland may pay prices that embody the cost of power and telephone services supplied in Texas. This procedure demonstrates the capacity of accounting to affect the material well-being of millions of people.

Let us look a little more closely at the calculation. Imagine that you are a divisional manager of a utility company that is just one division of a multiproduct conglomerate that evaluates, rewards, promotes, and fires divisional managers according to the level of profit they generate. When you borrow money for new investment, you must pay a rate of return that is competitive with market rates. Through the parent company, you are ultimately accountable to a shareholder group, composed mainly of large financial institutions. These investors are predominantly interested in dividend and capital growth and will either have you removed—or will achieve the same result by selling out to someone who will do the same—if you fail to achieve an adequate profit return. In these circumstances, what opportunities does the rate-fixing procedure afford you?

The calculation shown previously suggests that a rate increase may be achieved by inflating the value of the rate base or by padding total costs, or both. The desired result—increasing profits by increasing charges to customers—is attained by any of these options. Using the data from the previous example, let us assume that, for rate-fixing purposes alone, we create a "phantom expense" of $40 million. This expense is a "phantom" in that it never involves an actual cash payment of $40 million. We assume, however, that this is allowed as part of the total expenses used for establishing customer charges for 1981.

If this was the only change from the previous example, then according to the described procedure, total allowable expenses would increase from $170 million to $210 million, the estimated total revenue would rise to $220 million, and with the same 60 million units of production, the rate charged to customers would increase to $3.67 per unit. Since the additional "expense" requires no cash outflow, the utility's cash inflow increases by the full $40 million.

We can show how a phantom expense might arise by using the example of a utilities tax expense. If the phantom expense is a tax liability incurred in 1980, the payment to the IRS may be deferred: that is, the money is not paid over to the IRS until a specific set of contingencies arises. In some cases, these contingencies never arise, and therefore the tax liability may never be paid even though the "expense" might have been included for rate determination purposes in 1980.

Some states insist that utilities arrive at their rate by deducting future deferred tax liabilities from the total value of the assets. In the example, the rate base becomes $60 million ($100 million minus $40 million); the estimated profit allowed becomes $6 million; the estimated total sales revenue becomes $216 million ($210 million plus $6 million), and with 60 million units of production, the rate charged to customers becomes $3.6 per unit of service. The utility's cash inflow increases by $36 million through the increased charges to its customers.

If the rate base is unaffected by the deferred tax liability, the year-by-year rates charged to customers vary directly with the total expenses allowed—including the annual deferred tax charges—in this case, the full $40 million. The increase in customer rates will always be offset eventually, when some of the deferred taxes are actually paid over to the IRS, because the cash payment reduces the assets in the rate base which, in turn, results in a smaller total profit allowance for inclusion in the sales revenue which, finally, lowers the allowable rate per unit. As the rate base is permanently lowered for years subsequent to the payment to the IRS, customers eventually enjoy lower rates but, in the interim, future customers are being subsidized by current customers.

Even if all the deferred tax liability is eventually paid, current customers are being overcharged because the real cost of the deferred tax expense in 1980 is not the monetary value of the obligation, but the amount that the utility firm would need to invest in 1980 in order to realize the monetary amount when it falls due. For instance, if Manhattan Gas and Light owes the IRS $500 million in taxes in 1980, but payment is deferred until the year 2000, then, at an interest rate of 12 percent, the real present cost of these taxes is only $52 million, because this is all Manhattan Gas and Light need set aside and invest to provide for its future liability. Manhattan Gas and Light's current customers, however, are paying rates that were arrived at by adding the full $500 million to expenses in the 1980 rate calculation.

These observations apply only when the utility has to pay the deferred taxes at some future date. If for some reason the utiliy never pays over any of its accumulating deferred taxes, then customers' charges will be cumulatively inflated by this accumulating fictitious expense. This was a concern of the public utilities commissions in the states of New Mexico and Maine, where the rate base is not reduced by deferred tax expenses and, at the same time, these "expenses" appear to have little likelihood of falling due.

The real difficulty in this area is knowing if a current tax expense item is fictitious or real. In relation to deferred tax expenses, difficulties arise when a current expense item never actually materializes into a cash payment, or if it does materialize, it does so at such a distant date that its present cost is small and difficult to determine. Such possibilities arise, for example, in accounting for the investment tax credit and for accelerated depreciation. The accounting ambiguities in these areas create ample opportunities for excessive pricing by utilities.

The Investment Tax Credit

The investment tax credit is a reduction in a corporation's tax liability, earned by undertaking capital investment projects. The credit was introduced as an attempt to stimulate investment and to improve the productivity level of U.S. industry. A firm may recover up to 10 percent of expenditures on new capital projects in the form of tax credits.

From our viewpoint, the crucial issue is to determine when tax credit should be recognized in profits. Does it reduce tax costs in the year the credit is received? Or should the credit be amortized over the asset's life?

In support of the former, some accountants argue that as the credit is a reduction in the current tax liability, it should be applied against the current tax expense and thereby increase current profits. Advocates of spreading the benefit over the life of the capital project contend that the tax credit is really a reduction in the cost of the asset, and therefore should be amortized over each of the future years in which the asset is active in producing profits. The first approach is called the flow-through method, and the second is termed the deferral, or normalization, approach. Both approaches conform to generally accepted accounting principles. Those utilities seeking higher rates from their customers generally elect to use the normalization approach because spreading the credit-benefits over several years results in a higher current tax expense. Following the calculation procedure described previously, the normalization method gives a higher rate charge than the flow-through method in the early years.

Accelerated Depreciation Allowances

The rate determination procedure described in Figure 6.1 requires an estimate of the total expenses for the period. Included in these total expenses are two items that are of interest here: a depreciation expense, which is an estimate of the diminution in the value of plant equipment and other fixed assets, and a tax expense, which pertains to payments to the IRS.

Neither of these expense items need involve an immediate cash payment in the period in which they are recognized as expenses: depreciation expenses correspond to assets that may have been paid for many years ago; tax expenses are related to cash payments that are expected to be made to the IRS sometime in the future. The main characteristic of an expense is that it is a cost incurred in generating the revenue for a period, and there is no reason why a period's expenses need to have been actually paid for in cash in that period.

It is in this context that what is called the deferred tax expense arises. A public utility's expense—for rate determination purposes—consists of two components: that which is payable now (the tax payable) and that which is payable in the future. For example, for 1982 rate determination purposes, the tax expense allowed in 1981 may be decomposed as follows:

tax expense for 1981	=	tax payable in 1981	+	deferred tax expense payable in, say, 1999
$500,000	=	$100,000	+	$400,000

In this example, 1981 taxable profits are assumed to incur a total liability of $500,000. This is payable in two parts: $100,000 now and $400,000 in 1999. The full $500,000 is included for rate determination purposes, even though $400,000 may never be paid. Even if it is paid in 1999, its present cost is quite modest. The formal method for calculating the amount by which a utility can defer payment of its current tax expense is called the accelerated depreciation method. Accelerated depreciation affects the timing of payment of tax: the $100,000 and the $400,000 above. The accelerated depreciation method involves some complex and lengthy calculations; for our purposes, however, the important point to remember is that the technique opens up new vistas for utilities seeking to overcharge their customers.

Accelerated depreciation is used by market economies throughout the world; ostensibly to stimulate new investment. In parts of the Common Market firms are allowed to write off 100 percent of capital expenditures against taxable income in the year in which the expenditure is incurred. For example, a $20 million plant with an expected life of 40 years would generate tax deductible depreciation allowances of $500,000 per year if the plant's value declines by equal amounts in each period. With annual taxable income (before depreciation) of $1 million per year, a firm's tax liability would be $250,000 per year with a corporate tax rate of 50 percent. If, instead of tax deductible depreciation of equal amounts each year (straight-line depreciation), the firm used accelerated depreciation of 100 percent in the year of purchase, then the entire $20 million depreciation allowances could be offset against taxable income in that year. Since, in our example, this income is only $1 million, the remaining $19 million in depreciation can be carried forward and offset against taxable income in each succeeding year until it has been used up. Thus our firm could defer paying taxes for 20 years—until the year 2001—provided it continued to earn a predepreciation taxable income of $1 million per year. Ceteris paribus, the firm would begin paying $500,000 per year in tax from 2001 through 2020.

The choice between the two depreciation alternatives is clear: a tax payment of $250,000 per year for 40 years starting now, or $500,000 per year for 20 years starting in 2001. The total of tax payments is the same in both cases; they differ only as to when they are paid. Thus accelerated depreciation reduces the current tax liability by increasing long-term tax depreciation expense. The two streams of tax expense add up to the same amount—$10 million—but under acceleration, tax payments do not begin for 20 years. Thus, compared with the nonacceleration (straight-line) situation, the firm has the tax money available to reinvest during the period in which payment is deferred. If, for instance, the firm could invest the deferred tax monies in projects that earned 15 percent on average after taxes, then compared with the straight-line situation, the firm would accumulate approximately $368 million in interest by the end of the 40-year period.*

---

*These figures are arrived at as follows:

If $250,000 per year is invested for 20 years at 15 percent net per year, this will accumulate to $250,000 x 102.44358 = $25,610,895.

If, in the year 2001, this amount is reinvested for a further 20 years at 15 percent, it will compound into $25,610,895 x 16.36654 = $419,161,740

These figures highlight the profitability of accelerated tax depreciation for public utilities. What these calculations indicate is that the real, present cost of taxation declines dramatically when acceleration is used for tax purposes. For instance, a liability of $250,000 incurred in 1981, but not paid until 2001, does not cost $250,000 in 1981, but considerably less. If the $250,000 incurred in 1981 is not paid until 2001, then, at a 15 percent discount rate, the present cost of the 1981 tax expense is only $15,275 (250,000 x 0.0611). If $15,275, rather than $250,000, were included as part of the total tax in the 1981 rate determination calculation shown previously, then substantially lower rates would be charged to current customers. If the $250,000 is used however, the rates suffered by current customers would be considerably higher. Current accounting principles do not sanction the use of the present cost of the tax expense (i.e., $15,275); rather, the amount of the expected cash payment (i.e., $250,000) must be used.

The above vehicles for overcharging customers are joined by the prospect that the tax may never have to be paid. There are circumstances in which a firm can avoid paying taxes almost indefinitely. Suppose, in our example, that the company invested an additional $20 million in the year 2000. Additional depreciation expense would then be available to reduce taxable income in 2001 and each year thereafter. Thus even when a firm experiences zero capital expenditure growth in real terms, tax liabilities may be postponed. Furthermore, with inflation a firm is likely to pay a great deal more for replacing the plant in the year 2000 than it paid for the plant back in 1980. At an inflation rate of 12 percent per year, the cost of a plant doubles after 6 years; after 20 years, it costs 9.6 times its original cost. These increasingly inflated amounts will be available to reduce taxable income and to defer taxes in future years. Consequently, a firm may be static or

---

From the year 2001, annual tax payments of $500,000 must be made for 20 years. If this 20-year annuity was invested at 15 percent it would compound to $500,000 x 102.44358 =   51,221,790

Compound interest earned by the year 2021, resulting from the investment of tax savings from accelerated depreciation, after paying tax expense of $500,000 per year from 2001.
$367,939,950

even declining in terms of its real output, and yet, due to inflation, successively growing waves of accelerated depreciation that arise from the replacement of the old plant may be more than sufficient to "roll over" tax liabilities indefinitely. Finally, deferred tax liabilities may never materialize if corporate tax rates continue to decline at the rate they have in recent years.

These three future conditions—a firm's real growth in investment expenditure, the effect of the rate of inflation, and changes in tax rates—make it very difficult to estimate whether a firm will ever be required to pay over its deferred tax liabilities. These difficulties are in addition to problems of estimating the present cost of the future payment, a calculation that, as we have seen, is sensitive to the rather arbitrary choice of a discount rate. Uncertainties as to the future values of these three factors make the deferred tax expense a highly subjective item. As the deferred tax expense helps make up the tax expense, and the tax expense is part of the total allowable expenses that, in turn, are used to calculate the rates charged to customers, the utility prices end up being based on rather controversial and sometimes dubious assumptions. The question of whether deferred taxes should be included in the tax expense—and therefore the rates—is an accounting question that hinges on subjective estimates as to whether a payment to the IRS will eventually have to be made. With these considerations in mind, we can now explore the scale of overcharging that could be induced by accounting practices.

Power and Telephone Companies

Federal tax laws were revised in 1954, 1969, and again in 1981 to encourage industrial investment in new plants and equipment. The congressional legislation of 1969 resulted in a major income tax break for public utilities, with many telephone and power companies obtaining large amounts of interest-free money in the form of deferred taxes. By 1978, this interest-free loan had reached $20 billion, and by 1980 it exceeded $25 billion. Congress enacted the legislation for the investment tax credit in 1962. The initial credit of 3 percent of investment expenditures was raised to 10 percent in 1975 and to 11.5 percent in 1976 for those companies that offered their employees stock ownership plans.

Between 1955 and 1975, electrical utilities collected $7.1 billion from their customers for income taxes that were included in their total costs—

and hence rates—yet never paid over to the U.S. government. The 50 percent increase in electrical bills in the two years ending 1975 corresponded with substantially larger charges for deferred taxes. Prior to 1955, power companies paid an average of $1 billion per year in federal taxes. By 1975, annual tax payments had declined to less than $800 million, even though sales revenues had multiplied fivefold. Income taxes paid as a percentage of revenues had declined from 12.7 percent to 1.8 percent for the period. In 1975 alone, 150 of the largest private power companies billed their customers $2.2 billion for federal income taxes. Only $728 million was actually paid over to the U.S. treasury. Of these 150 companies, 134 charged their customers more than they paid over, 31 received tax refund checks totaling $82 million, and 12 paid no federal taxes at all. These disparities are due to the difference in timing between when a tax liability is incurred and when it is paid. As we have seen, accelerated depreciation allowances may allow payment of existing tax liabilities to be deferred indefinitely.

By far the largest benefactors from deferred tax allowances and investment credits are the telephone companies. Bell Telephone, then a subsidiary of American Telephone and Telegraph Company (AT&T), had accumulated deferred tax reserves of $11.3 million by 1978, twice the amount for all power companies combined. By 1982, Bell Telephone's deferred tax reserve reached 20 percent of its market capitalization. A Bell Telephone insider forecast that the deferred tax reserve would continue to grow until at least 1991. In 1977, AT&T collected 6.5¢ out of every dollar from its customers (a total of $3 billion) for federal taxes. Only $617 million was paid over to the authorities in 1977; the remainder was carried forward as deferred tax liability. Two thirds of the total amount carried forward was attributable to accelerated depreciation; the remaining third was made up of investment tax credits.

The history of the relationship between the telephone companies and the State of California highlights the entanglement of utility accounting and the social issues it raises. Pacific Telephone, then AT&T's California subsidiary, and General Telephone of California, the West Coast subsidiary of General Telephone and Electronics Corporation, were so opposed to the flow-through of the benefits of accelerated depreciation and investment tax credits to their customers (by reducing total costs and therefore rates) that they refused to claim these tax breaks throughout most of the 1950s and 1960s. In this way, the companies avoided the entire controversy by paying high levels of federal taxes, losing the tax relief for credits and accelerated depreciation, but passing the full cost onto the customers.

Although the members of the California PUC found this policy arrogant, it was not until 1968 that they ordered the two companies to take full advantage of the tax breaks. The PUC proceeded to set allowable rates as if the utilities had taken full advantage of the relief. The PUCs in 18 other states took similar action, and it looked as if the telephone companies would eventually concede the point.

Instead AT&T went to Washington, and through the powerful utility lobby, it secured legislation to the effect that any company that began taking accelerated depreciation and investment credits after 1969 would be required to make full provision for the deferred tax item in its tax expense for rate determination purposes. In this way, the legislation precluded companies from passing on the full benefits to customers in the form of lower rates. To add teeth to this legislation, any company that passed on the benefits to customers would forfeit the tax advantages and would be liable for repayment of back-taxes. This last provision angered members of California's PUC, who considered it a cynical move by Bell to resist reforms by placing a gun to its own head. The whole legislation has come to be known as "Bell's bill."

The PUC challenged the 1969 congressional law in the California Supreme Court in 1977, and the telephone companies compromised. By February 1980, 12 years after legal struggles had begun, the California PUC had ordered Pacific Telephone and General Telephone to refund to their customers $381 million and $111 million respectively. As these belated flow-throughs may be in contravention of the 1969 legislation (Bell's bill), Pacific Telephone and General Telephone could be liable for back-taxes of $1 billion and $111 million respectively. This issue is currently before the courts. If the utilities manage to avoid these back-taxes, the California PUC wants an additional customer refund of $100 million per year.

Implications

The tax incentives created by accelerated depreciation methods and the investment tax credit have been criticized by economists for leading to excessive capital investment, surplus power capacity, and, through overinvestment, an unnecessary loss of jobs. The effects of accounting standards and practices are much more difficult to evaluate. As utility services eventually become embodied in other goods and services, mispricing of them may create efficiency imbalances that affect an entire economy. Such an imbalance would be reflected in a misallocation of national resources, as well as a maldistribution of income to different factors of production.

Accountants do not possess magical skills for predicting future rates of inflation, corporate tax, and company growth. Yet any charge against current income for deferred taxes—even a zero charge—requires a prediction about these and other variables. As accounting principles are clearly incapable of providing a resolution to these problems, we have to ask what really caused the accountants to take the sides they took. For instance, a senior partner of the accounting firm Arthur Andersen, in opposing the flow-through method in the California dispute, argued that the tax deduction for a new piece of equipment is as much a company asset as anything else the company owns. With flow-through, he claimed, the company is giving the asset away. This argument displays a profound misunderstanding of the matter. The problem is not one of giving assets away; the issue is whether deferred taxes will ever actually be paid to the IRS and therefore result in an expense for rate determination purposes. To quibble about the accounting technicalities would be to risk losing sight of the crucial question: With so much uncertainty surrounding the amount of the current expense, what part do—and should—accountants play in determining the distribution of income through rate determination?

Questions such as the above cannot be dispatched in a simple and direct fashion. In order to understand why accounting deals so badly with the kinds of controversies raised in the previous paragraphs, it is necessary to understand why contemporary accounting practice and theory are constituted in the way that they are. This, in turn, requires a review of the development of the subject—historically and socially—in order to determine the allegiances that the subject has formed (and rejected).

The undue influence of neoclassical economics (marginalism) will be seen to be crucial in understanding the discipline's present predicament. By stressing marginalism, and neglecting other theories of value, accountants have become impotent in analyzing coherently the types of controversies discussed previously. We will review the villain—marginalism—together with the other theories of values that accountants have neglected, and then return to contemporary scandals (like those outlined previously) in order to ascertain which value theory is best suited for dealing with today's problems. First, however, as accountants rarely consider value theory, and its relation to their discipline, these matters must be discussed.

Part II
Preconditions for Accounting
and
Other Value Rationales

7

Value Theory and Accounting

Professional activities, together with beliefs that supported them, evolved as part of a broader process of economic and social change. Materialistic considerations are relevant because they help us understand the role of professional activities in producing the necessities of life (psychic, aesthetic, material, etc.). Social factors are important because they underscore the link between professional activities and the context of social conflict; they focus attention on struggles over the creation and division of economic wealth. Once conflict is recognized as an important ingredient in the context of accounting, it is no longer sufficient to accept at face value the profession's official version as to what accounting is or does. What part does accounting play in social conflict? Whose interest does the subject promote?

These questions set clear limits on the definition of accounting practice that is sought here. A definition that falls within these limits—and that is subsequently developed—is that accounting practice is a means for resolving social conflict, a device for appraising the terms of exchange between social constituencies, and an institutional mechanism for arbitrating, evaluating, and adjudicating social choices. Four aspects of this definition require elaboration. First, it is unlikely that many accounting practitioners or academics would define accounting in this manner, nor would one necessarily expect them to. The aim here is to offer a unique view of accounting, one that situates the activity in a social and historical context and, in doing so, provides new and valuable insights.

Second, accounting practices only assist in the resolution of certain kinds of social conflict, principally those related to economic production and exchange (so-called economic events). Thus accounting is a member of a battery of belief-forming institutions, including the law, education, the media, religion, and the family. The exact function of any one belief-shaping institution, relative to others, may vary from one social context to the next.

Third, the definition of accounting as a social conflict resolver does not commit the subject to any one side of the social conflict: there is nothing inherently and irrevocably conservative, reformist, or radical about accounting practice (even though, it will be argued, that much contemporary practice assumes a reactionary and conservative posture). This aspect of the definition acknowledges that it is possible to develop forms of accounting all along the political spectrum. Just as it is possible to have alternative forms of education, legal services, medicine, bookshops, psychotherapy, and legal firms, so is it possible to construct a socially critical and radical accounting practice.

Finally, the definition highlights the link between the practice of accounting and theories of value, that is, theories about how the terms of economic exchange are determined in different social systems. This linkage is mediated through the body of academic and professional theorizing that seeks to provide the rational underpinnings of accounting practice. Contemporary accounting thought—and hence, contemporary accounting practices—has been overwhelmingly influenced by one particular theory of value: marginalist economic theory. Yet few accountants appreciate the controversial history of marginalism and its tenuous and questionable status as a theory of value. Most importantly, many accountants are unfamiliar with the alternative value theories that exist in economics, which could provide an intellectual foundation for alternative accounting. Accordingly, what follows is a critical review of the history of value theory that seeks a new theoretical rationale for understanding the part played by accounting in the case studies presented earlier.

Figure 7.1 depicts the relationships between value theory and accounting thought that are explored in the following discussion.

The base of figure 7.1 represents economic exchange transactions. An economic exchange transaction is defined broadly as a transfer of economic use-values (i.e., the transfer of a capacity to affect human well-being). This broad definition encompasses the "second-order" aspects of exchange, known as "externalities." An externality is either a positive or negative effect on the well-being of parties to an exchange, apart from the immediate buyers and sellers. An example of an externality is the effect of pollution on beach-users that results from the production and sale of offshore oil.

Figure 7.1.   The Relationship Between Value Theory and Accounting

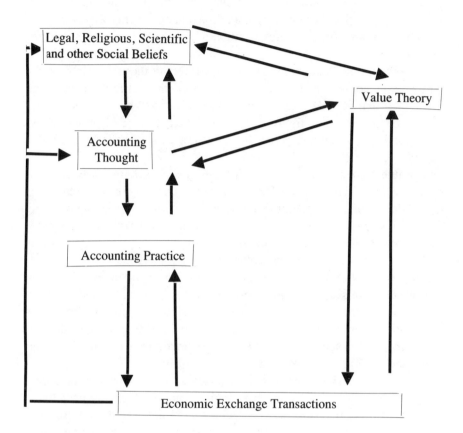

"Accounting Practice" (in figure 7.1) is shown to deal with only a sub-set of all economic exchange transactions. For example, an accountant's income statement and balance sheet would register transactions involving the cost of extracting oil and the revenue from its sale, but it would proba-bly ignore the business lost by the tourist industry because of polluted beaches.

In addition to reflecting economic exchanges—albeit partially—ac-counting practice also helps effect economic exchanges. Accounting state-ments are used in making decisions about the purchase of a company's se-curities, in assessing a firm's tax liability, in determining the rates a public utility can charge its customers, in deciding whether an employer can afford to pay a wage increase, and so forth. This is not a passive and representational role for accounting; ultimately accounting is part of that exchange process itself—as an informational commodity that promotes exchange. If accounting practice did not participate in exchange in this way, then presumably, competitive pressures would eradicate it as an unnecessary cost of production.

"Accounting Thought," in figure 7.1 refers to those attempts to systemize and comprehend accounting practice through intellectual and theoretical activity. Accounting thought is shown to be influenced by a variety of factors in the figure, including the experience of economic exchanges; legal, religious, scientific, and other social beliefs; and value theory.

Value theory is concerned with the terms of exchange between producers under different kinds of social systems. The scope of value theory is quite wide, ranging from, for example, studying how specialist producers from different tribes in parts of East Africa establish a rate of exchange for their products to examining how a modern conglomerate prices its products and, therefore, establishes terms of exchange with its customers. Accounting shares many of the same concerns as value theory: it measures and appraises the terms of exchange between different social constituencies, helps effect an allocation of resources, and simultaneously determines a distribution of income. Most importantly, in helping to effect decisions, it often arbitrates in social conflict over the production and distribution of income and wealth—the economic necessities of life.

Before embarking on the sociohistorical analysis of accounting, there are a number of considerations that require attention. First, we need to cement still further the links between value theory and accounting. Second, we need to give some attention to identifying the conditions under which value theory and accounting play a social role. Through their common interest in the terms of exchange between social members and institutions, accounting and value theory both implicitly assume the existence of a basic set of social and economic conditions: circumstances of specialization (division of labor) and market exchange. Without economic specialization, the problem of determining the terms of exchange would not exist and neither would the need for value theory and accounting. The "value rationales" of value theory and accounting thought are only relevant to those social systems in which integration and cooperation have developed enough to enable social members to devote part of their efforts to producing, not for personal consumption, but for a market exchange (i.e., commodity production). Part of the subsequent discussion attempts to delineate "Preconditions for Specialization and Exchange," because these are also the preconditions for the development of value theory and accounting thought and practice.

Consider the following examples provided by Ernst Mandel (1962, pp. 15–17, 62–68):

1. A caste holds a monopoly over the blacksmith craft in certain Indian villages and, at the same time, owns and works land holdings in order to feed caste members. When a farmer or villagers from outside the caste requires a weapon or a farming implement, he provides the raw materials and works the blacksmith's land until the commodity has been produced. Here the basic unit (or numéraire) of exchange is governed by an equivalence in work-hours.

2. An accounting system, in terms of work-hours, existed in Japanese villages in the Middle Ages. Agriculture was primarily a cooperative activity, with harvesting, farm construction, and stock breeding done in common. The village accountant maintained a comprehensive record of the hours spent by each villager on the farms of other villagers. By the year's end, all villagers were required to balance their accounts with others. Such systems recognized that children contributed less than adults by valuing a child-hour at one-half of an adult-hour. Once again, the basis of exchange was an equivalence in terms of labor time.

3. In Japan in about eighth century A.D., two kinds of nonagricultural labor were compulsory: *cho* and *yo*. The statute of Taiho specified these obligations in quantity of work-time (ten days), amount of cloth (26 shaku, i.e., approximately ten yards), and quantity of corn (one *to*, i.e., approximately two bushels) (Mandel, 1968, p. 62). These obligations were reducible to a common metric that made them comparable and equitable: the average amount of labor time embodied in each.

4. In European feudal society, obligations to the feudal lord were often discharged in one of three forms of rent: rent in the form of labor (usually involving working on the lord's land or demesne), rent in kind (wheat, livestock, etc.), and money rent. Mandel notes that "the landlords . . . were careful to see to it that when the conversion was made between the different forms of rent, they were closely equivalent" (1968, p. 96).

Can we regard the above as examples of early accounting practice? Are the rationales underlying ancient record keeping instances of early accounting theory? To answer these questions, a number of contemporary cases will be added to the previous list of historical examples and the commonality between the past and present examples will be investigated. Consider a typical accounting system that

- informs shareholders as to what they have received (e.g., earnings, dividends, and growth prospects) in exchange for their initial investment;
- allows the IRS to decide whether the tax paid by an individual is sufficient;
- allows creditors to assess the security of their claims;
- helps public utilities commissions decide whether the profit earned by a public utility, calculated according to generally accepted accounting principles, is consonant with the community's interests and represents a reasonable return in the light of the monopoly status endowed on the utility;
- helps the federal agencies, such as antitrust investigatory units, assess the social worth of a corporation's activities;
- aids management in gauging whether the resources they commit to particular projects (in terms of manpower, machines, materials, etc.) will be matched by the benefits that will accrue in exchange for such commitments.

Both the historical and contemporary examples involve exchange situations. The accounting information facilitates the valuation of what is—or what might be—received through a configuration of exchange transactions. A shareholder provides an initial investment, together with contracts of hire for directors and managers, in exchange for dividends and capital growth; a creditor lends money in exchange for safeguards, assurances, and eventually the return of the principal with interest; the SEC (on behalf of the community) gives social legitimacy and support to a corporation in exchange for behavior that conforms to certain laws and norms. In all cases, accounting information helps parties to social and economic transactions assess the adequacy of the value of their returns or entitlements.

Two levels of decision making are involved in the examples on the two lists: an individual level and a social level. Accounting and value theory operate at both levels; they examine alternatives from the viewpoint of each individual party to an exchange—as buyers, sellers, producers, merchants, etc., and they seek a rationale for appraising exchange possibilities for the collective parties to an exchange. Examples of exchange decisions at the collective (social) level are illustrated by the barter agreements found in precapitalist societies, by the way the goods of the modern private firm are priced, by the processes by which wage rates are established in a particular locality, and by the manner in which a firm determines its level of dividend payout. In all these cases, the problem is essentially the same: How are terms of exchange determined and how should they be resolved between different social constituencies (customers, sellers, labor, shareholders, etc.)?

Common to all items on the two lists is the notion that a value rationale is needed for making decisions and, therefore, resolving dissonance or conflict, at both the individual and the social (interpersonal) levels. Accounting and value theory have each evolved value rationales—some in common and others that differ—for making decisions and resolving exchanges. At an individual level, modern investors are encouraged by the theory of finance to appraise investment opportunities in relative terms; here the yardstick of value for evaluating a particular alternative is what is given up by foregoing the next best alternative. At the social level, rationales for resolving exchanges are multifarious, frequently appealing to custom, convention, ritual, or law for a solution. In tribal societies, barter exchanges are often settled using the concept of a "just price," in which labor time spent in production forms the basis for equalizing the quantity of goods exchanged. A similar social logic or rationale existed for determining the sufficiency of a payment to a feudal lord, the division of the proceeds of sale of a merchant's cargo after a voyage, the justification for an electrical utilities application for a price increase, the fairness of an exchange price between a fisherman and a weaver at a medieval market, or the adequacy of the payment by a Tibetan shepherd to a local healer.

Value theory and accounting are not universal to all forms of society; they are limited to specific economic and social conditions. As these conditions evolved into new forms, the prevailing forms of value theory and accounting adapted and changed to accommodate the new circumstances. The appearance of specialization and exchange signifies an increase in the mutual dependency between society members, whereby production for consumption is relinquished for production for exchange. The social cooperation implicit in a division of labor was considered to be the source of the "wealth of nations," according to Adam Smith. Specialization not only led to greater wealth, but through heightened interdependency it increased the need for a rationale for dividing the product of the new cooperative enterprise. Value theory and accounting represent sophisticated rationales for resolving exchanges, distributing income and resources, and dividing up the social product. The need for these social rationales originated with specialization and exchange, and it is these origins, therefore, that will be considered next.

8

The Emergence of
Specialization and Exchange:
Preconditions for
Value Theory and Accounting

The Creation of a Social Surplus Product

Accounting and value theory provide a means of arbitrating in economic exchanges. Not all types of exchange employ arbitration as a method of conflict resolution: exchange by plunder or by piracy does not depend on arbitration between the parties in order to be implemented. Similarly, value theory and accounting, as value rationales, represent only a subset of the many kinds of rationales, beliefs, and ideologies that are instrumental in resolving social conflict. Religion, science, the law, and mythologies all contribute social logics that resolve exchange decisions and thereby encourage further specialization in production. Value theory and accounting are therefore socially relative in this specific sense: specialization and exchange are necessary, but not sufficient, for value theory and accounting to emerge as social adjudication processes.

The emergence of economic exchange and the division of labor are intertwined; they represent conditions in which individuals no longer aim to be self-sufficient by producing for all their personal needs, but redirect their efforts toward producing items that can be exchanged. Historically, specialization in production is not typical. Humanity has existed for approximately one million years; for 985,000 of those years, the bulk of humanity has experienced little other than extreme poverty and hardship (Mandel, 1968, p. 25). Indeed to this day, deprivation and malnourishment are the common conditions of most peoples. Under such circumstances, food production is the only possible economic activity. Apart from specialization between the sexes, each member of a tribal society engages in the full range of activities necessary for survival.

A range of discoveries, inventions, and fortuitous events helped raise productivity above subsistence level, thereby providing communities with a surplus that permitted a degree of specialization. The invention of the bow and arrow and the harpoon were among these improvements, as was the transition from a nomadic to a settlement existence, which permitted an investment in permanent tools, the establishment of a form of agriculture (around 15,000 B.C.), and the domestication of animals in the neolithic period (approximately 10,000 B.C.). These transition periods were followed by a range of metallurgical discoveries that augmented labor productivity still further: copper (in the Euphrates, Tigris, and Nile river valleys in about 6,000 B.C.).

The most important effects of the metallurgical revolution were felt in agriculture with the introduction of the iron plough on the heavy soils of Europe from around the eighth to the seventh centuries B.C. Benefits from the development of agriculture were a long time accruing because little was initially known about farming techniques. Irrigating, maintaining soil fertility, rotating crops, and allowing land to lie fallow all contributed to agricultural productivity and the creation of agricultural surpluses as a regular and reliable phenomenon. A permanent surplus in foodstuffs enabled numerous workers to be released from the agricultural sector and allowed to engage in specialized and autonomous craft occupations. Agricultural development led to the appearance of European towns; similarly, the introduction of metal implements in Japan in the eighth century A.D. led to a great increase in agricultural production and a commensurate increase in population (Mandel, 1968, p. 37).

The smith was one of the first craftsmen to work exclusively for the market in medieval Europe. The original meaning of the word *smith* in both Latin (*Faber*) and German (*Schmied*) was "craftsman" (Mandel, 1968, p. 39). Partly as a result of craft development, the town emerged and separated itself from the country to become an independent economic entity.

For many historians, agricultural development is seen as an important precondition to civilization. This was the view of the ancient Greeks at the time of Homer. The Chinese of the classical period associated the invention of agriculture with the mythical emperor Chen-Nung. In Aztec mythology, the society's prosperity is attributed to a communication received by the high priest in a dream; the communication instructed the Mexicans to dam a large river in order to distribute the water over the plains (Mandel, 1968, pp. 35–45).

There is no one factor that explains how societies come to produce a surplus. Different natural endowments may cause a surplus to emerge at different stages of social development. The inhabitants of Central America were able to generate a substantial agricultural surplus even before metal tools came into use because of favorable climatic conditions and low population density. In contrast, in Western and Central Europe, urban communities did not emerge until the iron plough appeared.

There are, however, a number of important events in history that were germane to the emergence of a social surplus. The neolithic and metallurgical revolutions were important because they signified a transfer of control over the means of subsistence from nature to humanity. Instead of being passive victims of the whims of nature, people began to be able to assert a degree of order and control over their environment. This new direction was reflected in the ways in which the surplus was deployed. The surplus permitted foodstuffs to be stored in anticipation of periods of shortage, a greater division of labor, which led to the first signs of crafts specialization in the production of articles not needed for immediate consumption, and an increase in family size, which in turn further expanded productivity.

The social surplus generated by these early communities was insufficient to allow private property to evolve in any significant way. Indeed, Marx referred to such societies as instances of primitive communism because of their general opposition to personal accumulation, status, and reward differentials—whether due to special aptitudes, skills, or social position. Thus, when Levi-Strauss asked the Nambikwara Indians what special privileges and advantages their chief enjoyed, they replied, "He's the first man to march off to war" (Levi-Strauss, 1963, p. 330). Mandel notes that this is the same reply that was given four centuries earlier to Montaigne in response to a similar question to an American Indian (Mandel, 1968, p. 41).

There are numerous examples of customs and ceremonies that prevented excessive wealth accumulation by individuals. This belies arguments that wealth accumulation is an innate and invariant property of rational human behavior, found throughout the universe of human experience. Margaret Mead, in describing the feast organized among the Papuan people of Arapesh, considered it an institution that was "an effective measure against any one man accumulating wealth disproportionate to wealth accumulated by others" (Mead, 1937, p. 445). Asch, in his field studies of the Hopi Indians, observed that all individuals are treated alike, without discrimination. Those who seek praise for themselves are resented and criticized. Most Hopi men refuse the position of foreman; even the play of

children exhibits these characteristics: they will play basketball for hours
without keeping score, not knowing who is winning and who is losing
(Thompson, 1950, pp. 94–95).

Silent, Simple, and Ceremonial Exchange

Although various kinds of exchange have evolved, only certain types
of exchange require a value rationale for their resolution. Plunder and exchange are two ways that tribal societies can acquire foreign products and
thereby expand their means of subsistence. Encounters between tribal
groups not related by blood are rarely between parties of equal strength.
Such encounters are frequently accompanied by violence (potential or actual). These circumstances quickly teach the weaker groups to flee before
the arrival of the more powerful group, and the latter not to kill the weaker
groups if they wish to maintain the supply of certain products. For example, the trade partners of the headhunters of New Guinea include the swamp
peoples from the east who specialize in the production of cooking pots and
baskets. The headhunters do not kill the swamp people because they would
lose their source of pots (Mead, 1952, pp. 170–71). These conditions
typify one of the earliest forms of exchange: *silent exchange,* in which the
weaker group leaves its products in an established location and returns only
after the other group has left its own goods in the same place.

Silent exchange takes place on a regularized basis, in contrast to *simple exchange,* which occurs occasionally and casually between hordes enjoying differential yet complementary natural endowments (for instance,
between fruit gatherers and hunters). Levi-Strauss has shown that when
groups united by a common ancestry become large and dispersed, they frequently maintain a degree of cohesion and solidarity through *ceremonial
exchange,* the exchange of presents and gifts made from products drawn
from the different territories. These exchanges reinforce weakening blood
ties and express the real, material dependence of each group on the other. If
the harvest times of different groups differ for example, then ceremonial
exchange ensures that a continuous source of food is available for all
groups (Mandel, 1968, p. 51). The repetitive and routinized character of silent and ceremonial exchanges sets them apart from the more primitive
form of simple exchange. Silent exchange and ceremonial exchange are
transitional forms in the evolution of developed exchange.

Developed Exchange, Commensurate Reciprocity, and the Need for Accounting

Developed exchange is distinguished from traditional exchange in two ways: first, by the extent to which it has become routinized, and second, by the need for customs and practices for establishing a determinable reciprocal payment.

Developed exchange involves transactions between communities on a regular basis. The more frequent such exchanges become, the more pressing the need for a criteria for adjudging the appropriate level of reciprocity (i.e., the terms of trade). It is in these circumstances that a rudimentary form of value rationale and accounting evolves.

A number of conditions must be fulfilled in order for developed exchange to materialize. These include an increase in labor productivity, the formation of regular surpluses among neighboring tribes, and the professionalization of craft activity. Even if these conditions are met, exchange may only operate at a rudimentary level in that it may take many years for the craftsmen to become fully independent of agricultural work. In the case of the Kafflitcho and Gougo tribes in East Africa, for instance, some craftsmen are fully independent, and others are not. In the former case, the village members denote specific quantities of clothing, food, and ornaments in return for their work; in the latter case, village members work the craftsmens' land in order to repay their obligations (Mandel, 1968, p. 55).

Reciprocity applies only among groups; it does not govern relations among members of the same family group. The service that members owe to their community is usually predetermined according to social custom, tradition, or religious rite. Service obligations to the family within the system of consanguinity vary according to age or sex; they are not directly related to a member's contributions to the group's welfare. In the case of the modern family, for instance, personal services, such as child rearing, housekeeping, cooking, gifts, presents, and income obtained from laboring outside the home are given and received by family members without precise calculations of equivalent values.

Developed exchange often coexists with other types of exchange in the same community. This is so in Indonesian villages where two forms of economic activity take place side by side: *sambe sinambat,* unpaid work aimed at satisfying essential needs, and *toeloeng mensoloeng,* activity devoted to personal needs, for which a return—commensurate in kind—is expected. In the case of institutionalized ceremonial exchanges, it has been found that in the majority of cases, a principle of equivalence links the magnitude of the gift with that of the "counter-gift" (Mandel, 1968, p. 53).

Developed exchange is accompanied by greater craft activity, and for many social members this represents a major change in the meaning and significance of work. Persons who produce for their own consumption (i.e., produces use-values) live on the direct product of their own labor. Production and products, exertion and consumption, outlay and benefit, means and end, sacrifice and return, are all identical to them; all form a coherent and indivisible totality, in theory and in practice. Production for market exchange (commodity production) violates this unity: producers are separated and alienated from the results of their labor and receive, as compensation, a "ticket" to the maze of commodities in the market place.

Commodity production not only exemplifies developed exchange but also presages a new economic and social order. Craft emerges as an independent economic activity once some community members are released from agriculture and are able to produce articles exclusively for market exchange. Unlike their predecessors, craft producers no longer live directly on the products of their own labor; rather the reverse is true: they live only if they can get rid of their products.

The commodity producer's dependence on market exchange is part of a more generalized interdependence at the tribal or clan level. In areas where there is a true regional division of labor and a regular network of exchange has evolved—through local markets for example—local tribes no longer rely on direct consumption of their own production, but depend on foreign products in order to reproduce their existence. In this fashion, specialization and its corollary, commodity production, represent a quantum jump in interdependence at both individual and societal levels.

Coincidental with the growth in social interdependence is the emergence of the need for orderly ground rules for exchange. How many cooking pots should a weaver receive for one blanket? How many coconuts should an itinerant smith obtain for a cooking utensil?What are the appropriate terms of exchange for a Menimel potter of the Amazon basin?

Such problems are, in essence, problems of valuation and choice. Modern variants of exactly the same problems are studied in university courses on financial analysis in which students are taught to assess what constitutes a reasonable return on an outlay. "Return" is conceived in the broadest sense here to include current dividends and earnings, growth prospects, the riskiness of financing policies, working capital priorities, liquidity policies, business practices, and so forth. The only difference is that exchanges between the potter and the weaver are likely to be consummated within a few hours, whereas exchanges between corporations and their stockholders usually continue indefinitely. This complication aside, determining whether a commensurate reciprocal benefit has been obtained is as much a problem for the potter as it is for the corporate investor. Estimating the benefit value of a cooking pot (relative to its cost) is likely to be just as imprecise an affair as gauging the income likely to accrue through an investment.

While the uncertainty of future events causes serious difficulties in valuing returns in contemporary exchange, it does not disturb the validity of the view adopted here: value theory and accounting are closely tied to developed exchange because they provide value rationales for determining the degree of reciprocity commensurate in an exchange, from both an individual and a societal point of view.

Value Rationales for Resolving Personal and Social Conflict

Accounting, as a value rationale, attempts to resolve the degree of reciprocity appropriate in an exchange. A diverse range of examples highlights this role. Shareholder or potter, coachmaker or SEC, what is required in each case is a yardstick for appraising the terms of trade and determining the degree of reciprocity commensurate with what is contributed. Placing this construction on events reveals a hitherto unrecognized ancestry of accounting thought and practice. We have a coalescence of ideas that binds the needs of the itinerant smiths of equatorial Africa with the services of the CPA: a linkage that will be presently explored.

Once a consistent division of labor and means of exchange are established in a society, the labor time spent producing a product is frequently used to determine the relative worth of the goods produced. When product exchange is based on labor-time equivalences, "equal exchange" is ensured and, at the same time, the emergence of privileged and underprivileged groups—a development that might undermine the system of labor cooperation and specialization—is prevented. Indeed, failure to establish exact exchange equivalences between commodity producers could lead to complete dissolution of the community: producers would stop making products that were "underpriced" relative to the labor content of the items received in exchange. In this way, a value rationale based on labor-content equivalences in determining exchange values helps maintain social integration and an economic equilibrium.

In order to ensure a proper allocation of labor time between essential and nonessential activities, some tribes have devised what is, in effect, an accounting budget that distributes time between different products according to importance, to ensure a desired level of subsistence. Society members are able to dispose of remaining free time as they wish. Boeke, for example, notes that Indonesian villages organize their economies by allocating scarce labor time in this manner; in Japanese villages, where several families may work together to transplant rice, a record is kept of the cumulative obligations between the families in terms of labor hours (Boeke, 1940, p. 39 cit. Mandel, 1968, p. 61).

Examples of communities that economize on scarce labor time are ubiquitous: the major enterprises of China, Byzantium, Europe, and Arabia in the Middle Ages, as well as those found in antiquity, all used publically known rules that specified the amount of labor time to be invested in making each product, its length of apprenticeship, its cost, and the exchange rate between one commodity and another (Espinas, 1933–49, pp. 118, 140–42 cit. Mandel, 1968, pp. 63, 66, 68). Our everyday language clearly shows the influence of labor time as a yardstick of value: the word *acre* in medieval English meant the amount of land a man could plough in one day; in France the term *carrucata* has the same meaning, as does *pose*, the Swiss unit of area (Mandel, 1968, p. 62). Tributes imposed by one race on another were often designated in labor time, and as these dues were frequently interchangeable, equivalences were also specified. The records of the Chinese Tang dynasty detail how much work was to be devoted to growing millet (283 days a year) and wheat (177 days a year) and the land tax payable in kind (Mandel, 1968, p. 63). In the medieval commune, there was a direct link between the working day and the amount of tribute required (Espinas, 1933–49, p. 140 cit. Mandel, 1968, p. 56). Mandel lists numerous examples of what he calls "economic accounting based on the duration of labor." Such calculations were reflected in the determination of the payment-in-kind required of the forced labor of the Indians in Spanish America. Similarly, in Indonesia at the time of the "cultuurstelsel," the population was required to allocate one fifth of its land to crops to be sold to the government (those without land had to work 66 days per year on government land), and in Vietnam, loans made during the dry season were repaid in working days during the busy period (Mandel, 1968, p. 63).

Since the very beginnings of petty commodity production, estimated to be around 3000 B.C., all forms of labor have usually been considered equivalent, regardless of specific character. On the tables found at Sasa, inscribed in a Semitic language, the wages in a prince's household were fixed at 60 qua of barley for the donkey man, the shepherd, the cultivator, the smith, the cobbler, the cook, the engraver, the tailor, and the carpenter (Huart and Delaporte, 1952, p. 83).

As petty commodity production developed and crafts became more specialized and complex, the cost of apprenticeship was transferred from the community to the apprentices and their families. The exchange terms obtained by the craftsmen for their products were adjusted accordingly to compensate them and their families for the period of abstinence from production while developing skills. In this way, a unit of skilled labor may be viewed as composite, made up of the time spent directly producing the product and a fraction of the hours spent training to acquire the necessary skills. Without compensation for hours invested in training, there would be no incentive for society members to become craftsmen.

In simple commodity production, in which the primary producers alone exchange their products in the marketplace, exchange takes place in terms of equivalent quantities of labor time. As a system of specialization and exchange becomes more widespread, producers from more distant villages and regions introduce a great diversity of techniques of production and natural advantages. Under such circumstances, it becomes infeasible to use the specific labor content—the actual time spent—as a basis for the exchange price. Instead, the average amount of time spent producing a commodity—the societal average—becomes the primary basis for establishing the exchange value of the product. In this manner, producer, production, and exchange are regulated not by the personal idiosyncracies and nuances of each individual expressed in the labor time actually expended (commodities would truly be incommensurable under such a system) but by the societal average and therefore the labor that is socially necessary to make the product. Consequently, producers who are slow, wasteful, or who use obsolete methods are penalized under these arrangements because they receive, as compensation, products with a lower labor time content than they themselves have expended. Thus as commodity production expands, it disciplines each producer to strive for greater economy in terms of labor accounting in order to maintain the exchange value of the hours devoted to production. As we shall see, the discipline imposed on each individual by socialized commodity production was, according to Marx, the primary source of alienation under capitalism.

Value Rationales that Authenticate Unequal Exchange

What distinguishes barter exchanges based on labor time is that they may be regarded as forms of "equal exchange." But in many social systems, "unequal exchange" is the rule rather than the exception, and a considerable amount of energy has been expended by value theorists and accountants in devising rationales for explaining, arbitrating, and authorizing unequal exchanges. The next step therefore is to define "unequal exchange."

As long as a community can barely produce enough to keep itself alive, and as long as there is no surplus above this necessary product, it is impossible for a division of labor to occur, and therefore for specialized trades, such as retailers, scholars, artists, lawyers, and artisans to make their appearance. In these circumstances, all people are producers and are held to the same economic level; little social differentiation is possible.

But once the productivity of a society's labor has increased beyond subsistence level, and there is a surplus of products, the conditions are established that permit specialization through a divison of labor. Specialization is only possible however, if specialists are able to exchange their products for other commodities, and thereby acquire the necessities of life. In this sense, specialization and exchange require coordinated and concerted action. They are not merely "individual" acts of self-interest—as contemporary, orthodox economics would have it—but they are fundamentally social and communal acts requiring cooperative social action.

Specialization and exchange are probably the most basic expressions of a society's communality. In addition, they are always accompanied by one further trait in a developing society: the existence of a social surplus product that becomes the focus of a class struggle as to its division. A community whose subsistence level is 100 units of agricultural products faces an immediate problem if its productivity is doubled as a result of labor specialization: should the surplus be invested or consumed? If invested, should it be ploughed back into agriculture or into industry? If consumed, should it go to labor or to a sovereign class?

Precapitalist societies answered these questions in different ways. In Europe in the Middle Ages, villages were governed by a strict economy of labor time. The old laws of Bavaria, for example, specified that the "serfs of the Church" had to spend three days a week on the demesne of their Lord, and do "three days work for themselves" (Mandel, 1962, p. 61). Similarly, peasant women had to work for a fixed number of days in the workshops of the manor. The basic necessities for peasant life were met out of three days labor; the surplus produced above this level, generated by work performed on the lord's estate, was appropriated by the lord in its entirety. For both serfs and peasant women, the exchange was "unequal" because for contributing six days labor they received goods worth only three days.

The phenomenon of extracting surplus production is exemplified by cases of plantation slavery, as it existed in certain regions and periods of the Roman empire, or as may be found from the seventeenth century in the islands of Portuguese Africa and in the West Indies. In these tropical areas, slaves usually provided their own food from a tiny plot of land that they worked on Sundays. The products of this labor provided the slaves with a store of food: the necessities of life. The remaining six days of the week were devoted to working on the plantation for which the slave received no compensation. This labor produced the social surplus product that belonged to the slave owner as soon as it was created. These two periods correspond to what are termed "necessary" labor time, in which the necessary product is produced, and "surplus" labor time, in which a social surplus product is created. Surplus value is simply the monetary form of the social surplus product. When the surplus product is appropriated exclusively in monetary form, then the term "surplus-value" is applied instead of "surplus product."

The unequal exchange appropriation of the surplus is fairly transparent in feudal and slave exchanges. We have seen how, in accordance with the customs of these particular societies, something analogous to accounting rules existed for establishing equivalencies and adjudicating claims between conflicting social members. In short, even in precapitalist cultures, measures of value existed that quantified the rights (assets) and obligations (liabilities) of members of one class to another. The valuation practices and theories provided practical guides in the exchange of products.

Under capitalism, where specialization has advanced to a much greater degree than under previous social systems, exchange takes place between social members who freely enter a marketplace. While capitalist market exchange differs from the modes of exchange of earlier regimes in several important respects, it fulfills essentially the same adjudicating role in appropriating a surplus social product. And as in previous societies, theories of value—contemporary accounting theories—provide a social logic, a rationale, a set of guidelines, a social ideology, for completing exchanges and hence resolving the appropriation involved in unequal exchange.

When cast in the light of the history of value, accounting assumes special social significance, not just as a mechanical bookkeeping of events and transactions, but as a logic for appropriating material production through economic exchanges. As such, accounting is reflective of the ideology prevailing in each historical period. It is ultimately ideological because it facilitates the appropriation of surplus value, a process that has no ultimate logical foundation. Without such a logical foundation, accounting is exposed as an ideology, a way of rationalizing or explaining away the appropriation of the production of one social class by members of another. Our historical review will show that the theoretical task of explaining away social appropriation has been a complex and abstract affair that has taken on different forms throughout history. However, ultimately, the role of accounting remains the same to this day: an intellectual and pragmatic tool in social domination.

Part III follows, and it begins by cementing the links between value theory and accounting. It shows how modern financial statements are used to try to answer exactly the same questions that have occupied value theorists throughout the ages. The answers sought and given are rarely nonpartisan; accounting rules and conventions do not merely reflect, they also affect, the way income is distributed. This proactive aspect of accounting is evident from the subsequent review of the sociohistorical development of value theory, which shows the particular value theories prevailing in each era to be ideologically attuned to the priorities of antagonistic social interests.

Marginalism, the theoretical godfather of modern accounting, is the latest in this sequence of social ideologies; it was preceded by labor, mercantilist, canonist, and other theories of value. With the historical, intellectual lineage of accounting presented in this light—as a history of social ideology—we become more appreciative of the subject's partisanships and biases, and more aware of its malleability. In consequence, the historical perspective provided by Part III helps us construct a radical approach to accounting in Part IV, one based not on marginalism, but on Marx's theory of alienation. This new formulation is then used to reexamine the kinds of contemporary disputes introduced at the outset of the book.

Part III
Theories of Value

9

Antecedents to
Theories of Social Value

Introduction

There is a widely held view among accounting historians that the history of accounting lies predominantly in early uses of bookkeeping, and that the subject's development is reflected in its movement beyond these "primitive" origins, to the "rigorous" theories and research techniques that we find today. The previous chapters reject this view outright. Reconstructing accounting history in such narrow terms offers minimal insights into the power and potential of the subject. Instead, an alternative lineage for accounting is proposed, one that stresses its historical social context of specialization and exchange, competition and conflict, and the need for social beliefs, ideologies, conventions, and practices that resolve conflict and help reproduce a social order. Accordingly, arbitration in conflict over economic exchange is singled out as the one distinguishing trait that offers special insights into accounting's social role.

The role of accounting as an arbiter in social conflict is evident from the financial statements of any corporation. Consider the income statement and balance sheet for a hypothetical firm, Big Ate, shown in Exhibits 9.1 and 9.2. The income statement shows the value of exchange transactions that have occurred within the accounting period; the balance sheet lists the unexpired consequences of these transactions at the end of the accounting period. (The exact economic definition of these terms is not the issue here.) The exchange relationships in the financial statements link the corporate entity to social constituencies: wage labor, suppliers of raw materials and electricity, customers, suppliers of capital (shareholders and bondholders), and state and federal authorities.

Exhibit 9.1. The Big Ate Corporation:
Income Summary for the Year Ended 1984

	$ Millions		$ Millions
Material	20	Sales to Customers	800
Electricity	70		
Wages	100		
Pension fund contributions	60		
Depreciation of plant	200		
State taxes	40		
Federal taxes	30		
Bond interest	80		
Dividends paid	90		
Retained profits	110		
	800		800

Exhibit 9.2. The Big Ate Corporation:
Balance Sheet as of December 31, 1984

	$ Millions		$ Millions
Cash	20	Shareholders Equity	400
Accounts Receivable	370	Retained Profits	150
Inventory	110		550
	500		
Plant and Equipment	830		
Accumulated Depreciation	350		
	480		
		Bondholders	200
		Taxes owed	40
		Interest owed	70
		Dividends owed	50
		Accounts Payable	70
	980		980

The relationships shown in the financial statements are reproduced in Figure 9.1 with the income statement expense and revenue values attached to their respective arrows. Notice that when a corporation is viewed as a nexus of exchange relationships, accounting performs a role that is directly analogous to that served by theories of value in earlier periods. Thus accounting conventions and rules arbitrate and resolve conflict over the value of taxes owed, of pension obligations to employees, of customer debts, and of liabilities to the suppliers of materials and utilities. Once the values of such exchange relationships have been estimated, it is possible to compute their overall impact on the exchange relationship with the residual legatee: the shareholders. In the example, accounting conventions adjudge that a $200 million shareholder entitlement transpired as a result of the year's trading.

Figure 9.1.   Accounting Exchange Relationships Between Big Ate Inc. and its Social Constituencies

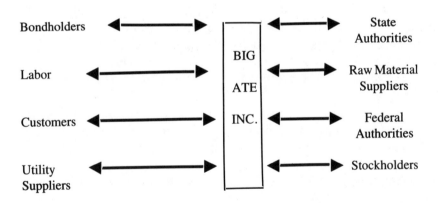

Note: Arrows denote two-way flows of funds and commodities.

There are several parallels between the arbitration role illustrated in the example and the processes of arbitration existing in the relatively simple economies, referred to in the previous chapter. First, characteristic of all situations under consideration are a division of labor, mechanisms for exchange, competition, and conflict over the terms of exchange. Second, accounting, which is no more than a social artifact, acts to resolve conflict in exactly the same way as, for example, the mystics and god-kings of earlier periods. Third, although accounting conventions and practices may sometimes produce unambiguous exchange values, in many situations they are ambiguous and arbitrary. These ambiguities are highlighted by the numerous disputes over accounting practices, such as over the amount that should be provided for deferred taxes or employee pension benefits, or the amount of profit earned for shareholders during a period.

The perspective on accounting history as the history of adjudicating in economic exchanges offers a new slant on accounting problems and questions. No longer does accounting appear as the immutable, ineluctable, technical mechanics of "bookkeeping"; instead, the subject assumes a flexible character in that it may be refashioned to suit changes in the balance of power between conflicting classes and groups in society. This is not to say that we must expect to find dramatic shifts in what we usually call "accounting"; rather, it is in the social practices of adjudicating and resolving conflict that the radical shifts occur, in which accounting is merely one particular apparatus that has evolved in specific social conditions and circumstances. (It is less significant for the argument here, but I contend that substantial variations *within* accounting theory and practice are also responsive to changes in the struggle between different social constituencies.)

If accounting and other social arbitration processes are to be regarded as malleable, adaptive, and, most importantly, socially relative, then a significant corollary follows: the rationales, logics, beliefs, theories, and ideologies that legitimize the arbitration processes prevailing in each era must also be periodically transformed to meet the dictates of the new social regime. Thus, just as religious beliefs are regarded as socially relative (catholicism bolsters feudalism, protestantism promotes capitalism, etc.), so accounting theories and other adjudication ideologies must also be socially conditioned (as well as socially conditioning).

This last proposition is not only central to this chapter; it is probably the most important one in the whole book. In what follows, we will see that accounting has been co-opted and straightjacketed by one particular theoretical ideology: marginalism. I hasten to add that I am not suggesting that accountants are merely thoroughbred neoclassical economists. Obviously accounting practice has been shaped by many forces other than formal economic thinking. But marginalism has monopolized accounting thought in one specific sense: of all the theories of value available, it is the one that has been given serious consideration to the virtual exclusion of all others.

To proceed, therefore, we will examine the affinity between marginalist value theory and accounting. The chapter then reviews the history of theories of value. This review serves several purposes. It shows the variety of rationales available to support alternative and radical accounting practices, thus opening up political possibilities for the subject, and it shows the socially partisan biases of marginalism (and thus those of contemporary accounting). Finally, these biases point to the reasons for the breakdown in current accounting practice, as shown in the controversies presented at the outset of this book.

Marginalist Value Theory and Accounting Practice

Two themes run continuously through the history of accounting thought. These themes maintain the subject's commitment to marginalism. The first is the emphasis on individualism (whether the individual owner or the corporation as a legal "person"). This individualistic emphasis serves to preempt questions about the class affiliations of individuals and the part accountants play in class conflicts (Macpherson, 1962). The second theme has been a concern to present an image of objectivity, independence, and neutrality by shunning "subjective" questions of value and confining accounting data to "objective" market prices (historical and current). This image is often extended to portray the accountant as a disinterested, innocuous historian. The need for the imagery stems from a desire to deny responsibility for shaping subjective expectations which, as we will see, affect decisions about resource allocation and income distribution between and within social classes.

The importance of both an individualistic focus and an emphasis on "objective" historical cost was emphasized by Fisher (1906, p. 70), who wrote that "cost, at the time of purchase, is a market estimate of future earning power."[1] As such, he continued, it can be assumed "to reflect expected future returns to a *specific* individual."[2] The sovereignty of the individual owner was adopted by Sprague (1908), Hatfield (1909), and Canning (1929), who ignored the separation of ownership and management by focusing on the individual owner-manager.

Neither Fisher's view of cost nor his individualistic focus went unchallenged. For instance, in the 1960s and 1970s we find accountants questioning the relevance of Fisher's individualistic focus to a world of large corporations run by managers who are not owners (see, e.g., Rayman, 1972; Edwards, 1962; Lee, 1974, 1975; Taylor, 1975; Sterling, 1970; Chambers, 1971). These criticisms of Fisher's work hardly rival those of economists such as Veblen who contended that the concentration of corporate control favored the vendibility of capital relative to the vendibility of goods and services (Veblen, 1904, p. 146). Instead of viewing the rise of corporatism as a radical shift in the distribution of power and income between classes, accountants have persisted with their individualistic focus, using the legal model, which reincarnates, out of individual shareholders, a corporate "being," with its own rights and responsibilities.

Those accounting theorists who recognized the separation of ownership and management (e.g., Paton and Stevenson, 1981; Sweeney, 1930) contended that the firm itself had a "right" to maintain command over a given level of resources. Thus income was not earned by the owners unless a given productive capacity and/or level of purchasing power had been attained. Edwards and Bell (1961, pp. 48–56, 31–109) provide a further reconciliation between accounting and its utility-based, marginalist foundations. First, they espouse a concept of accounting wealth and profit that reconciles with subjective present value; second, they propose that the corporate entity should retain sufficient resources to allow the maintenance of physical capital.

The second theme in the history of accounting thought is the view of accounting as an impartial record of historical exchange values, with the corollary that the accountant bears no responsibility for affecting expectations, decisions, and ultimately the distribution of income within and among classes. I do not mean to suggest that accountants have rested easily with historical objectivity as their dominant objective. Rather, the protection offered by appearing as mere historians, together with the desire to measure subjective Fisherian-type income, has presented accountants with a dilemma. On the one hand, Fisherian and Hicksian income are faithful servants of marginalist value theory in the way that they install capital as the "producer" of value and legitimize profit as the reward for marginal productivity in production. On the other hand, the affiliations of accounting to these subjective notions of value have drawn accounting into a number of bitter disputes about the way accounting data influences income distribution within and among classes. Most disputes have centered on re-distributions of income within the capitalist class (i.e., among groups of investors) that accounting data has affected. The incidents involving Equity Funding, National Student Marketing, Slater Walker, Leasco-Pergamon, and the more recent affair involving Investors Overseas Services and Arthur Andersen all exposed the distributional impact of accounting, discrediting the profession's image of objectivity and impartiality and undercutting its authority and credibility.[3]

The long attachment of accounting scholars to historical objectivity needs to be considered in the light of the above. Kester (1918), Couchman (1929), and Littleton (1928, 1929) argued that accountants merely traced "unexpired costs," factual evidence, in and out of the firm. Littleton (1929, pp. 148–49) went further in asserting that cost and value were, in fact, unrelated.[4] Accountants, he wrote, deal only with the "supply side" of economics; "cost furnished the limiting factor to prices." "Value," he contended, "was subjective." Citing Böhm-Bawerk, who wrote that the value of the means of production is "regulated in the last resort by the amount of marginal utility of their finished product," Littleton argued that utility and value were mental concepts based on desiredness and had no place in accounting. Paton and Littleton's (1940) cost allocation model is the first coherent, authoritative view of the accountant as recorder, classifier, and matcher of costs with revenues. This view has provided the rationale by which decades of accountants; cloaked in pseudoobjectivity, have restricted the profession's vision of its responsibilities and the agenda for accounting research.

This restricted view of accounting research ignored alternative perspectives that were available both in accounting and in economics. Scott (1933) argued that accounting theory was based on marginalist premises, and thus was biased and socially dysfunctional. Scott recognized that "subject to conditions fixed by prevailing institutions, the machinery of the market controls economic activity, determines income and adjusts conflicts of economic interests between different classes and individuals of society" (1925, p. 191). He chastised his colleagues for their uncritical acceptance of the market model, noting that it had a pervasive effect on theorizing, that is, it did more than allow the theorist to accept market valuations for measurement of goods and services; it justified limiting the profession's role by assuming the viability of "regulation by competition" (Scott, 1933). Scott decried the blind reliance on the efficacy of competition and argued that if accountants did not recognize the noncompetitive nature of the corporate economy, accounting would become a useless "vestigial appendage" of society.

Veblen (1909, 1923) and later Keynes (1933) noted the dysfunctional nature of contemporary accounting, criticizing accountants for focusing solely on monetary returns. Keynes, for example, wrote that under the peculiar logic of accountancy, the men of the nineteenth century built slums rather than model cities, because slums paid. Veblen (1904) stressed the dangers of the growing separation of ownership and control. For Veblen, management's support for the vendibility of capital (through high profits), rather than the efficient manufacture of goods, reflected a conflict between the interests of capitalists and those of society at large. One result of this disharmony was that exchange prices no longer reflected value, but rather were a reflection of existing power relationships (or to use alternative terminology, were a reflection of the appropriation of income by one class from another).

Veblen directly influenced the subsequent work of Berle and Means (1934), Brandeis, and Landis (who played a substantial role in drafting the Securities Act of 1933) (Dorfman, 1973). Unfortunately, both Veblen and his student Scott, have been virtually ignored by accounting theorists and this has been reflected in the questions that subsequent accounting theorists have chosen to ask (and not to ask). Accompanying the individualistic focus, research has excluded inquiries into the class underpinnings of economic phenomena, the role of accounting in regulating economic activity, and the possibility that "accounting data has superseded competition as the chief arbiter of society's resources" (Scott, 1933, p. 225). The reluctance of accountants to address such questions and their acceptance of market prices (and hence their implicit commitment to particular distributions of income and social resources) are reflected in the persistent notion that accountants are historians.

Recent contributions to accounting theory have not modified the marginalist preconceptions and narrow focus of the discipline. While the market of competing interest groups has replaced that of competing individuals, and the utilitarian calculus has been extended to incorporate transaction costs, the basic marginalist assumptions remain unchallenged. These are vividly illustrated by recent work in agency theory, implicit in which are the following assumptions: that the primary (and perhaps sole) rationale for and objective of contemporary financial reporting is to serve the capital market; that competitive market forces can be relied upon to protect all interest groups (and that all interest groups are represented in the process); that members of each interest group are equally capable of processing information and discerning management's (homogeneous) utility function; that only government possesses coercive power; that all behavior is motivated by economic rationality; and that public interest arguments are always a sham to mask self-interest (Benston, 1979–80, 1982; Fama, 1980; Watts and Zimmerman, 1979).

Keynes's remark that "every practical person, who feels he is free of intellectual influences, is usually the slave of some defunct economist" is especially applicable to accountants (Keynes, 1936, p. 383). Most accounting practice has achieved a harmony with marginalist value theory without much conscious deliberation. This is mainly because marginalism is the only value theory with which most accountants are familiar; thus they reduce all economics to marginalism. When accountants do reflect on the nature of economics, they often perceive it to be so different from accounting that they often label approaches either as "economic" or "accounting." These differences turn out to be more apparent than real, however, because whenever an accounting problem of income determination or wealth measurement arises, all appeals to theoretical reason are framed exclusively within the marginalism domain and its conceptual linkages between market prices, cash, consumption, utility, and wealth.

Marginalism has virtually monopolized all accounting reflection about value theory, notwithstanding the fact that in order to resolve technical problems of concept operationalization and measurement, accountants have deviated from the marginalist model. These deviations and compromises have all been in terms of the fine print however; even the much vaunted area of "social accounting" is nothing more than marginalism with externalities. The obliviousness of accounting to all other theories of value is sufficient reason for concluding that accounting is unabashedly marginalist in its intellectual affiliations.

An array of value theories will be explored subsequently; each value theory will be examined relative to the conflicts and social interests that constituted it. Against this background of the social relativity of ideas—the role of theories as weapons of social conflict—we may gain a clearer appreciation of contemporary accounting. Accounting theory, like any social belief, is not merely a passive representation of reality, it is an agent in changing (or perpetuating) a reality. Marginalism provides accounting with a slanted picture of reality that affects both how the latter misperceives, and how it acts on, reality. This slant is ideological insofar as it misconstrues circumstances and events in order to promote certain partisan interests.

Placing accounting in its social and value-theoretic contexts is a necessary preliminary to the review of the public controversies introduced at the outset of the book. While the reader may have had a clear sense that something was wrong in each case, these problems were either misperceived or ignored by accounting reporting practice. What we require therefore is a systematic analysis of this accounting myopia, one that locates the source of the bias and offers some broad suggestions as to how it might be remedied.

The following table links the previous discussion of the marginalist origins of accounting with the subsequent discussions of the history of theories of value. The social and historical evolution of value theories is displayed in the variations from the top to the bottom of the table.

The table is divided vertically into two parts. The first shows value theories that are predominantly atomistic, individualistic, and private in their focus. (Such an emphasis may or may not be appropriate, depending on the society to which the theory is being applied.) In keeping with the earlier discussion, contemporary accounting and marginalist value theory are shown in the private or individualistic category. The right-hand portion of the table shows value theories that go beyond a concern about the equilibrium-contracting conditions for the immediate parties to the exchange.

Three types of social value theories shown in the table will be of particular interest to us: accumulationist theories, distributionist theories, and alienation theories. Each of these social theories examines the impact of exchange, not just in terms of the impact on the contracting individuals but also in terms of the impact on a specific notion of social development. Thus for example, accumulation theorists, such as Adam Smith, were primarily interested in how specific exchange contributed a "surplus" that permitted a greater division of labor and ultimately increased social productivity and wealth. Distribution theorists, such as Ricardo, theorized that social productivity would increase if, through individual exchange, surpluses were redistributed away from the land-owning and laboring classes to the new class of capitalists. Finally, alienation theorists, such as Marx, contended that social instabilities and crises would ensue from expropriative redistributions of income effected through individual exchanges.

The details of these social value theories will be pursued subsequently. However, a major proposition of this book is now clear: the absence of any social perspective in accounting disqualifies it from having anything authoritative to say about the public character of corporations; worse, by systematically excluding all social content from its theoretical agenda, and by persistently disenfranchising certain groups and social constituencies, accounting stands accused of partisanship and bias.

Table 9.1. The Private and Social Character of Value Theories*

Social Era	Private or Individualistic Value Theories	Social Value Theories
Feudalism	canonist theory of a "just price" (Aquinas, 1250)	
Mercantilism	mercantilist theory of the conventional price (Barbon, 1690; Cary, 1719)	
Early capitalism		classical political economy and the value theory of natural prices: accumulationist and distributionist theories (Smith, 1776; Ricardo, 1817
Capitalism	marginalist value theory (Bailey, 1825; Read; 1829; Jevons, 1871)	Ricardian socialist theory (Hodgskin, 1825; McCullock, 1825)
	Austrian school (Menger, 1871; Böhm-Bawerk, 1880; Wieser, 1880)	Marxist value theory as a theory of alienation, (Marx, 1840–52)
State and monopoly capitalism	Lausanne school (Walras, 1874; Parero, 1896)	Neo-Ricardians and Sraffians (Robinson, 1954; Sraffa, 1960; Keynes, 1939)
	conventional accounting practice	

---

*The dates in the table denote the times of major initial literary contributions by each school or viewpoint.

Canonist Value Theory and the Just Price

Two distinct concepts of value dominated the late sixteenth, seventeenth, and eighteenth centuries: the canonist approach and its successor, the mercantilist theory of value. Canonist theory was the most dominant theory of value in the centuries prior to the publication of Adam Smith's *Wealth of Nations* in 1776. The need for such a theory arose because producers of different commodities required a logic for determining their rates of exchange or terms of trade. According to classical political economy (a period ranging from Petty to Ricardo in Britain, and Boisquillebert to Sismondi in France) the main task of value theory was to explain what determines the power of purchasing over other goods that the possession of a commodity normally conveys to an owner. *Normally* was intended to connote an exchange rate set under long-term competitive conditions that were free of temporary fluctuations in supply and demand. The normal (or natural) price was considered to be equal to the costs of production (including costs of material, and labor and a customary profit) that, when added up, provided a monetary measure of the value of a commodity.

While most contemporary Western economists would not accept this view as a definition of the value of a commodity, few would consider it unreasonable, in an economic setting of small commodity producers, or unfamiliar. What would appear unreasonable to many today is the centrality that the classicists ascribed to labor in the determination of value and their "stubborn refusal to grant consumer demand and subjective utility the status of determinants of value and price" (Meek, 1975, p. 11).

The canonist concept of value may be traced to thirteenth century philosophers, such as Thomas Aquinas and other early canonist writers. They were concerned with the price at which small independent producers sold their products on the market and purchased commodities with the proceeds. Scholars and clerics were frequently involved in adjudicating trade disputes as well as other matters of distributive justice; consequently there was a need to develop a concept of an ethically just price.

As the proceeds of sale usually accrued to the direct producer the idea that the rewards should be commensurate with outlay and effort expended in production provided an obvious definition of a just price (Lekachman, 1976, pp. 19, 21). The constituent elements of the medieval just price included compensation for labor expended and risks taken, raw materials purchased, and transport costs incurred. A reasonable measure of distributive justice was probably attained by the concept of a just price in Aquinas's time because trade took place in small, static, and relatively self-sufficient communities, in which the efforts and expenses of various direct producers were known and could readily be compared (Meek, 1975, p. 13).

Canonist theorists contributed one of the earliest theoretical articulations of the concept of value and, through the medium of the church, their ideas about a just price and a fair value in exchange permeated all spheres of economic and social life. It is not that canonist theorists were the first to distill a rationale for conducting exchanges—clearly something analogous to this already existed in early communities in order that consistent customs and practices could be transmitted and adopted in different geographical locations and across generations. Rather, what distinguished the canonist era from earlier ones was the scale of the operation. First, specialization had reached a point where European society was able to employ, on a full-time basis, individuals devoted exclusively to "thinking about" valuation and related matters. Second, at no time previously had such a unified concept of value been present in public thought, and therefore in public action and affairs. Canonist value theorists were to medieval Europe what the god-kings and high priests were to ancient Egypt, in terms of their effect on social order and social control. Indeed, in this specific respect, canonist writers may be viewed as one of the first accounting ideologues in that they supplied the social beliefs and rationale for resolving matters of value and exchange for an entire social and economic order.

Mercantile trade transcended the boundaries of small communities and therefore posed some difficulties for value theorists, even in the time of Aquinas. Trade between merchants differed fundamentally from trade between direct producers. Merchants entered into exchanges in order to expand their capital; they required a premium on transactions—otherwise there was no incentive to trade. Direct producers, in contrast, exchanged commodities for money and then used the money to acquire additional commodities: a circular process represented by $C \blacktriangleright M \blacktriangleright C'$, in which C is the product measured in terms of labor hours, M is the money obtained, and C' is the labor hours embodied in the products obtained for the money. In the long run, an equilibrium will prevail when $C = C'$

These circumstances do not apply to the merchant; indeed Marx and other theorists have shown that the circular process is the reverse for merchants. They start with initial money (M), invest it in commodities (C), and then realize the commodities for M' (i.e., $M \blacktriangleright C \blacktriangleright M'$). For merchant activity to remain viable as an economic phenomenon, M' must be greater than M after all additional expenses, otherwise there would be no inducement for the merchant to enter into the exchange.

Merchants were viewed with considerable animosity, especially by the feudal lords with whom they conducted much of their business, because they were involved in "selling a thing for more than was paid for it" (Sewall cit. Meek, 1975, p. 13). Because merchants and traders usually came from afar (in England they were often referred to as "dusty feet"), their production costs were not known to local communities, and thus canonist principles could not be used to regulate the terms of trade between those merchants and their customers.

Mercantilist Value Theory and the Conventional Price

The growth of merchant trade initiated a major transition in the concept of value. Gradually, scholastic theoreticians began to articulate a concept of value that was more in keeping with the interests of those who dominated the new social structure. In order to account for the needs of expanding trade and commerce—and in particular the need for the gains of merchants and traders to be recognized as just—scholars retreated from the cost-oriented basis of the canonist's just price and redefined *just* in terms of what has been called the conventional price approach.

Meek (1975, p. 14) suggests that the conventional price (the price customarily paid and received) was reconciled with Aquinas's just price without too much difficulty by arguing that the value of a commodity was partly dependent upon its utility to the purchaser and, therefore, the subjective valuations of the individual consumer.

The medieval concept of a just price gradually lost its power over men's minds with the emergence of mercantilism. It did, however, leave a residual habit of thinking of value in terms of producer costs that became firmly rooted in the social consciousness. This was later to become one of the most influential intellectual legacies of the canonist tradition: the labor theory of value (Meek, 1975).

With the development of the idea of a conventional price in the mid- to late seventeenth century, several important subsidiary concepts emerged that were to play an important role in future theorizing. The ideas are well illustrated by Nicholas Barbon's pamphlet *A Discourse on Trade* written in about 1690, when classical value theory was beginning to supersede mercantilist value theory. Barbon's pamphlet links the value of a commodity—its current market price—with the strength of its demand and its level of supply. Moreover, he introduces the concept of the intrinsic value of a commodity—its utility value or subjective value—and suggests that this is causally linked to the market value, thereby anticipating marginalism and its causal ordering by nearly 60 years.

The emphasis on demand, and therefore utility, was understandable in the mercantilist period, as merchants were struggling for control over production, which still resided in the hands of direct producers. Similarly, the focus of merchants on market prices (as Petty wrote, "the excellency of the merchant lay in his judicious foresight and computation of market prices" [1899, p. 90, cit. Meek, 1975, p. 16]) reflected the prevailing view that it was consumers, not producers, who were the source of the merchant's gains.

The transition in economic thinking from mercantilist value theory to classical value theory involved concomitant changes in both the social context and the state of economic theorizing. Several intellectual innovations were contributory: the evolution of a concept of a "natural price," the development of the physiocratic school of thought, and finally, the emergence of Adam Smith's theory of value. As for the social context, we will see in what follows that changes in social circumstances demanded new theoretical contributions: especially ones that would fix attention on socially specialized labor as the prime source of material wealth.

The Social Context of the Transition to Classical Value Theory

The emergence of early forms of capitalism in the seventeenth century revived interest in a producer-cost orientation in value theory, especially in Britain, where we find writers such as Cary describing production costs as "true value" or "real" value" (Cary, 1719, pp. 98–99, 11–12 cit. Meek, 1975, p. 18).

The reversal in economic thinking mirrored a revolution that was taking place in economic practice. Many theoreticians of the times were spokesmen of the merchant-manufacturers and parvenu industrial capitalists of the towns, and these new entrepreneurs were increasingly concerned with costs of production. Competitive pressures on price differentials made it difficult for merchants to maintain their profit levels by their traditional methods and the merchant classes began to seek out new ways of exercising direct control over production costs. These methods varied from the "putting out" system (an early form of subcontracting in which production took place in the home) to attempts to increase productivity through technical improvements and the division of labor. The latter form of reorganization was often instigated from within the direct producer group. Dobb described it as "the rise from the ranks of the producers themselves of a capitalist element, half-manufacturer, half-merchant, which began to subordinate and to organize those very ranks from which it had so recently risen" (Dobb, 1946, pp. 128–29, cit. Meek, 1973, p. 19).

There was also an acute shortage of manufacturing labor during this period. Writings of the time were full of schemes for attracting foreigners by encouraging immigration and permitting naturalization, setting the poor to work, abolishing the death penalty in all but the most serious offenses, and so on. Production problems, together with greater competition in the marketplace, gradually helped divert the attention of economists and social philosophers from the sphere of exchange to that of production. These changes were accompanied by a growing belief that the wealth of nations (as well as private profits) emanated primarily from labor.

It was no accident that Adam Smith stated in the first sentence of *Wealth of Nations* that "the annual labor of every nation is the fund which originally supplies it with all the necessaries and conveniences of life which it annually consumes." Smith's view was entirely consistent with that of others of the period. It was not sufficient that labor be expended on a product in order to give it value. In order to impart value, labor had to be drawn from society's pool of specialized talents. There are numerous writings at the turn of the century that show how widespread these ideas were and how important they were in the early formulation of the labor theory of value (the classical value theory).

In essence, classicists regarded the interdependence between individuals, arising from specialization and the division of labor, as "the economic tie that binds people together" (Meek, 1975, p. 38). As Harris observes: "The mutual conveniences occurring to individuals, from their betaking themselves to particular occupations, is perhaps the chief cement that connects them together; the main source of commerce, and of large political communities (sic)" (Harris, 1757 cit. ibid.). Only a modest extension of these ideas is required to argue, as Petty and others did, that the real value of a commodity was more appropriately measured by the quantity of society's labor that had impregnated it than by its monetary value. Expressed somewhat differently, the quantity of socially necessary labor "regulates"—in Adam Smith's terms—the monetary value of a product. It would be incorrect to conclude that a fullfledged labor theory of value had emerged at this point; rather, while some writers continued to think of value in terms of market price, many were beginning to take an interest in the link between market price and production cost (Meek, 1975).

The Evolution of the Concept of a Natural Price

The concept of a commodity's natural price was one of the major intellectual breakthroughs of the eighteenth century. The classical notion of a natural price was probably most clearly discerned by Smith in his *Wealth of Nations* in 1776 but was anticipated in cruder form by Cantillon writing around 1730 and even earlier by Petty. A commodity with a natural price sold at a price equal to its "price cost" plus profit at the "natural" rate. The "natural" conditions were those of equilibrium, in which the profit level was such that there was no tendency for firms to leave or enter the industry: supply balanced demand.

In order for the idea of a natural price to evolve, two theoretical steps were necessary (Meek, 1975, pp. 25–27). The first was the development of the concept of a profit on capital—and later a period rate of return—as something distinct from rent on land or a premium paid to a supervisor of direct producers. This development permitted theorists to assert that prices were not arbitrarily determined, but behaved in a lawlike fashion in that, under long-term competitive conditions, they equilibrate to—in Smith's terms—prime cost plus a profit on the stock of capital.

The second theoretical strand needed to complete the concept of the natural price concerned the way socially necessary labor time imparted value to a commodity. Without a labor-based concept of value, the natural price was merely an additive theory, in which the overall price was obtained by summing the expenses incurred under the long-term, competitive conditions. But alone, such a view would be inadequate as an explanation of commodity prices because it simply substitutes one problem for another: instead of seeking an explanation of the price a commodity commands on the market, we now require an explanation of the prices commanded by the component resources of the commodity. Thus, classical scholars probed the causes of the component prices underlying the natural price (i.e., the wage rate, profit rate, material cost rate, etc.) (Meek, 1975, p. 32).

The reasons for this search for an explanation of the costs of production are to be found in the kind of problems that interested classicists. A theory of value based on supply and demand considerations and on an assessment of the tastes, preferences, and proclivities of consumers, would probably satisfy the needs of merchants and producers in their dealings at the market; however, it was hardly sufficient for scholars interested in the nature and causes of the wealth of nations.

Smith's Accumulationist Theory of Value

Adam Smith's theories become most comprehensible when placed in their historical context. Smith wrote at the dawn of the industrial revolution, 40 years before Ricardo, at a time when some of the most notable progress in capital investment was being made in agriculture rather than in industry (Dobb, 1973, p. 55). This was the period during which manufacturers were still identified with the "half-merchant" (a period characterized by Marx as one of "manufacture" in contradistinction to "machinofacture"). Moreover, Smith's declared aims were concerned with broad and fundamental issues of life in liberal society. He did not restrict himself to a narrow conception of economics but undertook the ambitious task of discerning the "anatomy" of civil society or, as Marx put it, penetrating "the inner physiology of Bourgeois society." Smith proposed to investigate "that system of moral philosophy wherein consisted the happiness and perfection of a man, considered not only as an individual but as a member of a family, of a state, and of the great society of mankind" (Smith, 1904, Vol. II, p. 259 cit. Meek, 1975, p. 45).

Smith's doctrine reflects a period of ideological transition marked by the problems of removing obstacles to industrial expansion. The regulations, practices, and sectionally protective impediments to free trade and competition were the objects of Smith's criticisms. He was especially critical of the mercantile school who, as he saw it, made a fallacious identification of wealth with money and an erroneous supposition that "to heap up gold and silver in a country is the readiest way to enrich it" (Smith, 1903, p. 163 cit. Dobb, 1973, p. 56).

For the early classicists, the natural price of a commodity was that which the market price or exchange price tended to gravitate toward in conditions of long-term equilibrium. The natural price was not the actual market price because the latter was the result of a range of fluctuations and inconsequential disturbances. The purpose of value theory, as Smith saw it, was to explain how the natural price was determined, that is, to delineate the forces by which it was governed.

What Smith needed was the factor that was the one predominant source of variation in the natural prices of commodities. This was to be the yardstick for ascertaining the real value of a commodity.

In *Wealth of Nations*—in contrast with the earlier *Lectures on Justice, Police, Revenue and Arms,* (the Glasgow Lectures)—Smith primarily attributes equilibrating movements (of actual prices towards natural prices) to the owners of capital in their desire to maximize profit. Of the "three great constituent orders," landlords, laborers, and capitalists, it was the capitalists and their drive to accumulate and expand their capital stock that formed the mainspring of economic growth and progress. Smith recognized that in a world made up of independent producers it might be legitimate to assume that commodities tended to be exchanged at rates that equated the labor power that they embodied. But under capitalism this rule of value no longer applied. Instead of small independent producers, capitalist society is made up of dependent laborers working under the direction of capitalist masters. The whole product no longer belongs to the laborer:

> As soon as stock has accumulated in the hands of particular persons, some of them will naturally employ it in setting to work industrious people, whom they will supply with materials and subsistence in order to make a profit by the sale of their work, or by what their labor adds to the value of the materials. (Smith, 1904, Vol. I, p. 50 cit. Meek, 1975, pp. 70–71)

At the center of Smith's analysis of the development of capitalism is the emergence of a social surplus and the appropriation of that surplus by capitalists for growth and development. These precepts were essential to Smith's basic theoretical mission: to show that the key to abundance lay in understanding how the surplus was appropriated, deployed, and then redeployed in successive time periods. For Smith, generation of wealth involved the study of economic dynamics, and this required an invariable means of measuring the flow of production over time that emanated from a particular sequence of employments (distributions) of surpluses.

Smith subscribed to the notion that it was the amount of socially necessary labor expended on the product that was a real measure of the value of a commodity. Smith uses the notion of a real measure in a special sense; it not only captures the magnitude of a commodity but it also embodies, inheres to or composes the product. Thus Smith states in the *Glas-*

gow *Lectures*, ". . . [It] is to be observed that labour, not money is the true measure of value" (Smith, 1896, p. 190 cit. Meek, 1975, p. 51).

Given the intellectual climate of Smith's era, a period of transition from the mercantilist's concerns about exchange to the early capitalist concentration on production and the division of social labor, it is understandable that he regarded socially specialized labor as the motivating force behind progress and abundance, and therefore as the quintessence of a commodity's value. Socially necessary labor gives a product its exchange value by virtue of the fact that the product was created in a society whose members exist by mutually exchanging the products of their labors. In this sense, all exchange is not only an exchange of labor, but ultimately an exchange of social activities. As Meek puts it: "The value relationship between commodities, which manifests itself in the act of exchange, is in essence a reflection of the relationship between men as producers" (Meek, 1975, p. 63). Marx also argued that value is ultimately a social relation.

While the labor expended on a product was the source of a commodity's value, it was Smith's opinion that it was not necessarily a measure of the extent of its value. This was a point of departure for subsequent labor theorists because Smith was looking not to the conditions of production for his ultimate metric of value, but to the conditions of exchange. It seemed to Smith that the appropriate measure of value was the "actual power of purchase of other goods" that the proceeds of a sale of a commodity conveyed to its owner. This he termed the "commandable labor value" of a commodity.

Smith's value principle of commandable labor value may be properly understood when placed in the context of his entire system of thought. In Meek's view (or his "guess" as he puts it) Smith's choice of commandable labor reflects his basic interest in the processes of capital accumulation, and his belief that these processes could only be understood in terms of the employment of "productive" wage-labor by capitalists in successive time periods (Meek, 1975, p. 65). Commandable labor value reflects the growth in the number of workers that can be hired and is a measure of the rate of capital accumulation, both for the individual capitalist and for society as a whole.

Smith appreciated that in order to properly evaluate the process of accumulation, it was necessary to take different sequences of reinvestments in heterogeneous goods and services and reduce each path to a common factor, in order to compare their relative wealth accumulation potential. For Smith, a suitable common factor was suggested by the situation of the individual capitalist: capital accumulation for the individual was indicated by growth in the number of laborers that could be hired. In this way, Smith settled on commandable labor (rather than labor hours expended in production) as his metric value.

From a theoretical perspective, a subtle but nevertheless important shift had taken place between the value theory espoused in canonist times and that developed by Smith. In the view of canonist theorists, the exchange of equal amounts of labor time formed a prescriptive policy foundation of the just price. Smith's concept of commandable labor value anticipated that capitalist appropriation would cause commandable labor time to exceed the labor time needed to replenish inputs. Indeed, it was a primary thrust of *Wealth of Nations* that this was a desirable situation. Hence, for the first time, a persuasive value theory argument in favor of unequal exchange was advanced: the argument that accelerated accumulation by capitalists would enhance the community's productive capacity and, therefore, its means of subsistence over time.

Notes

1. The attraction of subjective accounting income concepts is reflected today in contemporary generally accepted accounting principles and Financial Accounting Standards Board rules, in which present value procedures are used in valuing leases, pensions, goodwill, bonds, fixed assets (when payment is deferred), and oil and gas reserves.

2. Irving Fisher (1906), a self-proclaimed marginalist, has had considerable influence on the works of early accounting scholars (e.g., Canning, 1929; Rorem, 1928; Paton, 1922; Paton and Stevenson, 1918). Canning's acknowledgment to Fisher was explicit: "I need not declare my obligation to Professor Fisher for the influence of his writings upon my thought—that obligation appears throughout this book" (1929, p. iv). The influence of Canning can be seen in Vatter (1947) and subsequent funds flow theorists. The utility-based foundations of Fisher's work, as articulated by Hirshleifer (1970) and Fama and Miller (1972), are also widely acknowledged in the accounting literature, even the "standard teaching texts." Thus for instance, we find open acknowledgments to this intellectual heritage in Hendrickson (1970); May, Mueller, and Williams (1975); Edwards and Bell (1961); and Parker and Harcourt (1969).

3. Veblen (1904), regarded the value of large, managerially governed corporations as a psychological concept that was dependent on the expectations and confidence of investors. Those in control, he argued, attempted to promote the interests of capital by creating illusions (manipulating output, disseminating false reports and information, or withholding positive news) that affected exchange

prices. In this manner, he recognized the power of accounting to affect the distribution of income between and within social classes.

4. Those wishing to retain the link between historical cost and subjective consumption possibilities did so by arguing that future income is determined at the time of purchase (measured by the owner's implicit discount rate), and as Alexander (1950) was to contend at a later date, any future deviations from that income were due to faulty expectations and, as such, were not income or loss but merely revisions of initial cost.

10

Accumulationist and Distributionist Theories of Social Value

Criticisms of Smith's Theory of Value

The evolution of Ricardo's theory of value is best understood in the context of his critical reviews of Smith's ideas on the subject. First and foremost, Ricardo, like Smith, was a labor theorist in that he believed that the creation of commodities of value involved the depletion of society's necessary labor. The exchangeable value of a commodity represented the purchasing power over other goods (not a monetary value) that the possession of the commodity in question confers to its owner. Hereafter, "exchangeable value" will be used to refer to a commodity's potential exchange value with other nonmonetary assets; "exchange value" will denote a commodity's value in terms of money, or a generalized money equivalent. The labor expended in the manufacture of a commodity—"the difficulty or facility of production"—was supposed to regulate its exchangeable value.

Smith's focus on exchangeable values is as appropriate today as it was in his own time. Exchangeable value not only defines the terms of trade between commodities—and therefore commodity producers—it specifies the distribution of income among individuals and classes. In short, Smith was seeking to explain and evaluate the division of social wealth.

As we have seen previously, two concepts of value may be found in the writings of Adam Smith. The first, reflected in the first sentence of *Wealth of Nations,* attributes a commodity's value to the quantity of social labor consumed in the commodity's production. The efficient deployment of socially specialized labor is the genesis of the wealth of nations according to this view. The second concept of value to be found in Smith's writings is the quantity of labor that could be hired from the proceeds of sale of a commodity (called the commodity's commandable labor value). Thus, both of Smith's concepts of value were expressed in labor time; the first, and primary, one being a measure of the labor input to a commodity, the second being the labor quantity that could be acquired, or commanded, after realizing the commodity in question.

Ricardo's critique of Smith's commandable theory of value appeared initially in the first edition of *Principles*. In Chapter 1, Ricardo reaffirms his belief that socially necessary labor is the source of all value: "The value of a commodity, or the quantity of any other commodity for which it will exchange, depends on the relative quantity of labor which is necessary for its production, and not on the greater or lessor compensation which is paid for that labor" (Sraffa, 1951, Vol. 1, p. 11).

Ricardo criticized commandable labor as an unreliable measure of value because the quantity of labor that may be acquired from the proceeds of the sale of a commodity may fluctuate with the market wage rate—a variable that may be totally unrelated to the labor effort expended in producing the commodity. Thus, according to Ricardo, Smith's commandable labor value contradicted the more fundamental value of labor imputed to a commodity during its production.

Ricardo's criticism, that Smith had erected in commandable labor a second measure of value that stood in stark contradiction to the labor expended measure, is reinforced in his critique of Malthus's support for the commandable labor measure. Ricardo contended that commandable labor was an inadequate metric of value because it failed to reflect genuine improvements in efficiency. Ricardo shows this by using an example in which labor remunerated out of the corn produced:

> If by improvements in husbandry, corn could be produced with half the expenditure of labor and capital, it would, by Mr. Malthus, be said to be unaltered in value provided the same quantity and no more was given to the laborer in wages. . . . In Mr. Ricardo's measure, everything to which such improvements were applied would fall in value. . . . (Sraffa, 1951, Vol. IV, pp. 372–73)

In essence, Ricardo was arguing that Smith had already made a convincing exposition in favor of labor expended as the basic determinant of exchangeable value in early societies, and that he had offered no logical reason why this measure should be abandoned in favor of commandable value under capitalism. This was underlined by the fact that commandable value, at times, would not correspond with the labor embodied in a product. Ronald Meek (1975) has argued that Ricardo's criticism of Smith's concept of commandable labor value is rather ungenerous on several scores, not least of which is that he fails to appreciate the importance of accumulation to Smith's way of thinking and the way that commandable labor value matched neatly with this perspective.

The second part of Ricardo's critique of Smith's concept of value was that while the labor expended in the production of a commodity might regulate exchangeable value in simple commodity production—in which the direct producer owned the entire product—the same relation no longer held under captalism, in which part of the product was appropriated by the owners of land and capital. Specifically, when capital-labor intensities vary across firms, labor expended in production is no longer proportional to the equilibrium exchangeable values of products. The divergence of a commodity's exchangeable value from Smith's expended value had not passed unnoticed by Smith; indeed, his favorable disposition toward commandable labor value may have been motivated, in part, in a rather negative way, by the failure of labor-expended measures to fully explain current exchangeable values.

Such ambiguities in Smith's labor theory were not likely to please Ricardo. He was seeking a yardstick to measure the effect on total output of redistributing income away from landlords and toward capitalists. But the ambiguous relation between the labor expended on a commodity and the rate at which it will exchange for other commodities on the market means that a specific level of aggregate physical production has an infinite number of exchangeable values, each corresponding to a particular distribution of income. Thus a commodity may, at two points in time, use exactly the same quantity of human and physical resources in its production, yet its "value" can differ if the distribution of income between labor and capital has changed.

Accordingly, any given level of production of a commodity may have associated with it a range of possible income distributions, and each income distribution would give a different exchangeable value for the commodity (relative to other commodities). This was the essence of the second part of Ricardo's critique of Smith's concept of value: that Smith failed to provide a measure of value that was invariant to alternative income distributions, that is, there was no unique, one-to-one correspondence between the amount of socially necessary labor consumed and a commodity's exchangeable value.

In summary, Ricardo criticized commandable labor value because it was unreliable, and exchangeable value because it was always predicated on a given distribution of income. Both criticisms of Smith's value theory amounted to the same thing: Smith had failed to provide an invariant measure of value that society could use to adjudge the relative worth of different systems of economic organization, together with the commodity bundles that each produced. As noted earlier, modern accounting also faces these questions (c.f., pp. 85–87, 105–106) and has been no more successful than Adam Smith in obtaining answers.

From Accumulationist to Distributionist Value Theory

Adam Smith's ideas on value challenged the ethics and beliefs of mercantilism. His notions were not merely controversial but revolutionary inasmuch as they helped clear the way for the inception of capitalism. Similarly, David Ricardo's theory of value helped initiate a further revolution in social ideology by providing intellectual sustinence to the new social order (of capitalism) and, at the same time, supplying a theoretical basis for its overthrow (by aiding inchoate forms of socialism).

Inherent in the work of Smith and Ricardo, as well as in that of the classical economists who followed them, are concepts of value that are diametrically opposed to the value theory underlying much contemporary accounting practice and research. We may gain a better perspective on the partiality of our own accounting notions of value by examining the way in which the early marginalists, the forefathers of the notion of value in accounting today, systematically distorted and mystified classical notions of value.

Ricardo's writings spanned some three decades to his death in 1823. His work underwent considerable maturation during this period, something that should not be underrated either in interpreting Ricardo or when reading this perfunctory account of his ideas. The evolving form of Ricardo's ideas, together with the occasions when he changed direction and emphasis, provides ample ammunition for politically motivated attempts to discredit or remold his writings.

With the important exception of a recently discovered paper called "Absolute Value and Exchangeable Value" that he was working on in the last few weeks of his life, Ricardo's *Principles* represented the climax of his thinking. *Principles* first appeared in 1817; this was followed by two subsequent editions (both with modifications and improvements) that appeared before the author's death. In celebrating the publication of *Principles*, James Mill noted, in an article written in the *Edinburgh Review*, that between 1776, the publication date of *Wealth of Nations*, and 1817, "not a single treatise on political economy appeared in England. Adam Smith remained the only authority and he was little heeded" (Halevy, 1928, pp. 264–65 cit. Dobb, 1973, p. 65).

The reasons why *Wealth of Nations* lacked authority are not hard to find. Smith's work is full of anecdotes and illustrations; it does not provide a coherent theoretical system for political economy, nor was it Smith's intention that it should. For many readers, the primary virtue of *Wealth of Nations* was that it illuminated history from a new perspective and elucidated that perspective with numerous specific examples. These antecedents, in the view of contemporaries such as James Mill, only served to underline the importance of Ricardo's *Principles*: it provided the first integrated theory of value, profits, rents, income distribution, and economic growth, expressed and argued in a fashion akin to a mathematical demonstration, to which forceful corollaries as to economic and social policy were persuasively attached (Dobb, 1973, p. 66).

The differences between Smith's and Ricardo's concepts of value are reflected in their different conceptualizations of the economic problem and the ways they chose to analyze it. Both scholars subscribed to the view that the primary task of political economy was to discover the laws that governed the wealth of nations and to explicate those laws in a way that would delineate the areas of decision that were open to policy-makers (Sraffa, 1951, Vol. 1, p. 106). Smith's legacy to economists of the late eighteenth and early nineteenth centuries was his identification of the accumulation of capital as the primary cause of wealth. His theoretical focus therefore, especially as regarded value, dwelt mainly on the processes of accumulation. What particularly interested Smith were the institutional hindrances that impaired wealth accumulation as well as certain outmoded attitudes and beliefs that were incompatible with the expansion of capital.

The means by which the accumulation of wealth and abundance might be achieved appeared rather differently to Ricardo than it did to Smith. While the distribution of income between the constituent orders of landlords, capitalists, and laborers was of only secondary interest in Smith's study of accumulation processes, it assumed major proportions in Ricardo's work. Meek noted that in Ricardo's time, there was a widespread recognition that "pervaded business and financial circles and became the veritable milieu of economic thought": that profits were by far the most important source of capital accumulation and that "England's power depended on the flourishing condition of her manufacturers and upon the maintenance, undiminished, of industrial profits" (1975, p. 84). To this end, it was generally assumed that the social surplus was better distributed as profit rather than rent (Sraffa, 1951).

Ricardo is renowned for his trenchant attacks on landowners. He argued that a conflict of interest existed between landed property and industrial capital: "The interest of the landlord is always opposed to the interests of every other class in the community" (Sraffa, 1951, Vol. IV, p. 18). Ricardo felt that it was necessary to show, in much greater detail than Smith had, the part played by the distribution between rent and profit. Income distribution was, to Ricardo, the single most important problem facing political economy: "The most difficult, and perhaps the most important topic of Political Economy is the progress of a country in wealth and the laws by which the increasing produce is distributed" (Sraffa, 1951, Vol. VII, p. 24).

The theory of value played a central role in Ricardo's master plan. It was to provide a yardstick for assessing the alternative paths of national production that progressive redistribution of national income generated. Uninterested in the comparative statics of contemporary economics, Ricardo investigated economic dynamics: the path an economy took over time in terms of aggregate national income, income distribution among social classes, employment, savings, and investment. Income distribution—and therefore the distribution of property and wealth—were central to Ricardo's studies, and evolving a distribution theory was thus the principal problem in political economy in his view.

Ricardo saw economic activity as a loop in which, once continuing net investment and growth are introduced, a significant form of the outputs are ploughed back as fresh inputs before they have a chance to emerge as final consumer goods. Ricardo sought a methodology to determine the trajectory an economy would follow over time if it began from a particular distribution of income between laborers, capitalists, and landowning classes. This methodology was to be supplied by value theory. In this fashion, Ricardo aimed to provide a "conditional forecast" as to the patterns of growth and employment that would ensue in a succession of time periods from an initial distribution of income.

Absolute Value, Exchangeable Value, and Monetary Value

The search for an invariant measure of value was to occupy Ricardo up to the last few weeks of his life. An uncompleted paper titled "Absolute Value and Exchangeable Value," written in 1823, summarized his deliberations on the subject (Sraffa, 1951, Vol. 1, pp. 62–63). The discovery of this paper laid to rest speculations that Ricardo had abandoned the labor theory of value because of the difficulty of devising an invariant measure of value. It is now clear that, to the end, Ricardo viewed this matter as one of the most crucial facing economic science.

Ricardo was very clear in what he required from an "absolute" measure of value and why labor expended was central to any formulation of it. In a letter to Malthus, he unequivocally rejects the market price or monetary value of a commodity as being of central concern:

Nothing to me is of so little importance as the fall and rise of commodities in money. . . . It may be curious to develop the effect of an alteration of real value on monetary price, but mankind are only really interested in making labour productive in the enjoyment of abundance, and in a good distribution of the produce obtained by capital and industry. I cannot help thinking that in your speculations you suppose these much too closely connected to the money price. (Sraffa, 1951, Vol. IV, p. 83)

The relegation of monetary value to a secondary position relative to labor expended in production is also emphasized in a letter to James Mill:

They [my readers] must know that the prices of commodities are affected in two ways, one by the alteration in the relative value of money, which affects all commodities at the same time, the other by an alteration in the value of the particular commodity, and which affects no other thing. . . . This invariability of . . . value from particular causes relating to themselves only . . . is the sheet anchor on which all my propositions are built. (Sraffa, 1951, Vol. VI, pp. 348–49)

A compelling reason for preferring labor expended to a monetary value is its invariable character. Suppose, for example, that we are interested in discovering more economical ways of producing a particular type of beer and that we wish to compare two different beer production systems operating in different localities and in different points in time. We find that one of the beers retails for $1 a pint while the other sells for $1.15 a pint. In addition, the beers could be purchased for one half of an ounce, and three quarters of an ounce, of silver respectively.

Here we have two measures of value: dollars and silver. We could use either to evaluate the two beer production systems. But how are we to interpret the value ratios? Does the $1, compared with the $1.15, signify that the first production process is more economical? It could be that the $1.15 reflects the ravages of inflation and is a depleted currency compared with the $1. Certainly this might be the case if we discovered that $1.15 was expressed in Canadian dollars while the $1 was a U.S. dollar. The same might apply if we found that we were comparing New York dollars with Boise, Idaho, dollars. (A dollar goes much further in Boise, Idaho.) Similar confusion would ensue if one amount was expressed in 1975 dollars, and the other in 1984 dollars. Using a monetary measure of value, we can never be sure whether differences are attributable to production efficiency differences, or differences due to the unstable monetary yardstick.

Silver, gold, oil, or any other commodity presents similar difficulties. Can we conclude by comparing the two silver valuations of beer that the cheaper one has been produced more economically and will eventually drive the other from the market? It is possible that the difference has nothing to do with the economics of beer production and that it is the economics of producing silver that has changed. Again, when value is defined as an exchange ratio between two commodities—or one commodity and money—it is impossible to determine whether a change in the ratio originates with the commodity of interest (the relative form) or the value yardstick (the equivalent form).

Unlike monetary value measures, the labor embodied in a product is specific to that product alone. In the beer example, if the first production process required half the labor effort of the second, then, in terms of society's most vital resource, labor, we could say that the first process was more economical than the second. This statement would pertain regardless of fluctuations, for whatever reasons, in the money price of a pint or in its rate of exchange with gold, silver, wine, or gin.

We may summarize this discussion by referring to Maurice Dobb's "Requirements of a Theory of Value," since it so clearly states Ricardo's aims and concerns (Dobb, 1937, pp. 1–33). Dobb argues that a good theory of value must use independent constants or known parameters to determine a commodity's worth. For instance, to assert that a unit of commodity A is worth two units of commodity B (which may be either another commodity or money) tells us nothing; it merely shifts the focus of inquiry to the worth of commodity B. Now the worth of commodity B must be resolved before commodity A's value can be determined. Dobb likens the problem to that of an equation system: the form $x = y$ is not informative because we can only come to know x through y, and y can only be known from x. If however, x were defined in terms of constants or parameters whose values could be arrived at from outside the equation system, then we could come to know x. (For instance, in the equation $x = 32(y!) + 50$, x is in the position of a falling body, and $y!$ is the factorial of time in seconds that the body has spent falling.)

This is an entirely different kind of equation system than the previous one. In this latest case the constants (32 and 50) and the independent variable y are known and are of an entirely different character than x, and the latter's value can easily be determined. This is not so with the earlier formulation, in which the value of x depends on the value of y, because the relation merely replaces one problem with another.

To the requirement that a theory of value have constants that permit independent determination, Dobb adds that a value theory must provide a single metric that allows comparisons to be made. Thus Marx criticized utility as a measure of value because it did not permit interpersonal and intertemporal comparisons. Similarly, Dobb (1937, pp. 18–19) notes that the quantities of land and capital consumed are inadequate measures of a commodity's value because they represent an "essential dualism" (i.e., they cannot be reduced to a single ratio of value).

Reactions to Ricardian Value Theory

Ricardo wrote at a time of transition that involved not only the demise of the landowning classes, but also the emergence of working class movements that became more powerful under the socializing influence of capitalist production relations. Ricardo's ideas were used selectively: they were deployed initially in an offensive position against landlords and were subsequently attacked and rejected for the encouragement they gave to socialist movements of the working class.

To many working class spokesmen, the support that Ricardo's concept of value gave to their cause was direct and unequivocal. "Labour produces all" was the logical precursor to questioning why labor did not receive all—or at least considerably more than it had received in the past. These writers and pamphleteers are often described as "Ricardian socialists," although they added little to Ricardo's original formulation and frequently misinterpreted, vulgarized, and popularized the ideas to the point of making them easy targets of criticism.

Included among the Ricardians were Thomas Hodgskin, J.F. Brey, John Gray, and William Thompson. Hodgskin was a considerable influence in the insipient trade unions and working class educational establishments such as the Mechanics' Institutes. His work did not pass unnoticed by gentry economists. James Mill once wrote of Hodgskin's ideas that "if they were to spread they would be subversive of civilized society" (Robbins, 1952, p. 135, cit. Dobb, 1973, p. 98). Hodgskin propounded a rather underdeveloped concept of exploitation in which "profit and rent were alike filched from labour" (Dobb, 1973, p. 137). Like Hodgskin, William Thompson was also taken with Ricardo's view that only labor and nature were the originating sources of wealth. In his *An Inquiry Into the Principles of the Distribution of Wealth,* he deduced the right of labor to the whole produce from the postulate that labor is the sole active creator of wealth. Even before Thompson and Hodgskin, Piercy Ravenstone elaborated an appropriation theory of property income in which he wrote of "the pretension of the landowner . . . as being the basis of property of every description. . . . From this moment labor ceases to be free. A man cannot exercise his faculties . . . make use of his limbs without sharing the produce of his labor with those who contribute nothing to the success of his exertions" (Ravenstone, 1821, pp. 199–200, cit. Dobb, 1973, p. 139).

Marx was among those who severely criticized the friends of the working class who popularized Ricardo's ideas. Marx's reaction was of a distinctly different order than that of conservative economists; he argued that although the labor theory can be used to study the laws of motion of capitalism and the appropriation of the product of one class by another, it is unscientific, idealistic, and utopistic to then argue that such appropriations are unjust and that a redistribution back to the working people is in order.

A vociferous attack on Ricardo came from conservative economists whose criticisms were aimed at the emerging revolutionary socialist movements. Ronald Meek observes that the majority of establishment economists "were very much aware of the dangerous use to which radical writers were putting Ricardian concepts. . . . Their fundamental approach was determined by the belief that what was socially dangerous could not be possibly true" (1967, p. 71, cit. Dobb, 1973, p. 111). In commenting on the same conservative reaction to revolutionary variants of Ricardianism, Marx saw 1830 as the end of Ricardian economics and, indeed, not only Ricardian but also classical and scientific economics. From then on, he commented, "scientists were obliged to give way to hired prize-fighters" (Meek, 1967, p. 52, cit. Dobb, 1973, p. 96). It was in reference to the ideological thrusts of these "prize-fighters" that Marx coined the term "vulgar economics."

Marx was referring to economists of the day such as Samuel Read, who considered Ricardo's notion that labor was the only source of wealth a "mischievous and fundamental error" at the heart of his system (Read, 1829, p. xxix, cit. Dobb, 1973, p. 110). Similarly, Poulett Scrope, author of *Political Economy for Plain People*, referred to the "mistaken hostility to capital" and "the Right of Profit on Capital" in a response to Hodgskin's "robbery of laborers" (Scrope, 1833, pp. 103, 105, cit. Dobb, 1973, p. 110).

The attack on Ricardo's ideas by establishment economists took several forms: the notion of absolute value was rejected or conflated with relative or exchange value; Ricardo's dismissal of the supply and demand apparatus as inadequate was challenged (as was his rejection of utility as the primary determinant of value), and Ricardo's contention that money prices were mere appearances and had to be reduced to their "real" cost of socially necessary labor was dismissed by a number of economists.

Critics of absolute value did not challenge the concept directly, but chose to conflate it with other notions of value—principally exchange value. Bailey, one of Ricardo's most vociferous critics and a thoroughgoing relativist, begins by defining "exchangeable value" and then asserts that it is the only form of value: "[All] value denotes nothing . . . but merely the relation in which two objects stand to each other as exchangeable commodities. . . . Thus, Ricardo's search . . . was pointless because there was no way of defining 'unvarying value'" (Bailey, 1825, p. 4–5, cit. Dobb, 1973, p. 99). Bailey's criticisms were quoted approvingly as being decisive, in such influential and distinguished circles as London's Political Economy Club in 1831. However, even Malthus, who was frequently at odds with Ricardo, pointed out in defense of Ricardo's thesis that to reject one concept of value because it does not resemble another is hardly a justifiable dismissal.

Other attacks from the cloisters of Dublin and Oxford emanated from misunderstandings and misrepresentations of Ricardo's concepts of value, especially absolute value. Similar misapprehensions applied—and apply to this day—to Ricardo's views on supply and demand analysis. Ricardo recognized the role of the "scissors" in short-term price fluctuations, however, he estimated their primary failing to be both descriptive and prescriptive: descriptively, they said nothing about the level at which supply and demand fixed prices in the "normal" (long-term) case; prescriptively, they said nothing about the optimality of prices in a general (dynamic) macroeconomic context. Both issues were at the head of Ricardo's research agenda, and the concept of absolute value was central in his strategy.

The highly politicized context in which Ricardo's labor theory of value was discussed should not be taken as unusual circumstances that violate the working conditions of normal scholarly activity. It is a central tenet of his book that these are the normal conditions in which social theorizing takes place, especially theorizing about value and, therefore, accounting. Indeed, it is naive to suggest that a value theory or an accounting theory could emerge from an apolitical, asocial, and ahistorical context. Such pretenses are less prevalent in economics today than they were a few years ago; however in accounting they are, and always have been, commonplace.

Even though it is only partially complete, the previous discussion of the evolution of value theories reveals important continuities with contemporary accounting. Smith, Ricardo, and others struggled to resolve problems analogous to the accounting dilemmas discussed at the beginning of this work. For instance, distributionist and accumulationist theories strive not merely to describe actual economic exchanges, they also aim to prescribe economic policy. This is not too distant from the aims of this work: to evolve a new theoretical structure for accounting capable of adjudicating the social worth of transactions entered into by (say) Slater Walker, National Student Marketing, Hooker Chemical, etc. Although Marx's contribution to these deliberations still needs to be considered, it should already be apparent that an intriguing relationship exists between the concerns of early value theorists and the problems that plague accountants today.

11

Marx's Value Theory

Introduction

In some respects we are fortunate that Marx was unaware of Ricardo's renewed interest, in the last few months of his life, in embodied social labor as the measure of absolute value. Marx's understanding of Ricardo's labor theory of value was based on an earlier version of Ricardo's work, which included a seemingly insoluble problem. In essence, Ricardo found what he assumed was a contradiction to his "law of value" in that under capitalism, in which the organic composition of capital (capital intensity) varied across industrial sectors, there was no longer a direct correspondence between a commodity's long-term equilibrium price (exchangeable value), and the amount of socially necessary labor embodied in it.[1] This disparity preoccupied Ricardo, and it was these preoccupations that attracted Marx's attention, thereby revealing a great deal about Marx's notions on value theory.

While Marx rejected Ricardo's conclusions about the flaws in the law of value, it is important to recognize the extent to which Marx concurred with Ricardo on essentials. Marx observed that "the great historical significance of Ricardo for the science [of political economy was that he established that] the foundation, the starting point for the physiology of the bourgeois system—for understanding its internal organic coherence and life process—is the determination of value by labor time" (Marx, 1951, p. 203, cit. Dobb, 1973, p. 143 and Meek, 1975, p. 118). Ronald Meek points out that "Ricardo held a deep-rooted feeling that, in spite of appear-

ances to the contrary, embodied labor did in some significant sense constitute and regulate the 'value' of a commodity" (Meek, 1975, p. 119). It was,
however, Marx's opinion that Ricardo only half-realized the full implications of "this one great insight."

Marx held the view that value conceived in terms of the socially necessary labor time embodied in products was the key factor in regulating existence under all commodity-producing societies, including capitalism. A
major aspect of existence that fell within the regulatory orbit of the law of
value was that primary producers receive products in exchange for their
own that contain an amount of embodied labor equal in amount to that contained in their own. This proposition was so important for Marx—and
Ricardo—that without it he felt that political economy would be without a
rational basis.

Marx's Analysis of Ricardo's Deviations
from the Law of Value

Marx developed his critique of Ricardo and, in doing so, showed that
what Ricardo had taken to be deviations and exceptions to the law of value
were, in fact, the key to a new theory of social alienation and exploitation.
In this way, Marx reasserted the law of value as an explanation of exchangeable values under capitalism.

Marx proceeded by contrasting capitalist commodity production with
what is termed simple, or "pure," commodity production. Pure commodity
production refers to circumstances under which a division of labor exists
and independent primary producers exchange the products of their specialized activities for their means of existence. Pure commodity production—
an "ideal" type—assumes competition between independent producers and
a situation in which producers own their tools of production: there is no separation of ownership of labor and capital.

Under pure commodity production, independent producers receive, in
exchange for their products, money that enables them to buy a quantity of
commodities, containing an amount of socially necessary labor equal to
that contained in their own. The law of value predicts that in long-term normal conditions, free of temporary fluctuations, equal values—in terms of
labor time—will be exchanged. This proposition is summarized as follows:

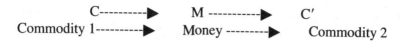

Competition between primary producers ensures that under pure commodity production, the labor time embodied in the commodity acquired (commodity 2) will tend to equal the labor time expended in the commodity initially sold (commodity 1). If primary producers were able to acquire commodities with a higher embodied labor content than that of their own, then two changes would be likely: first, the primary producers would probably be joined by others wishing to share in the favorable balance of trade enjoyed by the product; second, producers would probably curtail production of the acquired commodities until more favorable terms of exchange were restored. The equilibrating tendencies at work here are not in terms of the actual labor time spent in producing a product, but the amount of time that competitive conditions allow producers in the community to spend creating the product (Mandel, 1968). Thus obsolete technology or inefficient production methods will not be rewarded because for market exchange purposes, goods will be valued or priced by the standards set by the average producer in the market. This social regulation of private production is one of the most significant losses of individual sovereignty under capitalism; it is an alienating state for the individual because it amounts to a loss of control over life-activities.

In pure commodity production, the law of value operates in a direct and unambiguous way: commodities exchange in quantities that tend to equalize the labor quantities embodied in each. However, this relationship becomes complex under capitalist commodity production. This change in the relations between social members—from independent producers to capitalists and laborers—does not invalidate the law of value (as the early writings of Ricardo appeared to conclude) but modifies the form in which the law expresses itself. In either case, the focus on explaining exchangeable values betrays the more fundamental priority: to explain the distribution of income among social classes.

Capitalist commodity production differs from its pure counterpart in a number of important ways; it constitutes a change in the relations between social members, and it changes their relationship to nature. First, labor itself becomes a commodity that is bought and sold and, compared to the independent producer of pure commodity production, enjoys less control over production activities and the final product. Second, in contrast to pure commodity production, the direct producer loses control of the tools of production (material implements, machines, and other forms of physical capital). Consequently, human capital becomes "free" and physical capital is appropriated.[2] Under capitalist commodity production, it is the capitalist that hires labor, determines the method of work, establishes what is to be produced, and supplies the tools of production. Most importantly, it is the capitalist who, within the constraints of the market, establishes exchangeable values that are no longer directly proportional to the amount of embodied labor in the product. Under capitalism, the law of value still regulates a commodity's exchangeable value in that two labor costs affect exchangeable value: the subsistence cost of live labor and the rate of profit on dead, appropriated labor.

Pure commodity production involves a circulation of commodities, in which the exchange is carried out by the owners of commodities and consists of selling in order to buy. The reverse process is the case under capitalist commodity production. The circulation of money, that is, the successive operations carried out by successive owners of money capital (i.e., capitalists) involves buying in order to sell. Capitalists buy commodities, such as materials, machines, tools of production, and the commodity of human labor, not for immediate consumption, but as investments for productive purposes. We have, therefore, the following sequence:

$$M \longrightarrow C \longrightarrow M'$$
$$\text{Money 1} \longrightarrow \text{Commodity} \longrightarrow \text{Money 2}$$

The essential difference between the circulation of commodities ($C \longrightarrow M \longrightarrow C'$) and the circulation of capital ($M \longrightarrow C \longrightarrow M'$) lies in a comparison of the end points of each circulation process. In commodity circulation, an equivalence of $C = C'$ is an equilibrium condition because any divergence from the rule of exchange of equal values would activate competitive pressures to restore an equilibrium. In capital circulation, unequal exchange (i.e., $M' > M$) is an equilibrium precondition for circulation to take place because investors require a premium or profit to entice them to release funds (M) for a project.

Underlying the monetary relations in the circulation of capital is a corresponding circulation of labor time. Suppose, for example, that a certain plantation's slaves worked a full seven-day week and were allowed only on Sundays to grow and prepare food for their own consumption. In this case, the value of labor power (V) is one day, and what is termed the surplus labor (S), is six days. The surplus labor corresponds to what is appropriated by the slave owner and is calculated by taking the difference between the value of labor power and the value of the product of labor V', which in this case, is seven days.

Surplus labor is a quantitative expression of a coercive social relationship: it measures the systematic exploitation of one social class by another. The concept of surplus labor captures one of the most fundamental aspects of social existence because it measures that portion of life that an individual is compelled to give up in order to sustain others. Moral judgment is not necessarily implied here: the compulsion may originate in harsh natural conditions that will only support a disciplined and organized community. Alternatively, the compulsion could be a form of social oppression in conditions of plenty. The crucial consideration is the individuals' lack of control over time and life-experiences and, therefore, over the development of their capacities and potentialities (Ollman, 1976, pp. 73–126).

Surplus labor reflects exploitative aspects of social relations in that they represent an appropriation of labor time for which nothing is given in exchange. It is therefore a measure of unequal exchange, a phenomenon that occurs between slave and slaveholder, feudal lord and serf, and capitalist and worker. In a slightly amended form, we will see that this concept may also be applied to the relations between developed capitalist economies and "undeveloped" (Third World) economies, between large corporations and their customers and employees, and between national governments and their taxpayers.

In the previous example, the value of the labor product (V') was divided into two components: the value of labor power, or necessary labor (V), and surplus labor (S). One additional term must be added to the above in order to discuss conditions in a modern capitalist economy. The labor expended in producing a commodity includes not only current, or "live," labor, but also indirect "dead" labor, represented by the depreciation of time embodied in the machines, tools of production, and raw material used. If we denote "dead" labor hours as C (the constant capital), then we have the following relation:

$$C + V + S = V' \text{ in which:}$$

C is the constant capital (the labor time value of capital equipment depleted by production);

V is the variable capital or the value of labor power (the hours needed to reproduce current labor power);

S is the surplus labor;

V' is the value created in production (i.e., the total amount of socially necessary labor time spent in production).

In the above, V is designated as variable capital because it is the component of production that must be activated in order to create value and social labor. It is a payment in advance of production to laborers by capitalists, before value is realized in exchange, and it is an amount on which money profits are earned by the capitalist. (Capitalists would not make the advance without the prospect of earning profits.)

From the above equation, we can define one further quantity that is important to understanding the dynamics of capitalist commodity production: the exploitation ratio. The exploitation ratio is the ratio of surplus labor to the value of labor power: S/V. In the case of the plantation slave referred to earlier, the exploitation ratio is six days to one day (600 percent). The exploitation ratio is an especially meaningful characteristic of a society at large: it corresponds to the division of total national product between the classes, and it measures the average rate of exploitation of one class by another. It is also indicative of the rate of capital accumulation or new capital formation and, therefore, is a measure of the rate of growth of the productive forces. Most importantly, the labor theory of value, together with the derivative notion of the rate of exploitation, is germane to the analysis of all types of society in which one class lives from the produce of another. It is these fundamental relations of exploitation that Marx felt were underplayed in Ricardo's analysis. Categories such as rent, profits, wages, and capital are not eternal or universal to all kinds of society, but are specific to capitalism. In contrast, concepts of labor power and surplus labor are applicable to all wealth-producing societies and therefore qualify as a general theory of value.

The Transformation of Labor into Exchangeable Values under Capitalist Commodity Production

How does the law of value operate under capitalist commodity production? How are exchangeable values under capitalism regulated by the quantity of embodied labor time in a manner analogous to that found in pure commodity-producing society? Consider the following data pertaining to an economy consisting of three commodities:

Table 11.1. Deviations from the Law of Value

	Food	Entertain-ment	Accom-modation	Total
A Fixed Capital (used up) (hrs.)	20	70	60	150
B Variable Capital (hrs.)	60	40	80	180
C Surplus Labor (hrs.)	30	20	40	90
D Value Created by Labor in Production (hrs.)	110	130	180	$420 = A + B + C$
E Share of Profits ($)	21.8	30	38.2	90
F Exchangeable Value ($)	101.8	140	178.2	$420 = A + B + E$
G Deviations	8.2	(10)	1.8	$0 = D\text{-}F$

Table 11.1 shows an economy that produces three commodities: food, entertainment, and accommodation. Laborers worked a total of 270 hours during the period $(B + C)$. Of this amount, 180 hours were used to replenish the existing work force (variable capital), and 90 hours were appropriated by the capitalists who hired the labor, supplied the fixed capital, and owned the produced commodities. The value created by labor in production was 420 hours, consisting of the 270 hours expended by the existing work force in the current period and 150 hours expended by past labor in previous periods on fixed capital that was used up in the current period. The total surplus labor (90 hours) and the variable capital (180 hours) give an exploitation ratio of 50 percent; this is the same for the three sectors.

If the law of value operated in the same direct manner as was shown under pure commodity production, then the exchangeable values of the three products would be directly proportional to the current labor (variable capital) expended on each.[3] Row D in the table shows this distribution of social labor among the three commodities. These values are based on an allocation of surplus labor (Row C) and this depends on the overall 50 percent exploitation ratio. However, capitalists in charge of each of the three sectors would not earn profits in the same proportions as this surplus labor allocation, but rather in proportion to their capital invested. There is indeed a relationship between surplus labor and profits in that the two are equivalent in the aggregate, but they are distributed between the three sectors in different proportions. The total amount of capital in the economy is 330 hours and the total surplus labor available is 90 hours; the ratio of these two determines the rate of return on capital (27.27 percent). Through competitive pressures, 27.27 percent becomes the equilibrium rate of return for capitalists in the three sectors. The money profits that each commodity sector can expect to earn are obtained by applying the global rate of 27.27 percent to the capital invested (A + B) in each sector. The distribution of profits is shown in Row E and the resulting equilibrium market price (exchangeable value) for each commodity (including the profit allocation) is shown in Row F.

Notice that a discrepancy exists between the share of the surplus that each sector contributes to the total (Row C) and the share of the surplus that each sector's capitalists secure for themselves in the form of profits (Row E). For instance, workers in the food sector contribute 30 hours, while the capitalists in this sector only appropriate $21.8 in the form of profits. This shows how surpluses may be generated in one sector and, through economic interdependencies and competitive pressures, be appropriated by capitalists in other sectors. These discrepancies result in the deviations shown in Row G. Such deviations were taken by some theorists as a refutation of Marx's law of value: that labor-embodied values (Row D) regulate exchangeable values (Row F) at the individual commodity level.

The economy portrayed in the example is an extremely simple one in that the three commodity-producing sectors are independent of each other. If there were interdependencies between the three such that the output commodities of some sectors were required as inputs to other sectors, then the problem of determining exchange values from labor values for each commodity would become more complex, although quite soluble (see, e.g., Kregel, 1975). The above example, together with the more complex version, has come to be known as the "transformation problem" in the literature.

The transformation problem was regarded as insoluble for many years. Even in the simple case of independent commodity-producing sectors (as in the previous example), the deviations between values and prices (Row G) have led many critics to argue that the law of value was inapplicable to capitalist commodity production.

Marx's own analysis of the transformation problem was incomplete but, as it turns out, intuitively correct. Linear algebra had not been sufficiently developed in Marx's day to enable him to construct a watertight solution. Nor was it the custom among economists of that era to place great emphasis on mathematical models and proofs. The various attempts at solving the transformation problem that do appear in Marx's work are offered as examples and illustrations of a general line of argument, rather than as mathematical proofs.

As for the deviations between values and prices, shown in Row G of the table, it is not the case that these reveal an indeterminancy in the law of value. After all, exchange values can still be derived from labor difference (values), and the deviations are all calculable. More importantly, Marx saw labor as the first of a series of explanatory variables that theorists still had to elucidate. Maurice Dobb refers to these other variables as the "sociological datuum," consisting of political, social, and other extraeconomic forces that, together with labor, combine to determine exchangeable values and thus the distribution of income among groups and classes.

Value Theory, Crisis Theory, and Monopoly Capitalism

Concepts in the previous passages provide the essentials for developing an alienation-based theory of value that may be used in analysis of the dynamics of capitalist development, including the recessions and expansions that the system undergoes. The progress of a capitalist economy over time is subject to a number of internal contradictions that disrupt its path. The exploitation ratio (S/V) and the rate of profit ($R = S/(V + S + C)$) underlie one such contradiction. It is in the very nature of capitalism to strive for greater accumulation of capital, and therefore, according to the previous equation, the rate of profit (R) will decline over time as the fixed capital (C) expands, ceteris paribus. This profit decline may be temporarily offset. For example, by increasing the amount of Third World labor employed, corporations have increased S, which boosts both the exploitation ratio and the profit rate. Technologically productive machinery also counters the profit rate decline. Replacing expensive equipment with cheaper equipment reduces and maintains the same productive potential.

The profit rate and the exploitation ratio reflect two contradictory tendencies at work under capitalism. Increases in the exploitation ratio (S/V) only bring temporary increases in the profit rate (R). In the long run, increases in the exploitation ratio add to the stock of constant capital (C), which causes the profit rate to decline. This happens because there is a limit to the rate of exploitation that may be achieved, while there is virtually no limit to the process of capital accumulation. Accordingly, it is argued, the profit rate will tend toward zero in the long run. (Of course, the long run may be very long.) It is the interaction of these variables over time that accounts for some of the behavior exhibited by capitalist economies. Failure to achieve an expected rate of profit in one period may cause cutbacks in investment by capitalists in a subsequent period. This lower investment level translates into a drop in demand for the capital goods sector and this results in cutbacks and layoffs that will effect further reductions in effective demand in subsequent periods.

Sweezy and Baran have emphasized contradictions that are specific to monopoly capitalism—as distinct from competitive capitalism. While competitive capitalism struggles to extract a sufficient surplus from its workers in order to maintain the rate of profit, monopoly capitalism faces a rather different problem: that of realizing production, and therefore surplus value, in the market (Sweezy, 1942; Baran, 1957; Baran and Sweezy, 1966). Monopoly capitalism suffers from overproduction and excess capacity; crises arise not because of the falling profit rate, but because of imbalances between effective demand and production, either in the aggregate or between different industry sectors or departments. One consequence is what is called "the uneven development of capitalism," in which interdependent industry sectors transmit among themselves disruptive variations in demand and activity.

The motivation behind this all-too-brief digression into crisis theory and monopoly capitalism is to indicate what is, for many researchers, one of the important roles played by Marx's labor theory of value. As David Yaffe has pointed out, it is the social conflict beneath the market appearances—expressed in the exploitation ratio and the organic composition of capital—that drives the slumps and (progressively fewer) booms that feature in the crises of monopoly capitalism. (Yaffe, 1975). The underlying institutional and social forces expressed in those ratios must be understood if the determinants of inflation, growth, unemployment, and other aspects of social existence are to be explained.

With such a broad social agenda, Marx's value theory is qualitatively different from the individualistic variants posited by marginalism and contemporary accounting. Marx was also an accountant of sorts and could well have applied his value theory to the Big Ate corporation introduced earlier. Instead of restricting the analysis to the financial impact on those immediately connected to the venture, Marx's value theory would allow us to expand the terrain of analysis to examine alienating and appropriative social relations underlying the business enterprise. These relations are institutionalized in corporations such as Big Ate; they are the genesis of the antimonies and contradictions behind the crises and slumps experienced under capitalism.

By "crises," I am referring not only to catastrophic economic slumps, but also to the more pervasive forms of alienation that emanate from social conflicts that distinguish capitalism as a social system. Thus, the horrors of toxic dumping that are stimulated by competitive pressures to cut costs, the predatory activities of some managers and shareholders, the rapacious exploits of multinationals in poor countries, the overcharging of customers by public utilities and nationalized industries, all constitute forms of alienation. As a social theory of value therefore, these ideas provide a promising perspective for reexamining the controversies described at the outset of this book.

The term "alienation" lacks precise meaning at present. In order to sharpen its analytic focus for reviewing the earlier controversies, the following passages will explore the usage of the term by Marx and other social theorists.

Social-Structural and Other Forms of Alienation

In the view of many interpreters, the term "alienation" is used in two broad senses in Marx's writings. "Social alienation" is most commonly associated with the writings of the "mature" Marx. It refers predominantly to class-based forms of exploitation and appropriation, and in this sense, social alienation is built into the very structure of society itself (Mandel, 1971).

What distinguishes social alienation from other forms of alienation is that it originates from the class structure of the social system in question. For many theorists, this perspective is unduly restrictive and fails to account for many other kinds of alienation. Thus, for instance, the experience of many Eastern Bloc countries is that alienation does not disappear with the disappearance of social classes (McLellan, 1975). Women and minorities in those and other countries suffer special disadvantages that cannot be reduced exclusively to class exploitation. Furthermore, citizens in some societies enjoy a benevolent social structure, but because of harsh natural conditions, they may suffer extreme hardship and deprivation (Mandel, 1971, p. 159). Additionally, recent history in Europe has raised questions about the sufficiency of alienation conceived in terms of social class: The rise of fascism in the 1930s halted and reversed what was once thought to be an inexorable process of socialization, supposedly energized by resistance to social-structural alienation (Held, 1980). Finally, relatively recent theorizing has focused attention on the division of labor itself, arguing that greater specialization—in and of itself—cannot be taken uncritically as a symptom of social progress, especially when such specialization may involve tedious, boring, and dehumanizing work aimed at producing a large number of wasteful and destructive products (Braverman, 1974; Edwards, 1979).

The above considerations have led to a critical reexamination of the meaning of alienation. Some writers have discovered a humanistic and even idealistic concept of alienation in the writings of the "young" Marx (Fromm, 1961). Others have traced the concept's meaning from the Greeks through Hegel and Marx to reveal an anthropological root (McBride, 1977). Existentialists have emphasized the subjective aspects of alienation (Sartre, 1968).

Reasons for the controversy over the meaning of alienation are attributable in part to Marx himself. Marx's writings span 40 years, from the early 1840s to his death in 1883. A comparison of the works of the young Marx with those of the mature Marx exposes differences that, for some interpreters, merely reflect the natural progression and development of thought over a 40-year period. For others however, the differences reveal a fundamental and decisive break in the modes of analysis of the young and of the mature Marx. These difficulties were accentuated by the chaotic state in which Marx left his writings and by his work's never having appeared as a whole collection at a single publication date—new manuscripts were discovered long after his death, and were published in a piecemeal fashion.

To both Marx and Hegel, alienation involved a dependence, a lack of or loss of control. For Hegel, the concept was anthropological in that the alienation of humanity reflected its dependence on nature for its means of subsistence. Human labor is the process that expresses this dependence in all societies at all times. Through the labor process, humanity provides for its existence by applying and developing its abilities, powers, capacities, talents, senses, and potentialities. The development of humanity, as expressed in the development of potentialities and capacities, is always regulated by and through the process of labor. Nature always mediates labor, and therefore people are alienated or controlled by an external power. This form of alienation is anthropological insofar as it originates from a dependence on nature for survival. As Ernst Mandel has pointed out, even with massive technological developments, there is no likelihood of completely overcoming this anthropological aspect of alienation because humanity will always be dependent on nature for its existence. In this manner, humanity will always be alienated relative to some idealized existence in which people are no longer bound, through labor, to nature.

In one vital respect, Marx's concept of alienation went beyond that of Hegel. To Marx, alienation was not just anthropological; it was also social:

> At the same pace that mankind masters nature, man seems to become enslaved to other men or to his own infamy. Even the pure light of science seems unable to shine but on the dark background of ignorance. And our invention and progress seem to result in endowing material forces with intellectual life, and in stultifying human life into a material force. (Mandel, 1971, p. 178)

For many Marxists, social alienation derives from social conflict and domination. Social oppression, the exploitation of one class by another—through the unequal exchange of commodities, for instance—is viewed as the root of the individual's alienation. The development of the productive forces (i.e., the means for reproducing human existence) was expected to contribute to the ultimate decline of class exploitation. The contradiction in capitalism between increasingly socialized production and its private appropriation would ultimately instigate capitalism's collapse. Moreover, the development of the productive forces could help reduce anthropological alienation by releasing humanity from its subjugation to nature and transforming work into an enriching, self-fulfilling, and self-enhancing process of development (Mandel, 1971, pp. 155–61).

The relative importance of various forms of alienation is the primary source of contention between leading schools of contemporary Marxism. The ever growing power of Stalin after the 1917 revolution led to the formulation of a communist doctrine that, with a dictatorial party machine, became as oppressive and as alienating as anything found in the West. Stalin's reign of terror reduced the working class to passive recipients of doctrinal instructions that dominated every sphere of human affairs. Hegel was condemned as a reactionary thinker in this period, and the subjective, humanitarian tendencies found in Marx's early writing and Hegel's anthropological conception of alienation were all but eclipsed. In the world of the new Soviet state—which, it should be remembered, was under the threat of the invasion of over 13 foreign armies at the time—the interests of the individual were ruthlessly subordinated to the interests of the new state.

Even before the publication of *Grundrisse,* we find theorists rejecting the one-sided view of alienation propounded in the Stalinist era. Before the 1917 revolution, Lenin himself was beginning to appreciate the importance of Hegel to an understanding of Marx. But it was George Lukacs in 1923,

well before the publication of *Grundrisse* and *The Manuscripts,* who restored the strong Hegelian links to the whole of Marx's thought, especially
his economics. Lukacs rejected the rigid, mechanical vision of socially determined humanity that was popular in the Stalinist era: the abolition of
class would not automatically lead to the abolition of alienation in Lukac's
view. In *History and Class Consciousness* (1971) Lukacs, as a Hegelian,
stresses the role of subjective consciousness and social ideology in sustain-
ing existing social arrangements and their potential for eradicating alienation through revolution.

The erratic relationship between Jean-Paul Sartre's existentialism and
the various official Communist party doctrines illustrates the controversies
between humanist and social-structural views of alienation. Sartre's existentialism is intended to provide an effective counter to alienation in general, but especially to humanistic-subjective alienation. Sartre places the
ultimate responsibility on individuals for their own predicament and des-
tiny and that of others:

> Man is nothing else but what he makes of himself. Such is the first prin-
> ciple of existentialism. It is what is called subjectivity. . . . Thus, exis-
> tentialism's first move is to make every man aware of what he is and
> make the full responsibility of his existence rest on him. And when we
> say that a man is responsible for himself, we do not mean that he is re-
> sponsible for his own individuality, but that he is responsible for all
> men. (Sartre, 1957, pp. 15–16)

Sartre felt that Marxism since Marx had come to a stop. Contemporary
Marxism had retrogressed and stagnated because it had become institutionalized as an instrument in the hands of an opportunistic Soviet bureaucracy, which had divorced theory from practice and transformed a flexible
and heuristic dialectic into a petrified dogmatism (Novack, 1966, pp. 22–
23). Sartre contended that all of Marx's disciples had slighted the individu-
ality of facts and the originality of living history and failed to follow Marx's
example of treating every event, person, and process as a unique whole. At
the extreme, Sartre found the followers of Marx to be abstractionists who
"forced individuals and facts into prefabricated moulds, . . . eliminated
subjectivity and reduced men to robots or objects" (Novack, 1966, pp. 20,
23).

Apart from Sartre, other critics of an overreliance on class alienation
include "critical" theorists such as Adorno, Habermas, and Marcuse. The

critical theorists have developed a system of concepts aimed at conditions that have emerged since Marx's death. They emphasize human rationality and social psychology as means of exploring one of the major forms of alienation in the modern state: domination by an all-pervasive technocratic ideology. Marcuse himself was sufficiently pessimistic about the revolutionary potential of a proletariat so overwhelmingly dominated by a materialistic and technocratic ideology that he placed his hopes in the "misfits" and "deviants" on the periphery of society—students, blacks, and other exploited and persecuted minorities—to form a union of "the most advanced consciousness of society with its most exploited force" (Marcuse, 1966, pp. 256–57). This thesis is in direct contradiction to Marx's declared view that there was little revolutionary potential in a force outside society (in what is sometimes called an underclass and what Marx termed the Lumpenproletariat).

Attempts to go beyond class exploitation in understanding alienation have had the greatest impact in the United States and on those Western Europeans who are relatively wealthy members of the world community. Social alienation through class oppression is not as pronounced in these parts of the world as it is in others; indeed, many would argue that citizens of these developed countries are, for the most part, beneficiaries, rather than victims of, exploitation. Accordingly, the subjective view of alienation as "forlornness"—a term that both Heidegger and Sartre were fond of—as loneliness, and as poverty in conditions of plenty, is much more meaningful in the materially rich West than in the Third World, where social alienation is much more oppressive.

In this context we can understand the sharp rebuke delivered to Western Marxists by Samir Amin. Amin considers the subjective alienation experienced by well-heeled, middle-class Parisian intellectuals as little more than a mystifying fancy or whim, because it distracts us from the worldwide character of exploitation and, therefore, the social genesis of alienation (Amin, 1978, pp. 115–118).

The above paragraphs sketch some of the recent controversies aimed at finding a more relevant definition of alienation. Overall, the reader may have gleaned the impression that a state of intellectual chaos, rather than coherence, now exists as to the meaning of alienation. However, there are two reasons why the situation is not quite as bad as it might appear.

First, recent reinterpretations of Marx's writings reveal a considerable amount of unity to the concept of alienation; Ollman's work is especially pertinent here (Ollman, 1976). Ollman shows that our ethnomethodological biases cause us to systematically misread Marx: we distort his meanings by implicitly using a modern, philosophical way of interpreting his words and fail to recognize the importance of Marx's own philosophy—that of internal relations. Modern thinking is predominantly analytic: it decomposes and simplifies problems to render them more amenable to prediction and control. The separation of variables into mutually exclusive independent and dependent forms, the reduction of causality to unambiguous, unidirectional and usually linear relations, the neglect of dynamic interaction through time, and an overemphasis on equilibrium—rather than disequilibrium—properties are common examples of analytic "simplifications." While these simplifications might be appropriate in a laboratory, it is questionable whether they are valid for the study of society, in which, in the final analysis, we create our own history.

Ollman shows us that, in contrast with analytic thinking, Marx's philosophy of internal relations preserved the organic coherence of the subject of study. Instead of decomposing an entity into parts, this philosophy respected the totality and inner relations that provided the momentum for transformations through time. For Marx (and Ollman), alienation is a systemic property of capitalism that permeates all its manifestations and instances; thus rather than adding to the proliferation of concepts of alienation, this view underscores their unitary origins.

Second, it is antithetical to the spirit of Marx's work to ever expect to arrive at a finely finished and polished intellectual schema, especially for a term like alienation. This is not just because Marx saw his work as the beginning—not the finale—of an analysis of society (his preliminary view about the law of value evidences this). More importantly, ideas and theories could never be universal and eternal categories for Marx; they were always socially relative in the sense that the beliefs relevant for analyzing one social system are irrelevant, and even ideological, in dealing with the next. Marx's criticisms of "eternal categories" in classical political economy are well known in this regard.

The above suggests that it would be perfectly in keeping with the spirit of Marx's own analysis to refashion and attune concepts like alienation for particular circumstances and problems. This is exactly the approach adopted in the final part of the book, in which alienation is categorized into a range of types, each corresponding to a set of controversies involving corporate accountability.

Criticisms of Marx's Value Theory

The most spirited challenges to marxist value theory in recent years have come not from orthodox neoclassical economists, but from distributionists (mainly neo-Keynsians and neo-Ricardians). Led mainly by the works of Robinson (1953–54, 1980) and Sraffa (1960), these schools first attacked marginalism and exposed fundamental flaws in that mode of analysis (Kregel, 1973; Harcourt, 1972). They then proceeded to critique Marxist economic theory (Steedman, 1981; Steedman, Sweezy et al., 1981). Most of these criticisms foundered because they attempted to reduce Marx's labor theory to an asocial and technical calculus: the poverty of algebra, as Shaikh put it (Shaikh, 1981; Elson, 1979; Arthur, 1979).

As this book challenges the ideological underpinnings of accounting—and marginalism—the criticisms of marxist value theory are drawn largely from marginalist thinking.

Menger, Wieser, and Böhm-Bawerk were members of the so-called Austrian school, for whom the criticism of socialist doctrines was something of a preoccupation (as it was also with Pareto). Wieser developed Menger's imputation theory expressly as an answer to supposedly socialist claims that property income represented exploitation of labor; Böhm-Bawerk's theory of interest and capital, elaborated along Jevonsian lines, was intended as an answer to Marx's theory of surplus value. The Austrians are frequently described as apologists of the existing system, so much so that Schumpeter dubbed Böhm-Bawerk "the Bourgeois Marx" (Schumpeter, 1954, p. 846, cit. Dobb, 1973, p. 193).

Marxists—old and new—have shown more respect for Böhm-Bawerk than for virtually any other opponent. Bukharin (1972) characterized Böhm-Bawerk's work "as the economic theory of the leisure class" (Kay, 1979, p. 46) and, more recently, Paul Sweezy cites Böhm-Bawerk's critique of Marx's labor theory as a masterpiece that surpassed all other attempts. We will examine Böhm-Bawerk's criticisms of the labor theory because they represent the most serious challenge to the labor theory from the marginalist camp; if the labor theory is able to withstand these criticisms, then its plausibility as a value theoretic basis for modern accounting is advanced.

It was the publication of the third volume of *Capital* that persuaded Böhm-Bawerk to draw together his various criticisms of Marx into one volume; this was first published in 1896. Böhm-Bawerk showed an excellent appreciation of the issues at stake: Marx's theory of value stands at the center of his entire doctrine of political economy. Once that theory is discredited, so are all of Marx's conclusions as to exploitation, the class struggle, and surplus value. Böhm-Bawerk acknowledged that the central parts of Marx's arguments exhibited a "logical development and connection [that] present a really imposing closeness and intrinsic consistency." For this reason Böhm-Bawerk chose to concentrate his challenge on the premises found at the very outset of *Capital* (Böhm-Bawerk, 1975, p. 88).

In Böhm-Bawerk's view, Marx used an Aristotelian method to identify labor as the one factor underlying all commodities with an exchange value in the market place. Height, weight, size, smell, or other physical characteristics, for instance, are not shared by all commodities and therefore do not qualify. Using Aristotle's "method of exclusion," Marx gradually eliminated all contenders save one: the labor time expended in producing a commodity.

Böhm-Bawerk did not directly challenge Marx's criterion for choosing the one common factor, but rather the way the criterion had been applied. He proposed three arguments against labor time as the source of value: first, that certain commodities existed with an exchange value that did not require any expenditure of labor (e.g., land, minerals); second, that labor was not the only common property of commodities; and third, that the use-value (utility value) of a commodity could serve as well as labor could, as a criterion of value. We will consider each of these counterarguments in turn (see Kay, 1979, for a more detailed exposition).

Gifts of nature, such as land and natural resources, are a subset of a more general category of commodities that caused considerable theoretical difficulty for labor theorists. If labor determined exchange value, how was the market price of land or wood to be explained? Items other than nature's resources also created difficulties. Ricardo, for instance, struggled to explain the difference in price between old and new wine when both required the same labor in production. Sraffa, over a century later, was to deal with this problem by excluding "nonproduceable goods" from his analysis. Marx also explicitly excluded gifts of nature, however this only seemed to strengthen Böhm-Bawerk's contention that Marx had failed to provide a general theory of value.

The reason Marx excluded gifts of nature was that although they appear to exchange as though they were commodities, they do so only because of the intervention of property relations under capitalism. In precapitalist societies, in which access and availability of these resources was not restricted, these gifts were free, not bought and sold as commodities. Today there still exist many of nature's gifts that have not yet been assimilated into the system of property ownership (e.g., certain fishing rights, hunting rights during designated periods, the warmth of the sun, the air we breathe, land in the outreaches of Canada). It is the appropriation of these gifts by the intervention of property relations that makes them seem like commodities. Similarly with Ricardo's bottles of wine: a differential in the prices of mature wine relative to young wine arises because the investor in the mature bottle is able to extract a premium, not because of any personal contribution to production, but because without such a profit return, investors would withhold capital from the investment in wine.

The exchange value of gifts of nature and the profit component included in the exchange of labor-produced commodities are premiums required to entice capital into use. The premiums are sustained by the institution of property rights whereby gifts of nature and tools of production (accumulated labor) are protected and withheld from production until a payment is secured.

Gifts of nature were not really items of wealth—and were not therefore commodities—in Marx's view, because they did not depend on human labor for their production. Moreover, Marx's view was that labor time was only the starting point in explaining the exchangeable value of a commodity, and that a theory of capitalism was required that incorporated factors in addition to socially necessary labor into the explanation.

Böhm-Bawerk's second criticism was that commodities shared common properties other than their being products of labor and that Marx ignored these. Being composed of energy, being subject to gravity, or being located in time and space are examples of other properties of commodities. This criticism ignores, however, a further condition imposed by Marx: that the property must not merely be common, but that, in some sense, it must regulate or influence the exchangeable value of a commodity. This addition rules out those common properties that do not influence a commodity's exchangeable value. Ollman (1976) views this regulation or influence as a complex determination or creation; Shaikh (1981), in contrast, describes Marx's notion of regulation as "tendential," whereby exchangeable values are constrained to upper and lower limits established by the amount of labor expended in the production of a commodity.

Following his second criticism—that labor time is not the only property shared by commodities—Böhm-Bawerk proposed the alternative property of general utility as the governor of the exchangeable value of commodities. Böhm-Bawerk uses Marx's own mode of analysis in advancing this argument against Marx's position: If the labor of private, specialized individuals can be aggregated into a totality of socially necessary labor that is capable of imparting value to commodities, then why can't the same logic apply to utility? Namely, the utility of individuals can be aggregated into a general utility that is distributed among commodities according to their worth, and it is this distribution that causes the relative exchangeable values of commodities.

This last criticism is based on a confusion as to Marx's relation of the labor of individuals to social labor. Social labor, or more precisely, socially necessary labor, is not merely a simple summation of the labor time of individuals. Socially necessary labor is a systemic, organic whole, in which each specialist is integral to the whole. Individual specialist producers are not only indispensible to the totality, but their tasks are meaningless without the overall system of specialization. Labor expended on making buggy whips is only socially necessary relative to a very specific set of past technological and social conditions; in other circumstances (e.g., today) it would be superfluous. We must also remember that the amount of socially necessary time associated with a commodity is not necessarily the time actually spent working; rather it is the time that, on average, competitive and technological conditions allow for the production of the commodity in question.

The above considerations show that for Marx, the relation between individual and social labor was not merely a simple summation of the former into the latter. Socially necessary labor is something more, in the sense that it is a combined and concerted total social effect. In what sense can we conceive of general utility in the same light? Can the separate *utils* of disparate individuals be combined into the same kind of working entity as socially necessary labor? This would not appear to be the case: utility is an individualistic quality and hence cannot be aggregated across individuals. It remains so, whatever the level of specialization in society.

Notes

1. As indicated previously, there are two characteristics of socially necessary labor that are relevant here. First, such labor includes that which forms part of a division of labor that has evolved to meet the needs of the community in question. This defines labor in socially relative terms in that it is contingent upon the effective demand of a certain society. For instance, the labor time of a professor of finance might be socially necessary in modern capitalist society but would be socially unnecessary in a feudal society. Second, socially necessary labor is not the amount of time actually spent in making a commodity, but the social average time that competitive conditions allow. Wasted time is not therefore allowed in this

measure, as the long-term competitive equilibrium price would not reward inefficient use of labor time.

2. As Mandel and Morton have pointed out, the significance of this characteristic of capitalism is frequently poorly understood. If the lot of "free" labor
under capitalism is compared to that of the serf under feudalism, we can see that
freedom can be a mixed blessing. While the serf was bound to the soil, this also implied that the soil was bound to the serf, giving certain rights and entitlements to
the latter as to the means of subsistence for him and his family. Indeed, because of
his rights and entitlements, the serf held a superior social station under feudalism
than journeymen, for instance, who had no tie to the land (Morton, 1945, pp. 52–
54). Deprived of rights and access to nature, "free labour is coerced to sell her
labour services in order to obtain the means of subsistence."

3. The relationship between labor value (hours) and money prices ($) is as-
sumed to be 1 hour = $1. This definitional assumption in no way affects the final
results.

12

Marginalist Theory of Private Value

From Classical to Marginalist Concepts of Value

During the mid- to late-nineteenth century, the ideas that unified Smith, Ricardo, and Marx were gradually supplanted by a new theoretical orientation more in tune with the emerging capitalist social order. This new orientation, early signs of which appear in Malthus's work, was the vehement opposition to the Ricardian socialism—marginalism.

The transition from classical to marginalist views of value was completed by the elaboration of two catenations of ideas. The first related to the directional flow of the causal influences and determinants of value. Under marginalism, value originates not from the fund of labor that Smith termed "the wealth of nations," but from the utility-based subjective preferences of consumers. This reorientation was accompanied by a shift away from macroscopic problems of the economy at large, toward a microscopic emphasis on the behavior of utility-maximizing individuals, either as consumers, entrepreneurs, or employees. These were not individuals in the Ricardian or Marxian sense however, because all signs of class origins were carefully omitted from the theoretical picture and so, therefore, were the main sources of social conflict and social change.

The second aspect of the transition was an attempt to remove a number of social policy issues from the agenda of economics, mainly by expunging politics and sociology from political economy. This was achieved by confining economics to the study of the sphere of market exchange. Critical parameters molded by forces "outside" the market—such as the distribution of income—were treated as "given" because, in the words of one marginalist, "to do otherwise would be to ask economists to commit value judgments" (Robertson, 1930).

The foundation for marginalism was laid by Jevons.[1] In the second edition of his *Theory of Political Economy,* Jevons consciously shunts the "car of economic science," which Ricardo "had redirected onto the wrong line" (Jevons, 1879, preface, cit. Dobb, 1973, p. 166). At the beginning of his work, Jevons has a frequently quoted passage that provides the basis for the marginalist theory of value: "Repeated reflection and inquiry have led me to the somewhat novel opinion, that value depends entirely on utility. . . . In this work I have attempted to treat Economy as a Calculus of Pleasure and Pain" (Jevons, 1871, p. 2, cit. Dobb, 1973, p. 168).

Criticisms of Utility Theory

Space precludes a comprehensive exegesis on the various criticisms that have been leveled at Jevons's claim that utility is the central moment in value theory. Indeed, a flavor of these criticisms has already been provided in those passages devoted to Marx and Ricardo. Rather, we will confine our criticisms to three areas of specific concern: the relevance of utility, the nature of utility, and the meaning of utility as an aggregate social function.

Ricardo challenged the relevance of utility by arguing that it was effective demand, not merely utility, that affected the level of production and distribution of resources, thereby underscoring the need for a theory of income distribution that showed how effective demand was composed. Ricardo, like Marx, understood that in a very real sense, distribution preceded everything else, and therefore an "economic sociology" was essential to show how social and property relations affected income distribution and its translation into effective demand.

The meaning of the concept of aggregate utility has been questioned by many authors (e.g., Boulding, 1969; Kay, 1979; Arthur, 1979). Their criticisms relate to one of the primary functions of aggregate utility in neoclassical economics: as a criterion of social choice and efficiency. Social labor value does not suffer from the same drawbacks as aggregate utility, as it can be justified on the grounds that individual labor becomes additive and homogenized as labor evolves into a specialized cooperative entity. The same argument cannot be made for utility: the *utils* of individual consumers are not socialized into an integrated whole; they remain disparate, incommensurable, and, therefore, nonadditive (Kay, 1979; Arthur, 1979).[2]

The nature of utility, as conceived by Jevons and his followers, has been questioned because of its ambiguous form. Dobb notes that both Marshall and Pigou recognized that utility was ambiguous because desire (or in modern parlance, revealed preference) was used to represent satisfaction. Thus Marshall said: "We fall back on the measurement which economics supplies of the motive, or moving force to action, and we make it serve with all its faults, both for the desires which prompt activity and for the satisfactions that result from them" (Marshall, 1920, pp. 92–93; Dobb, 1937, pp. 27–28). This touches on an even more sensitive nerve in utility theory: that wants (desires) are distinct from needs (satisfaction) and that utility theorists may not be aiding the fulfillment of human satisfaction at all, but merely feeding the insatiable appetites created by advertising. Marginalists have to put forward utility as an independent and exogenously determined quantity in their theoretical system because if they admitted that desires and wants were socially created (by advertising and education for instance), then they would be forced to confront sticky questions about the degree to which advertising generates desirable wants.

Jevons further contributed to the development of marginalism by utilizing, as an analogy, the equilibrium-seeking tendencies found in the study of statical mechanics.[3] This turned out to be a particularly prophetic analogy, as it led to a manner of thinking (i.e., that an economy tended toward equilibrium) that contributed to the assumption that all factors and services would be fully employed at an equilibrium position, overlooking (until Keynes in the 1930s) the possibility that multiple equilibriums were possible, and not necessarily at the full employment level.[4]

Jevons's notions of utility-based theory, diminishing marginal returns, and the equilibrating tendencies of economies gave rise to the assumption that maximizing behavior by economic agents (i.e., entrepreneurs, laborers, and consumers) led to the maximization of the social welfare. This was an invalid deduction since such a summation is contingent upon the distribution of income—a further example of how the latter intrudes itself. Both Jevons and Walras often overlooked this qualification in their enthusiastic support of the capitalist social order (Dobb, 1973, pp. 175–76). The most flagrant claims for the "natural justice and order" of capitalism were made by J.B. Clark: "What a social class gets is, under natural law, what it contributed to the general output of industry" (Clark, 1899, p. 46).[5]

What Jevons's theory lacked was a comprehensive scheme for showing how the prices of goods in various parts of the economy were determined. Menger and his two disciples, Wieser and Böhm-Bawerk, provided this framework by conceiving of an economy in terms of goods arrayed in various stages of production, whose values are imputed indirectly from the preferences of consumers for final goods. That is to say, all resources and intermediate goods were valued in terms of the marginal productivity toward final consumer goods.

Walrasian General Equilibrium

Walras expressed marginalist value theory as a general equilibrium model of a capitalist economy, in which he embodied the same economic interpretations and causal implications as did Jevons and Menger. This model contributed a representation of society at large that enabled marginalists to claim they were pursuing policy prescriptions consonant with the social interest.[6]

The Walrasian system shares the problem that confronted Menger, Wieser, and all subsequent marginalists. In order to assess whether the distribution of income in an economy is at a social equilibrium, a production function analysis is employed, which requires quantity measures of factor inputs (e.g., labor hours, acres) (see, e.g., Arrow et al., 1961). In such an analysis, heterogeneous capital goods and tools of production are conventionally measured by present value methods.

The result of such an analysis is the optimal, equilibrium level of prices, profits, and wages, that is, the optimal distribution of income. But, in assuming the discount rate needed for the present value calculations, one is also assuming at the outset a distribution of income, and this is what the analysis is supposed to derive.[7] Consequently, in its attempt to show that an economy's particular income distribution is optimal, marginalism begins by assuming an income distribution!

It is important to note that these criticisms are directed at marginalism's ability, as a theory, to explain and appraise the prevailing discount rate or rate of profit. It may be that the "real" rate is indeed optimal, in terms of say, economic growth, employment, or inflation. However, the significance of the indictment lies in the fact that marginalism, as a theory, is incapable of demonstrating this social optimality. This, after all, was the original mission of marginal productivity theory: to show that the interest rate and wage were optimal in that, at the margin, these costs just offset the benefits they created. Modern marginalists have abandoned this original mission by taking the prevailing interest rate "as given" and plugging it into their analysis.

The theoretical flaws of marginalism that invalidate it as a macroeconomic theory also contaminate its intellectual dependents, such as accounting. For example, consider a management accounting problem of appraising an investment in a new factory in an area of high unemployment. According to marginalist rationale, the firm's best interests, as well as those of society, would be furthered by rejecting the investment if its net present value was negative. The authority for such a rule derives from marginal productivity theory. However, as the previous discussion has shown, the basic ingredients of a present value calculation (the discount or profit rate and the wage rate) are arbitrary or indeterminate quantities in marginalist theory.[8] Thus, although the prescriptions of management accounting may advance the interests of capital in such circumstances, they certainly cannot claim to be harmonious with society's interests.

Marginalism: Truth, Fact, or Ideology?

An important lesson from the historical review concerns the extent to which accounting theoreticians may be said to foster the social ideology of capitalism through their myopic adherence to marginalism (Katouzian, 1980; Abercrombie, 1980; Lowe and Tinker, 1977; Cornforth, 1971, 1980).

The recurring lesson from our history of value theories is that social theorizing is subordinated not to a quest for absolute truth, but to social conflicts that continually remold the social consciousness for the purpose of social order and control. Our focus on value theory underlines the dialectical pressures of social history: the conflicts, antinomies, and contradictions that spring from social conflicts (Amin, 1978). These provide the momentum for change, not only in the social structure, but also in the ideological apparatus through which social order and control is achieved. In this fashion therefore, economic, accounting, and other theories are not so much refuted by the facts as rendered obsolete by historical change. Thus canonist value theory was overthrown by mercantilism; the conventional price approach of mercantilism was rendered obsolete by inchoate forms of capitalism; Ricardian socialism was refuted by the ideological developments of capitalism and, currently, the revival of classical political economy appears to be a response to the difficulties of late capitalism (Mandel, 1975). Truth, in this view, is not an absolute to be discerned by logic and/or by facts, but a social truth, that only embraces those theories that are in tune with the prevailing social ideology. In focusing this materialist perspective on accounting, we recognize that accounting theories form part of social ideology and, as an ideology, are always changing and changeable.

Social Value Theories and Accounting Practices

Marginalism, which informs contemporary accounting, differs from the value theories of classical political economy in one vital respect: the treatment of the societal ramifications of exchange. Accumulationists, distributionists, and alienationists were, and are, unabashedly societal in their outlook. Accumulationists, such as Adam Smith, saw specialization and exchange—indeed unequal exchange—as the key to economic growth and abundance. Ricardo was also concerned with paths of economic development; as a distributionist he focused specifically on the redistribution of income away from the unproductive landowning and squandering laboring classes, to the new class of capitalists. Alienationist theorists also set unequal exchange as the cornerstone of their analysis; however, instead of just celebrating the positive development of the productive forces, they also stress the instabilities, contradictions, disharmonies, and deprivations likely to ensue.

Marginalism contrasts with classical political economy in the way that it elevates the individual to center stage and extinguishes class and other social-structural considerations. Societal ramifications of exchange are trivialized in such an analysis: economic actors are composed not of members of unequal classes, but of freely competing individuals; thus exchange is never "unequal" on a systemic level. It follows that there is for the neoclassicist no cumulative dynamic worthy of serious attention: real historical time, dynamics, accumulation, growth, all receive scant attention, as evidenced by the preeminence given to comparative statics and rational expectations (both of which reduce economic dynamics to an absurdity).

The dubious historicity of marginalism is matched by its simplistic treatment of problems of aggregation. Marginalism's theoretical universe is populated only by individuals; macroeconomic variables are simply derivative in this atomistic point of view. Macroscopic, aggregate, synergistic processes have no independent theoretical existence under marginalism: there is no equivalent of Smith's wealth accumulation or Marx's "state of development of the class struggle." Social value theories attribute to the economic aggregate an independence that is not merely a summation of the properties of individual society members.

One further lesson may be educed from the earlier exegesis of theories of value; it concerns the powerful influence that social conditions may exert on theorizing. Canonist, accumulationist, Marxist, marginalist, and distributionist perspectives all constitute thinly veiled exhortations to redistribute social income and power in favor of specific interest groups. Theorizing is inevitably partisan—a palpable fact that has yet to register on the accounting research agenda.

The previous considerations suggest that of all the theories of value marginalism is least appropriate for dealing with problems of conflict over the distribution of social wealth. This is not to suggest that social value theories offer instant solutions to accounting problems; it does imply, however, that by its very atomistic nature, marginalism disqualifies itself from offering relevant answers. For these reasons, the alienation theory of value is employed in subsequent chapters to reexamine the controversies that originally motivated this book.

Notes

1. Stigler describes Jevons as "the forerunner of neo-classical [marginalist] economics" (1946, pp. 13, 135).

2. Boulding points to lack of realism in marginalist utility analysis. For instance, it is assumed in general equilibrium theory that utility functions of consumers are independent of each other, thereby excluding the effects of greed and envy that intertwine the utility functions of individuals (1969). An equally unrealistic assumption of marginalist economics is that production and consumption decisions are independent, thus implying that advertising and other production decisions that attempt to condition consumption choices may be safely overlooked (Graaf, 1975).

3. Dynamic considerations are neglected by marginalist methods because it is assumed that an economy will gravitate to an equilibrium state. Unfortunately, the path of movement that an economy follows in this equilibrating process is undefined, as is the time frame in which it takes place (Dobb, 1973, pp. 168, 173).

4. Sir John Hicks has cautioned that "economists are so used to the equilibrium assumption that they are inclined to take it for granted, yet there are market forms, not necessarily unrealistic or unimportant, where mere existence of an equilibrium, even in a single market, is doubtful, and perhaps more than doubtful" (1965, pp. 15–16, cit. Dobb, 1973, p. 173).

5. This crude attempt to bless the existing order of things was subsequently disowned by Stigler (who remarked that "Clark was a made-to-order foil for the diatribes of a Veblen") but the approval bestowed by marginalism was still allowed to linger in many texts (Stigler, 1946, p. 297, cit. Dobb, 1973, p. 176).

6. An exhortation to apply general equilibrium theory to social choice issues facing accountants can be found in May and Sundem (1976) and the American Accounting Association (1977).

7. For readers interested in exploring these issues, see Sraffa (1960) for an economic analysis and Tinker (1980) for a discussion of the accounting implications.

8. This does not mean that these quantities are arbitrary in general. Several theories (particularly exploitation theories) have been put forward to explain the level of profits relative to wages. Kalecki for instance, emphasized the degree of monopoly; others have stressed the degree of unionization or the monetary policy of the state (Dobb, 1973). The point is that, unlike marginalism, these exploitation theories do not attempt to relate the existing distribution of income between profits and wages with the colorful language of efficiency, equilibrium, optimality, justice, etc.

Part IV
Expropriation by Unequal Exchange
The New Accounting Problematic

13

Marginalism versus Alienationist Value Theory

Limitations of Marginalist-Based Accounting

Accountants who have explored the economic foundations of their subject invariably appeal to neoclassical concepts of economic wealth and welfare and virtually ignore other theories of value. The previous chapters point to serious deficiencies in marginalist, wealth-oriented notions of welfare and the superiority of alienation-based approaches. In this final part of the book, a four-level hierarchy of alienation is explored, each level encompassing the levels below it and incorporating additional dimensions of alienation. This hierarchy will be used to explore new forms of accounting systems, each differing from the others in terms of the kinds of alienation it is capable of detecting.

Alienation-based value theory contrasts in several significant ways with the neoclassical formulation which, through conventional accounting systems, seeks to measure and disclose indexes of wealth accumulation—profit. Profit reflects welfare in terms of the size of the "cake" available to a social collectivity; it is the surplus of excess remaining after replenishing consumed resources.

Profit is an inadequate metric of performance in that we are usually interested not only in the total size of the cake, but also in how it is distributed. Although the "academic accounting literature has been most reluctant to acknowledge distributional problems, the modern popular financial press is replete with criticisms of accountants arising out of scandals involving distributional issues. Today we find numerous examples of such controversies: Have some shareholders and speculators made excessive gains at the expense of other shareholders by greenmailing (New York *Times,* June 13, 1984)? Have some managers paid themselves excessive salaries (*Fortune,* June 25, 1984)? Have insider traders abused privileged positions by making abnormal gains (New York *Times,* May 13, 1984)? Is the corporate income tax expense overstated, thereby helping to increase public pressure to reduce taxes and redistribute income away from the state to other constituencies (*Business Week,* November 28, 1983)? Are employee pension expenses sufficient to meet pension obligations (*Fortune,* December 26, 1983)?

Refining profit measurement will not help resolve these kinds of questions because the questions imply that an unequal exchange—an appropriation of income and a form of alienation—is occurring.

We will see that not only are distributional issues inextricably tied to problems of alienation, but more importantly, all accounting problems are really problems of income appropriation and alienation.

Alienation and Marginalism

Alienation, the state of being out of control, may occur in two specific ways. Anthropological alienation pertains to the struggle against natural forces for existence. Early periods of human development were characterized by a dependence on natural rhythms and elements. Nature is out of humanity's control in the sense that economic progress and the development of human potentialities are restrained by our limited ability to harness natural forces to our advantage. Developments in productive techniques (the forces of production) diminish anthropological alienation by transferring control of human well–being from nature to man.

Neoclassical economists and accountants are most acquainted with the term "alienation" in the anthropological sense: as a state of economic underdevelopment that can be remedied by a more efficient utilization of economic resources, a condition of deprivation that can be eradicated by technological progress and the accumulation of wealth. Indeed, some would argue that the primary social function of financial statements is to aid wealth (capital) accumulation and thereby minimize anthropological alienation.

Alienation theory differs from marginalism principally in terms of its second dimension: social alienation. Social alienation originates in the struggle between class and class. It incorporates all forms of deprivation and estrangement that are derivative of class rights and obligations. Masters and slaves, lords and serfs, and capitalists and workers are broad classes of citizens that are distinguished by their differing rights, obligations, and entitlements to social income and wealth (the means of subsistence). Inequalities in rights and entitlements are structural in that they are universal to all parts and members of the social system under examination; indeed, they are important enough to be used as a basis for defining social systems and distinguishing one system from another. Each social system is defined by what is termed the social relations of production. Under slavery, for example, the ruling class owns natural resources, tools of production, and members of the slave class, and these social relations may be distinguished from those found under certain forms of feudalism, in which the vassal maintains economic possession of the land and the tools of production as long as homage and service are paid to the lord.

The social relations of alienation are expressed in an appropriation of income and unequal exchanges among different social classes. Thus, a slave may spend six days producing commodities that are consumed by others and receive, as recompense for sustenance, commodities that require only one day's labor power to produce. In this social order, the slave exchanges seven days' worth of produce for one day's worth of sustenance.

Under the labor theory of value, exploitative relations are expressed quantitatively and objectively. Capitalism, for example, may be defined by a propertied class that secures its means of subsistence through property ownership, and a laboring class that survives through the sale of wage labor. The unequal relation between these two social classes is expressed—objectively and quantitatively—in the relationship between the labor time embodied in the commodities that each provides and receives in the sphere of exchange. Capitalists—qua capitalists—invest no labor in social production and receive, through exchange, goods that contain the labor time of other social members. Laborers, in contrast, qua laborers, receive through exchange commodities embodying less labor time than the amount they expend in production. The deficiency is the amount appropriated by capitalists. Unequal exchange refers to the exchange among social classes of commodities containing unequal amounts of social labor.

Anthropological and social alienation are similar in that both refer to the estrangement of man from his essence: the existence of obstacles—natural or social—that impede the realization of full human capacities and potentialities.

As we have seen in previous chapters, alienation is not restricted to its social and anthropological forms. Sexual and racial oppression are also instances of alienation, which coexist with structural forms of exploitation. Whatever its form however, alienation is an appropriation of the human essence, an obstacle to human growth and development, and this is frequently reflected in an unequal exchange: an appropriation of labor time from one social constituency by another. Alienation value theory focuses on questions regarding the manner in which the social cake is divided, not simply on increasing the size of the cake.

Accounting records transactions between different social constituencies; alienation theory is concerned with exploitation that results from such transactions. As we have seen, because of its dependency on marginalism, accounting has no way of adjudging the inequality or exploitiveness of exchanges. Despite this theoretical myopia, accountants have encountered social alienation in a number of recent controversies: expropriations from outside shareholders to insiders made possible by the latter's informational advantages; expropriations by greenmailing; expropriations from employees through inadequate health and safety provisions or through insufficient contributions to pension schemes; expropriation of a local community's environment by pollution (not unlike the enclosures of common lands in early Europe) and of racial minorities through discriminatory practices; and expropriations from Third World peoples through commodity prices and wages held low by coercion and repression.

Alienating transactions or unequal exchanges, may appear as quite profitable relationships on an accountant's income statement for an enterprise. And here is the root of the crisis in accounting: the subject has no way of detecting inequality and expropriation in exchange. Accounting not only needs a way to appraise "the bottom line," but rather every line, to see whether the underlying transactions represent equal exchanges or exploitative ones in the sense described previously.

Figure 13.1 shows a hierarchy of different levels of alienation and their relation to accounting. Anthropological alienation has an asocial and technical character that corresponds with the conventional accounting focus on profit and wealth accumulation. This asocial form of alienation is shown at the lowest level in Figure 13.1. Social alienation becomes the focus of higher levels in the hierarchy. Accordingly, the concept of alienation aimed for here is one that is sufficiently broad as to subsume the conventional focus on profit, earnings, and surplus increments to wealth—growth in the size of the cake—and, at the same time, allow us to examine degrees of conflict over income distribution—how the cake is divided.

Figure 13.1.   A Hierarchy of Alienation

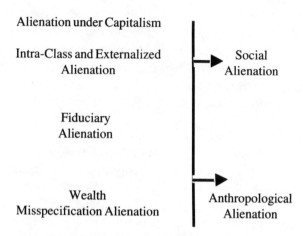

Alienation under Capitalism

Intra-Class and Externalized
Alienation

Social
Alienation

Fiduciary
Alienation

Wealth
Misspecification Alienation

Anthropological
Alienation

(The main focus of conventional wealth oriented accounting)

Alienation as a Hierarchy of Expropriation in Exchange

The first level in Figure 13.1, wealth misspecification alienation, recognizes misallocations in the corporation's real economic value as alienation. Such misallocations are a result of misperceiving the real economic value of a corporation's assets. Ultimately, these misallocations detract from the accumulation of wealth. Only perfect foresight as to a corporation's future could avert wealth misspecification alienation because only then would it be possible to discern the present, real economic value of corporate decisions. This form of alienation has earned more attention in the accounting literature than any other. It is included here because it is part—albeit a small part—of the total picture of alienation.

Fiduciary alienation represents the owner's loss of control arising from the separation of ownership and management in large corporations. In their fiduciary capacity, managers are entrusted with the owner's assets. In addition, they stand in a fiduciary relationship with trade creditors, banks, and other constituencies (some would argue society itself), all of whom have relinquished control over resources to management. Traditionally, conventional accounting counterbalances this loss of control—fiduciary alienation—by monitoring and regulating management's conduct.

The third and fourth levels of alienation shown in Figure 13.1 consist of intra-class alienation and externalized alienation. Intra-class alienation arises from the rivalry between factions of the capital-providing group. Insider trading exemplifies this form of alienation, whereby a group of stockholders expropriates the wealth of others by exploiting the informational advantages conferred by their privileged position as insiders (e.g., managers, auditors, bankers). Conventional accounting "overlooks" such appropriations because it chooses to treat the corporation as an entity, thereby failing to detect the gains and losses among fractions of capital. Indeed, the "entity principle" ensures that this myopia is institutionalized.

Externalized alienation reflects the side effects of corporate behavior, which fail to register in the corporation's profitability calculations, but nevertheless materially affect the well-being of other institutions and members of the community. These side effects—called externalities—would be detected by accounting systems that took an overall, societal perspective, but they are neglected by conventional systems that confine their attention to the corporate entity level of analysis.

Capitalist alienation, the final level in Figure 13.1, incorporates forms of alienation associated with the structural inequalities that define capitalism as a social system. From a sociological perspective, capitalism is uniquely defined by the rights and entitlements over the means of subsistence (economic wealth and income) that are enjoyed by society members. Insofar as society members hold rights in common, they form a class, and thus we may refer to their rights as class rights. In contrast with, say, feudal, slave, or Asiatic society, capitalism protects property rights (restrictions on access to, use of, and consumption of, property) and supports the property owner's claim to societal income without requiring any personal participation in the social production of that income. In contrast, "free" wage owners are denied guarantees of income or employment and must sell their labor power in order to survive.

The propertied classes and laboring classes differ in one important respect: their unequal opportunities for securing the means of subsistence. Property ownership is sufficient to provide income for capitalists; no personal labor is needed. For labor, access to natural and other life-sustaining substances is barred; work is a precondition for obtaining income, and there is no assurance that work will always be forthcoming. Specific inequalities in the rights of different classes is a defining characteristic of capitalism; it is also the primary source of capitalist alienation in that one class may restrict and deprive other society members of life-sustaining substances and conditions.

The above view of social conflict might appear to be an overly simplistic view of modern capitalism, in that citizens are not just workers or just capitalists, but both: income may be obtained simultaneously from working and from such sources as pension plans and savings accounts. Rarely do we find a "pure" capitalist; capital owners often labor in the management of enterprises.

Class analysis is not invalidated by these complications because it does not aspire to assign individuals to one class or another. It assumes that individuals will adopt a multiplicity of contradictory roles that create instability and conflict for them. For example, a class viewpoint recognizes that, as petty investors and consumers, people may take advantage of benefits from cheap offshore production of goods and services and, in so doing, help undermine their security as employees. Such examples illustrate the ambiguous role of the individual under capitalism: citizens may alienate themselves insofar as advantages secured in one realm may be attained at a cost to other realms.

Conventional accounting does consider alienation, but only obliquely and passively, by helping to perceive (report) misallocations and certain misappropriations of resources (shown by the two lowest levels in figure 13.1). But conventional accounting also plays a direct, proactive role in perpetuating alienation through its omissions. By giving a restricted picture of alienation, conventional accounting allows alienation to continue by default. The full impact of this selective perception is revealed by contrasting the focus of conventional accounting with its potential domain of interest, as done in Figure 13.1. The difference between the two reflects the ideological biases inherent in contemporary accounting.

14

Elements of
Radical Systems of Accounting

Overview of the Framework

Figure 14.1 extends Figure 13.1 by contrasting what accounting is with what accounting could be. Figure 14.1 envisages a spectrum of radical accounting systems, differing in their capacities to recognize various levels of domination and alienation. These systems are ordered approximately in terms of their sensitivity to alienation. The figure shows contemporary accounting tending toward the lowest level of sensitivity, and the most enlightening, emancipatory form of accounting at the highest.

Apart from conventional accounting, all the accounting systems in Figure 14.1 are hypothetical in that they still need to be developed and implemented. The aim of this book is not just to describe existing practice, but to delineate ways in which it might be enhanced. The hypothetical accounting systems are essential to this purpose because they direct our attention toward clarifying the nature of the alienation problems that accounting might help resolve. This is a way of defining what "improvement" in accounting practice means. Figure 14.1 will assist in exploring the degree of improvement that alternative accounting systems offer, in terms of their sensitivity to alienation. The figure is relevant because it posits an ascending scale of problems of alienation and a corresponding scale of radical accounting systems designed to combat each level of alienation.

The meanings of the hypothetical accounting systems and their capabilities become more concrete by exploring a number of contemporary accounting controversies and scandals and showing how these contemporary problems relate to the accounting systems and the types of alienation shown in the figure. The figure and its underlying propositions will be tested, therefore, in terms of its ability to make sense out of current events, disputes, trends, and developments. By closely examining instances of each level of alienation, we will see the kinds of accounting systems needed for detecting different levels of alienation. Fiduciary alienation will not be included in this discussion, so I may concentrate on those forms of alienation that conventional accounting ignores.

Figure 14.1.   Alienation and Accounting Consciousness

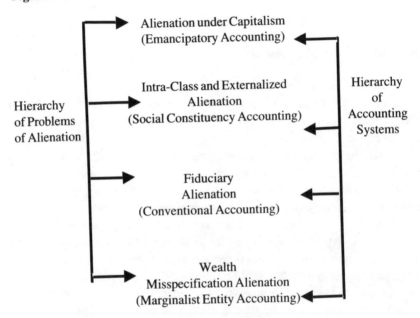

Note that in the hierarchies of cognizance of alienation in figures 13.1 and 14.1, conventional accounting (Fiduciary Alienation) is shown above Marginalist Entity Accounting (Wealth Misspecification Alienation). This ordering is significant because it suggests that conventional accounting practice displays somewhat greater sensitivity to problems of social alienation (in its concern for protecting the owner's assets) than that prescribed by marginalist economics. Here we see marginalism as asocial and technocratic, and playing a role as an ideological "ideal": aspiring to influence accounting practice, yet never being fully realized.

Wealth Misspecification Alienation:
Some Current Disputes

Wealth misspecification alienation is one of the most familiar forms of alienation. It is predominantly an anthropological (nonsocial) form of alienation, which occurs because conventional accounting measures cannot possibly reflect the "real" economic value of a corporate entity as anticipated by the marginalist theory of value. By "real" economic value, marginalists mean either the present value of the future cash flow expected to be earned for the firm's shareholders, or the firm's current stock market value—itself serving as the capital market's evaluation of the shareholders' prospective cash flow. Under certain conditions, the present value and the stock market value will be equal. (The details need not concern us here.) Both approaches originate in marginalist utility theory; they both value alternatives by summing discounted prospects over time and assume that cash is a monotonically decreasing function of utility, and they both depend on subjective preferences and expectations as to prospective cash flows and discount rates.

Conventional accounting ignores the cash flow implications of many decisions; thus it encourages wealth misspecification alienation. For instance, research and development expenditures are usually expensed in the period in which they occur; they do not rank as assets on a firm's balance sheet, even though such expenditures may produce substantial earnings in future periods and thus represent an unexpired asset at the balance sheet date. Similarly, the wealth impact—in terms of future cash flows—of employing superior management is rarely recorded in the conventional accounts, even though it is often crucial in valuing a company for a merger or a takeover.

Scorning conventional accounting's inability to produce measures that accurately depict a marginalist version of income and wealth is a celebrated, yet somewhat meaningless, pursuit for many accounting academics. (Criticizing something for lacking absolute perfection is a form of trivial idealism that has long since been abandoned in more mature sciences.) Marginalist entity accounting is the theoretical ideal that would remedy these problems, and it is illustrated in a multitude of textbooks and academic writings (see, e.g., Edwards and Bell, 1961; Parker and Harcourt, 1969; May, Mueller, and Williams, 1975; Hendrickson, 1970). All of these books treat the marginalist conception of value as a theoretical ideal and either offer policy proposals that would supposedly move ac-

counting practice closer to that ideal, or otherwise justify existing accounting practice as the best approximation to the ideal.

Marginalist value theory has more impact on the reporting practices of
corporations than any other theory of value. Present marginalist value
methods are used in valuing bonds, leases, pension liabilities, goodwill,
fixed assets when payment is deferred, and oil and gas reserves. Attempts
to align conventional accounting practice with marginalist principles seek
to reduce wealth misspecification alienation by an efficient allocation of
social resources. Accountants frequently invoke a form of wealth misspecification when they consider that the disclosed profit is inaccurate (or
not "true and fair"). National Student Marketing overstated its annual
profits by exaggerating revenues and understating expenses. Appended to
NSM's accounts was a footnote concerning $3,754,103 in profits from
firms acquired after the year-end. Omitted from current expenses were deferred product and start-up costs of $533,000 and the cost of prepaid sales
programs of $1,048,000, and a large unbilled receivables item was in-
cluded to inflate annual revenues. These items were regarded by many financial analysts as distortions of reality that, in our terms, increased alienation by failing to reflect the "real" marginalist economic income. Similarly,
it has been argued that the $2.2 billion in accumulated deferred taxes
charged against the 1980 annual profits of public utilities is a fictitious item
because, in the view of many analysts, it is unlikely to materialize. Its effect is to understate accounting profits relative to marginalist income and to
understate the wealth of the stockholder.

It is frequently difficult to draw the line between honest mistakes—
which is what is implied by wealth misspecification alienation, as a form of
anthropological alienation—and deliberate attempts to misappropriate the
income of others (social alienation). For example, few observers would regard the distorted profits of NSM or the public utilities as innocent errors,
but as attempts to appropriate the income of outside shareholders and customers using certified financial statements to authorize the acts.

Wealth misspecification alienation exists because conventional accounting does not possess the foresight required by marginalist entity accounting. This form of alienation hardly seems to warrant the extensive discussion that exists in the accounting literature. Furthermore, there are
grounds for believing it to be one of the least important forms of alienation
because it and the marginalist entity system that recognizes it fail to consider the deleterious effects on those outside the corporation (i.e., externalities and intra-class competition). In short, this form of alienation overlooks the fact that the corporation is not a monolith and does not exist in a

social vacuum. The corporation is an entity only in theory; it is a fiction—a reification—that masks an array of conflicting social interests. By treating the corporation as a working unit of analysis, conventional accounting and marginalist entity accounting neglect the differential impact of accounting practices on the individual constituencies that make up the corporation. Under the entity assumption, profits and losses among different fractions of capital are ignored. The kind of expropriation perpetrated at National Student Marketing is masked, and managers, insider traders, and directors— acting as shareholders—are free to make exorbitant profits at the expense of others by enticing new shareholders to invest in overvalued companies. And it is accounting information that is usually used to entice the victims. By focusing exclusively on the corporate entity, we turn a blind eye toward these conflicts and their consequences.

Marginalist entity accounting views the problem of alienation as essentially technical and procedural—seeking rules for income determination and asset measurement, for example. Social constituency accounting and emancipatory accounting (see Figure 14.1) stress the social and political contexts. Social constituency accounting is an extension of marginalist thinking that acknowledges social conflict within the restricted terminology of marginalism. Even with this narrow vocabulary, conventional accounting fails to adequately reflect the alienation inherent in corporate relations. Emancipatory accounting reaches beyond social constituency accounting to incorporate expropriations through unequal exchanges inherent in capitalism itself. The accounting literature is less informed about this kind of alienation than about any other.

Intra-Class Expropriations and Appropriation by Externalization

Introduction

Social constituency accounting, shown in Figure 14.1, surpasses marginalist and conventional accounting systems in its potential capacity to detect alienation. Specifically, it recognizes two forms of alienation not considered before: intra-class alienation and externalized alienation. The discussion of these types of alienation is organized into five sections, each dealing with a particular constituency that is subjected to the expropriation. The five sections deal with expropriations from, and therefore the alienation of, capital providers, local communities and neighborhoods, customers, labor, and overseas nations. Marginalist entity accounting was adjudged inadequate because it ignored many of the social contradictions raised by surrounding activity; thus we find that, in the final analysis, social constituency accounting, with its marginalist underpinnings, is similarly flawed.

Social constituency accounting recognizes conflicts of interest, both within the corporation and between the corporation and other interest groups. The latter conflicts, or side effects, of corporate behavior are often called externalities; they include the usually negative effects of corporate activities on the well-being of community members outside the corporation, in situations in which they cannot obtain compensation through legal, contractual, or other means. Pollution is a common example of an externality that results from corporate activities the costs of which are not impounded in the profit and loss calculations of the responsible firms, but are borne by those not otherwise associated with the corporation. An example is the acid rain created by industrial smokestacks, which has been linked with the destruction of large quantities of fish and plant life in the lakes of Canada and Scandinavia.

Corporations may be compelled to acknowledge their external effects by fines, taxes, compensation payments, and restrictions on the use of technology. These different practices result in the externalities' being internalized or impounded in the cost and profit functions of the offending corporation, thereby curtailing the antisocial (alienating) effects. We will call externalities that have been socially recognized in this way, institutionalized externalities. "Institutionalized" refers to the existence of social processes for recognizing and impounding negative externalities—a form of counter–appropriation.

Corporations are not always compelled to impound their negative externalities into their cost functions. Such cases are defined here as "noninstitutionalized externalities." Examples include the injury and loss of life among citizens of Third World countries who have purchased poorly described and extremely powerful over-the-counter drugs (e.g., steroids) supplied by pharmaceutical multinationals seeking to dispose of their surpluses. Other instances include the deaths of infants in poor countries that resulted from Nestlé's having promoted the sale of concentrated milk without giving adequate product use information to mothers. Few effective legal remedies are available to the victims in such cases. The only partial remedy of these negative externalities has been to increase the firms' public relations costs through public boycotts and sanctions.

Institutionalized and noninstitutionalized externalities are not mutually exclusive in that an externality that is impounded at one point may be disimpounded at a later date, and vice versa. For example, it is unlikely that the courts of a few years ago would have entertained some of today's product-liability suits. There is also evidence of the reverse trend, whereby externalities are given less attention by the courts, or "deinstitutionalized," as would seem to be the case today regarding racial and sexual discrimination and harassment. The recent Manville Corporation case also illustrates the recent tendency to reverse the institutionalization of externalities in the courts. Manville, faced with millions of dollars of legal claims by 16,000 workers suffering from asbestos-related diseases, filed for bankruptcy under Chapter 11. The effect of the filing was "to freeze all claims and not spend a dime defending them" (New York *Times,* December 10, 1982). Since the filing, business has been better than usual for Manville and its stockholders: the firm's share price rose from $4.5 to $9.5 between August 27 and December 9, 1982.

Conflict over externalities (positive and negative) is merely a further example of the struggle over the distribution of income. Fundamentally, there is little difference among a firm that seeks to avoid the cost of safe treatment of toxic waste, a firm that uses fictitious financial statements to raise capital, and a firm that successfully disposes of its pension obligations to employees (as with Harvester Company, considered subsequently). These situations are identical in that they exemplify the struggle among different social constituencies over the distribution of income, a struggle in which accounting plays an important and substantial part.

From general considerations as to the nature of intra-class and externalized alienation, we can now examine a number of current controversies. The discussion is broken down by alienation of five separate constituencies: capital providers, local communities, labor, overseas nations, and consumers. The inadequacies of the concepts of intra-class and externalized alienation are reviewed in the last section as a way of introducing alienation under capitalism.

Expropriating Capital Providers' Wealth

Appropriations from shareholders are at the center of many controversies surrounding conventional accounting practice. As we have seen, the entity principle ensures that the full impact of these unequal exchanges is obscured, thereby minimizing the exposure and criticism that these appropriative practices receive.

The dangers of the entity principle were dramatically illustrated by a recent spate of "greenmail." Greenmail—a play on the word *blackmail*—refers to the pressure on management to buy out a hostile takeover bidder at a price per share that is well in excess of the prevailing market price. Several things make greenmailing unsavory. First, members of management often buy out the predator to protect their own jobs, rather than because a more profitable future is in store for the existing shareholders. The intimidation of management is usually accomplished by the bidder's announcing plans to fire senior personnel if the bid is successful. Second, the predator frequently has little interest in actually taking over and running the target company; the main aim is to frighten the management to buy back the acquired shares at a substantial profit.

The real losers in greenmailing are the existing stockholders, because the premium on redeeming the predator's share is paid out of their funds. Other parties to the affair also do quite well: investment advisors earn lucrative fees by working both sides of the street, staid management members keep their jobs, and bidders are more than compensated for their speculative investment.

The bidder's profits are usually quite substantial. In June 1984, Saul Steinberg netted $52 million from his attempt to buy Walt Disney; two months earlier he had earned $10 million from a sortie into Quaker State. In March 1984, Bass Brothers of Texas earned $137 million from a buy-back from Texaco; they had already gained $21 million from an earlier attempt to buy Blue Bell. Rupert Murdoch netted $53 million from his foray into Warner Communications (*Fortune*, July 9, 1984; New York *Times*, June 17, 1984).

Details of some of the more controversial greenmailing incidents are shown in Table 14.1

Table 14.1. Profits from Greenmail

Date	Speculator	Target Company	Estim. Speculator's Profit ($M)
June 1984	S. Steinberg	Walt Disney	52
March 1984	S. Steinberg	Quaker State	10
March 1984	Bass Bros.	Texaco	137
Nov. 1983	Bass Bros.	Blue Bell	21
March 1984	R. Murdoch	Warner Communications	53
March 1984	J. Goldsmith	St. Regis	37
Sept. 1983	B. Pickens	Superior Oil	28

By June 1984, members of Congress began discussing plans for curtailing greenmailing. They were responding to complaints, not from small savers but from large institutional investors incensed by the buy-backs involving Rupert Murdoch and Saul Steinberg. Steinberg's reappearance in the financial press is especially prophetic since it was his takeover attempts of Reliance Insurance and Chemical Bank in the early 1970s that galvanized Congress into its last series of investigations into corporate mergers and accounting practices (Briloff, 1972).

The situation holds little comfort for stockholders however. If greenmailing is permitted to continue, it is the speculator who will profit, at the stockholder's expense; if greenmailing is curtailed, shareholders may fall victim to the extravagancies of an inefficient and overprotected management. In any event, as long as the entity principle is sacrosanct, shareholders can expect little protection from auditors (New York *Times*, June 13, 1984; *Barron's*, June 18, 1984).

The latest attempts by corporations to avoid proper accountability center on the accountant's newfound ability to circumvent time. The versatility of this discovery—to inflate earnings and thereby lull shareholders into believing that management members are efficient stewards—has been demonstrated in areas as far afield as insurance and oil.

Competition intensified in many parts of the insurance business in the early 1980s and so, therefore, did the pressure on management to employ creative accounting practices. In return for insurance premium income, insurance firms undertake to underwrite certain liabilities, should they arise in the future. These liabilities may materialize in ten, twenty, or fifty years. Insurance firms provide for these future liabilities out of their current premium income, and until recently, they would give an estimate of the full face value. Increasingly however, it is becoming customary to provide a smaller, discounted amount—a reasonable practice in that an estimated liability, with a face value of, say, $80 million, payable around 1995, has a present cost of $23 million at current interest rates of 13 percent. Thus if $23 million were set aside as an insurance loss reserve in 1984, it would accumulate to $80 million by 1995.

Accounting rules permit firms to change the way they account for their insurance loss reserves. Thus there is nothing wrong with a firm revising its reserves down from a face value of $80 million to $23 million. The difference would be a boost to accumulated profits, reflecting the overcautious previous reserving policy. What accounting rules do require, however, is full disclosure of the accounting change—lest shareholders mistake what is, in effect, an accounting correction for prior periods, for outstanding performance in the current period. Whatever the rules however, it is easy to see how a management with a dismal current profit record might be tempted to inject current income with excess reserves created in the past.

Selling loss reserves was an ingenious method devised by some insurance firms to accomplish just this. In 1982, Aetna Life and Casualty Company "sold" $80 million of its liabilities for $22 million to Fireman's Fund Insurance Company, a subsidiary of American Express. This transaction increased Aetna's pretax earnings by $58 million and the liability to the IRS by an estimated $25 million. (The increase in the tax expense is the only "real" transaction here.) Aetna did not disclose the exceptional nature of the transaction or the increase in the tax liability to its shareholders, but simply assimilated the "gain" into current profits.

Meanwhile, Fireman's Fund Insurance Company, Aetna's partner in the deal, was engaged in its own reserve swapping adventures with other insurance companies. (Reserve swapping is a slight variation on the basic game plan of selling loss reserves to create paper profits.) Fireman's Fund is a subsidiary of American Express who, in late 1983, boasted the awesome record of 36 consecutive years of earnings increases (*Fortune*, June 25, 1984). In this profit-hungry environment, Fireman's Fund entered into swapping arrangements with the Insurance Company of North America and created pretax profits of $142 million for itself in 1981 and 1982. The net result of this paper transaction—apart from window-dressing management's true performance—was to incur an additional $30 million in taxes on behalf of American Express stockholders (*Fortune*, November 28, 1983; January 9, 1984).

"Timing" is also an essential ingredient in another type of accounting magic that was beginning to emerge in the 1980s: "insubstance defeasance." Defeasance allows a firm to ostensibly retire its long-term debt and recognize in current income any gain on the transaction. Defeasance involves a firm buying high interest rate government securities and placing them in a trust committed to paying off the interest and principal on the firm's own debt. Because treasury securities issued today pay up to 12 percent interest—and much old debt yields no more than 6 to 8 percent interest—a company can retire a $1 million debt with a cash outlay of less than $700,000 (Los Angeles *Times*, January 22, 1984). Legally, the trust arrangement does not actually pay off the bondholders until the bonds actually mature, but because the firm has invested in treasury of other risk-free stock, it is allowed to remove the debt from its own balance sheet, thereby improving its credit rating.

For management however, the primary attraction of the defeasance transaction is the boost it can give to current earnings. In 1982, Exxon Corporation defeased $515 million in long-term debt, paying approximately 6 percent interest per annum, by buying $312 million in U.S. government securities yielding 14 percent. Exxon's quarterly earnings were increased by $132 million as a result of this transaction. Similarly, Kellogg Company followed with a defeasance involving $75 million in debt, and Atlantic Richfield Company defeased $88 million.

There are three redistributional effects of defeasance. The first is from stockholders to management if the transaction misleads shareholders into crediting management with better performance than it deserves (and this results in real wealth transfers to management). The second is from stockholders to bondholders in that the latter exchange risky debt for a secure trust arrangement—the stockholders bear the cost of providing this security by foregoing the use of the funds invested in the trust. The third is a transfer of accounting profits from future years into the present period because, without the defeasance transaction, future years would have benefited from the differential between the low-interest debt expense and the higher earnings from the funds committed to the trust. This third wealth transfer is from future to current shareholders, inasmuch as the defeasance leads to higher current dividends and stock prices.

Examples of the appropriation of shareholders' funds are numerous. Recent examples of Ponzi schemes include J. David in California, Home-Stake, and S-J Minerals. Accounting information did not play a central role in enticing investors to part with the $100 million to J. David, $130 million to Home-Stake, and $20 million to S-J Minerals, however these cases do illustrate how misleading information can create false expectations among investors and encourage them to part with their money. Investor losses in

National Student Marketing and Slater Walker (U.K.) exemplify appropriations from shareholders by management (intra-class alienation). Investors in NSM, who purchased at around $140 per share, watched their holdings fall to a low of $3.50. Had investors waited for the company's liquidation in late 1980, they would have received approximately $26 per share—a total possible loss of $114 per unit (New York *Times,* December 11, 1980, p. 56). These investor losses would not register in the firm's reports because they cancel out with investor gains at the level of the accounting entity.

Jim Slater, the managing director of Slater Walker, who ridiculed productive efforts by bragging that his company's objective was to make money, not things, shows us the folly of overlooking the links between accounting information, shareholder expectations, and the massaging of share prices. Lucrative gains were made by the firm's directors, not by manufacturing and selling but by manipulating share prices using investment client's funds.

Defeasances and other exotic techniques have not displaced the more mundane ways of expropriating stockholder wealth with accounting information. Reports of such appropriations continue unabated: In June 1983, the SEC filed charges against Fox and Company, one of the leading auditing firms in the United States, for using careless and improper auditing methods. The action arose out of irregularities in the accounts of three firms: Saxon Industries, Flight Transportation, and Apex Computer Corporation. Several months earlier, the bankruptcy trustee of OPM (standing for Other People's Money) Leasing accused Fox and Company of yielding to pressure to certify "materially false and misleading" financial statements. The trustee claimed that in 1976, Fox and Company had "miraculously changed losses and deficits into profits and a positive net worth" (New York *Times,* June 9, 1983).

In June 1984, a no-contest consent decree was issued against Datapoint, barring the firm from future violations of the Securities Exchange Act and SEC rules. The SEC accused the firm of overstating its revenues by $22 million and its net income by $5 million in the fiscal year ended in 1981. The SEC contended that the management of the company indulged in accounting irregularities and "shenanigans" to offset reduced demand for computers (*Wall Street Journal,* June 19, 1984).

Expropriating Community Wealth

The cleanup and relocation costs of the Love Canal tragedy were estimated by state and federal authorities to be $95 million. A further $2.65 billion in legal claims were then brought against the company (*Progressive,* November, 1981, pp. 35–42). Some commentators have suggested that Love Canal was one of Hooker Chemical's best-managed operations. To date, Hooker Chemical and its parent firm, Occidental Petroleum, have been prosecuted in Florida, Michigan, California, and New York. In Lathrop, California, Hooker Chemical workers have charged that the chemicals they worked with caused sterility. Hooker Chemical was fined $500,000 in New York State for dumping toxic material on a landfill next to the Gruman Aerospace plant. In Taft, Louisiana, Hooker Chemical's subcontractors sued the company, claiming that exposure to chlorine had left them sterile, impotent, and without taste and smell. Hooker settled out of court for amounts ranging from $7,000 to $250,000. In White Lake, Michigan, Hooker Chemical dumped over 20,000 barrels on a site that has now polluted a lake and killed large numbers of fish. The State of Michigan sued the company in 1979, and in an out-of-court settlement, the company agreed to pay for the $20 million in cleanup costs and over $1 million in penalties.

By focusing on the corporate entity, accounting practice ignores costs that corporations may externalize to other members of the community. Even when these costs are impounded in the firm's cost function (through fines, out-of-court settlements, special levies and taxes, etc.) accountants still become parties to an appropriation inasmuch as they never investigate the adequacy of such "expenses" from a noncorporate perspective.

Externalities may be intergenerational as well as cross-sectional. There has been a tendency to postpone confronting major environmental pollution problems, a tendency reinforced by the accounting practice of only recognizing environmental costs at the time a liability is imposed on the corporation. Environmental Protection Agency official Douglas Costle has illustrated how costs are "pushed into the next generation" with regard to the pollution of the James River with Kepone by the Life Science Products Company in Hopwell, Virginia, in 1975 (New York *Times,* September 27, 1980, p. 69). The pollution could have been cleaned up initially at a cost of $250,000, but the company delayed and has since paid out $13 million in damages claims. It is estimated that it will now cost $2 billion to clean up the river.

The pollution and long-term diminution of the vast underground water reservoirs (aquifers) that extend under several states is a further example of intergenerational wealth appropriations. Over half the U.S. drinking water requirements comes from sources of "fossil water" that has taken over 25,000 years to accumulate (New York *Times*, December 29, 1980). Since this water is not exposed to sunlight and moves very little, agricultural and other toxins take much longer to decompose than would otherwise be the case. The current usage of this water far exceeds its replacement rate in many parts of the country. In parts of California, intensive irrigation has so lowered the water table that the land has settled 30 feet in places. Overall, in the wet East 12 percent of the water used has not been returned to the aquifers; in the arid West, the quantity is 52 percent.

The subtleties of how accounting information participates in appropriating community wealth to private interests are well illustrated by corporate taxation. At first glance, financial statements convey the impression that corporate profits are subjected to approximately a 45-percent tax rate. But a closer examination reveals a somewhat different reality. Exxon, for instance, in 1982, declared a pretax income of $7.764 billion and an income tax expense of $3.578 billion—a 46-percent tax rate—yet the firm actually paid over only $2.032 billion (26 percent) to the IRS. The accounts of AT&T claimed a tax expense of $4.930—40 percent of its reported profits of $12.209 billion—even though it paid no taxes at all; indeed, the firm received a tax credit of $407 million. Similar discrepancies between the reported tax expense and the tax actually paid exist for other large corporations. Texaco, for instance, in 1982, reported a 51-percent tax rate, but actually paid 42 percent; for Dupont, the comparable figures were 68 percent and 59 percent, and for Sears, they were 21 percent and 10 percent.

The American Institute of Certified Public Accountants is well aware of the wealth distribution conflicts in this area. *Business Week* reports that "the AICPA has not taken a position, but some members worry that . . . [a change in the method of accounting for taxation] could plague companies with shareholder demands for bigger dividends and union pressures for higher wages, as well as direct political attention to how little income tax many corporations pay" (*Newsweek*, November 28, 1983).

Further examples of intergenerational and intracommunal appropriations of wealth will be explored in subsequent discussions. They include the bad loans owed to U.S. banks that the U.S. government has recently underwritten and the transfer of employee pension obligations from private companies to the public purse. These cases involve massive redistributions of income from the community to private corporations. Accounting practice collaborates in this appropriative act by neglecting the social impact of corporate activities.

Expropriating Customer Wealth

Overcharging by public utilities is an appropriation because, in a classical theory sense, it is an exchange of unequal amounts of embodied labor time. Even in relation to the norms of competitive capitalism, prices are "reasonable" only if they abide by those that would prevail in long-term, competitive conditions. Whatever theoretical criterion we use to assess the excessiveness of public utility prices, if accounting practices helped create exorbitant prices, then part of the responsibility for appropriation and exploitation falls on the accounting community.

A cost-plus-profit basis is frequently used to determine the prices of gas, water, telephone, and other utility services, and "cost" usually includes a provision for an item called "deferred taxation." In 1975, deferred taxation for the 150 largest companies amounted to approximately $1.5 billion. American Telephone and Telegraph had accumulated $11.3 billion in deferred taxation by the end of 1978; this was increasing by an estimated $2.4 billion each year.

Deferred taxation is an anticipated, rather than an actual, expense, and if the expense never materializes then, because this item has been included in the cost-plus utility pricing, customers will have been overcharged by the amount of the expense. In such cases, the accumulated deferred taxation item on the firm's balance sheet represents the appropriation of income from customers by the corporation.

The recent collapse of OPM dramatizes the part accountants and auditors can play in helping expropriate wealth from customers to other constituencies. One of the largest computer leasing firms in the United States, OPM was declared bankrupt in early 1981, amidst accusations of a $225-million fraud.

OPM specialized in buying computers and leasing them to large corporate customers, such as Rockwell International. Thus OPM effectively provided a financial service to its customers. These financial arrangements are advantageous to firms like Rockwell because they offer tax savings and a form of off-balance sheet financing that provides all the benefits of borrowing, without having such borrowings counted in new credit assessments.

OPM did not actually use its own money to buy the computers it leased out. It would first obtain a leasing contract from a firm such as Rockwell and then use the contract to borrow money from investment banking firms, such as Lehman Brothers Kuhn Loeb (New York *Times,* June 1, 1983).

It was through such arrangements that the owners of OPM discovered the secret to making their fortune; they re-presented the same leasing contract several times—with a few alterations and crude forgeries—to their investment bankers.

Its fraudulent methods were crude, but they were sufficient to outmaneuver the inadequate audit and accounting controls of OPM's lenders and customers. In forging the signatures of corporate officials on bogus leases, OPM sometimes mispelled names and gave incorrect titles. Myron Goodman, one of the OPM founders, who is now serving a 12-year prison sentence, spent several years looking for a "flexible" audit firm—one that would certify financial statements that would paint a rosy picture of OPM and that would not detect the lease frauds. In 1976 he found Fox and Company, who proceeded to use what the bankruptcy trustees' report describes as "a series of questionable accounting techniques" to produce "materially false and misleading" and "indefensible" financial statements. For example, when Stephen S. Kutz, Fox and Company's partner in charge of the OPM audit, drafted the 1976 financial statements and showed a loss, an enraged Myron Goodman told him to "get back to the grindstone and try to figure out a way to show a profit" (New York *Times,* June 1, 1983).

Rockwell International, OPM's largest corporate customer (who is reputed to have lost from between $30 to $40 million as a result of the fraud), did request a copy of OPM's financial statements at one stage but was reassured by Fox and Company's imprimatur, as was Lehman Brothers, which the company hired to replace Goldman, Sachs and Company as its investment banker in 1978, and First National Bank of St. Paul, which became its primary source of short-term "bridging" finance.

In separate suits, 19 banks and financial institutions that were swindled by OPM sued Rockwell, as well as investment bankers, auditors, and lawyers who lent authenticity and respectability to OPM. The total damage claim amounted to around $600 million; a settlement of $65 million has reputably been reached (*Wall Street Journal,* August 18, 1983).

Companies enjoying monopolistic advantages—like public utilities—operate in many sectors of the economy. In such cases, accounting practices may play an important role in pricing decisions and, therefore, in determination of the distribution of income among customers, the IRS, shareholders, and other groups in the community. Accounting practice attracts far less critical scrutiny in the private sector than it does in the public utility sector, yet its redistributive influence may be no less significant. This influence has been increased by the recent wave of mergers and takeovers and by the greater concentration in ownership and control that this has brought about. The above view of accountants contrasts dramatically with the popular view of them as timid bookkeepers and technicians, the alternative scenario suggests a prominent role for accounting in social choices, one of importance in forming redistributive politics on behalf of corporations.

Expropriating Employee Wealth

Many private corporations, city governments, and federal, state, and local authorities have promised generous pension benefits to employees without accounting for the cost of these obligations in a systematic way. Under existing accounting practice, employee pension benefits incurred in the current period are charged against current income, even though the pension may not be paid for 20 or 30 years. The difficulty is in determining the current cost of future payments. Accounting rules also allow corporations and other institutions to systematically understate the pension cost by not requiring them to make provision for all future payments. (Liabilities that are not vested need not be provided for.) The result is large unfunded liabilities; consequently, the firm's net income for the current period may be overstated.

The uncertainties surrounding pensions are illustrated by the fluctuations in the size of the debt owed to employees and the value of the portfolio of investments set aside to meet pension obligations. Corporations with some of the largest unfunded pension liabilities in 1979 and 1980 are shown in Table 14.2.

A pension liability is unfunded if no investments have been made to provide liability when it falls due. Under conventional accounting, unfunded liabilities are usually only footnoted. Moreover, the unfunded figures in Table 14.2 understate the liability because they only refer to vested benefits, benefits that the corporation is committed to pay.

**Table 14.2. Unfunded Pension Liabilities of Large
Corporations in 1979 and 1980**

Company	Unfunded Vested Pension Benefits ($M)		Percentage of net worth (1979)
	1979	1980	
General Motors	6,100	4,085	32
Ford Motor	1,920	0	18
Chrysler	1,200	1,275	66
Bethlehem Steel	1,191	420	46
U.S. Steel	1,000	0	20
Lockheed	391	0	117
LTV	624	62	87
National Steel	660	104	47

The above figures are only estimates of the present cost of the future
vested liabilities. Corporations have shown little hesitation in using
loopholes in the accounting rules to vary the pension expense to enhance
their profit performance (*Business Week,* August 25, 1980, pp. 94–95;
Dunn's Review, May 1981, pp. 78–82).

By the end of 1983, the 1979–80 situation had completely reversed:
only an estimated 10 percent of the some 100,000 private pension funds
were underfunded, compared with over 50 percent in the mid-1970s. Even
the notorious Lockheed Corporation pension plan, which in 1977 had a
deficit of $276 million, had a surplus of $702 million by 1983.

Two things had occurred to bring about this change in circumstances.
First, the stock market had risen and increased the value of the share
portfolios held to meet pension obligations. Second, high interest rates had
lowered the cost to firms of acquiring annuities for discharging their pension obligations (*Fortune,* December 26, 1983).

Companies were not slow to seize the opportunities offered by excess
pension assets, even though, as subsequent events have shown, it is very
imprudent to assume that stock prices will remain bullish. Since 1980, 138

pension fund "reversions" have been instigated on behalf of 128 companies. This has "freed" $515 million in excess assets. The Pension Benefit Guaranty Corporation (PBGC) is currently considering applications that would release well over $1 billion more (*Fortune,* December 26, 1983). Included among those who have successfully tapped excess pension assets are Kellogg ($58 million) Western Airlines ($29 million), Timex ($21 million), and Harper and Row ($10 million).

Pension reversions have stimulated a great deal of controversy. In many cases, employers have revised pension contracts to the effect that there is no longer an assurance that the employee will receive a defined amount on retirement. In the controversial case of Harper and Row, the company used the excess pension assets to purchase a block of its own shares for $20 per share. At the time, the company's stock was quoted at $13 per share.

Such incidents underline the complaint that companies are appropriating employee wealth and transferring it to management, shareholders, and other constituencies. In the Harper and Row case, a suit filed by District 65 of the United Automobile Workers Union protested that the pension fund was being used to entrench management and that the reversion violated management's fiduciary duty to employees. At the House Committee on the Aging, Representative Edward Roybal declared that "a proliferation of these self-interested employer activities is spreading unchecked like some insidious disease, striking down the retirement security of the worker, infecting one employer after the other . . ." (*Fortune,* December 26, 1983).

The absence of more realistic assessments of corporate pension obligations has serious consequences. Understating the current pension expense overstates current profits and may cause excessive dividend distributions, that is, dividends paid out of capital, not income. Ultimately, corporations may be unable to meet their pension commitments, and employees, other corporations, and the state will be required to make up the difference. International Harvester Company recently off-loaded $45 million of pension liabilities into the Pension Benefit Guaranty Corporation. The PBGC is financed by private companies whose pension plans it guarantees; thus, other companies—their shareholders and customers—eventually bear the cost of underfunded pension plans that fold. The PBGC is currently suing Harvester, contending that the sale of its subsidiary, Evirodyne, to Wisconsin Steel was a fraudulent attempt to avoid a pension debt of $86.2 million (*Wall Street Journal,* December 7, 1982).

Underfunding of pension obligations is commonplace in the state and local governments. Some 6,000 state and local pension plans are reputedly

ill-managed and have $300 billion in unfunded liabilities (Los Angeles
Times, November 19, 1978, Section 5, p. 5). As of 1979, the Fire and
Police Pension Fund in Los Angeles was underfunded by $2 billion, and the
New York Fire Department had pension obligations valued at $1.5 billion
and pension assets of only $0.5 million (*Wall Street Journal,* February 26,
1979).

Expropriating Wealth from Nation States

The genesis of the Foreign Corrupt Practices Act in the United States
illustrates the detrimental impact of appropriative behavior at the international level. The mid-1970s witnessed a series of bribery scandals involving U.S.-based multinationals, executives, military personnel, and politicians of foreign governments. News of these scandals destabilized the governments of Japan, South Korea, the Netherlands, Indonesia, and other nations. It was disclosed at Senate hearings in 1975–76 that Lockheed had
paid more than $106 million in secret "commissions" to promote foreign
sales, including $7 million to a well-connected Japanese agent who was
also the head of a right-wing youth movement.

Kakuei Tanaka, once Japan's prime minister and one of the country's
most influential politicians, was forced to step down from office after accusations that he accepted a $2.5 million bribe from Lockheed. After a six-
year trial, Tanaka's conviction in 1983 precipitated a general election and a
crisis for the Japanese government that simmers to this day (*Forbes,* January 31, 1983, p. 74). Lockheed made large secret payments to Prince Bern-
hard of the Netherlands to influence his recommendations, as inspector
general of the armed forces, concerning fighter-plane purchases by the
Dutch government. The subsequent scandal nearly deposed the Dutch
royal family. In Italy, Exxon paid more than $50 million to Italian political
parties and government officials to buy favorable tax and energy legislation
(New York *Times,* June 8, 1981).

The 1977 Foreign Corrupt Practices Act made it illegal to pay bribes to
foreign government officials. Corporations are now required to disclose
questionable payments, and as a result of such disclosures, 527 firms were
cited by the SEC (*Newsweek,* February 19, 1979). These included Boeing
($500 million), General Tire and Rubber ($41 million), Northrop ($34 mil-
lion), and many others.

During subsequent Senate hearings, Senator Frank Church noted that "morality in the business community is not our responsibility, nor is enforcing the law in other lands. What this government and this Congress must concern itself with are the very real and serious political and economic consequences that spreading corruption can have for U.S. interests both at home and abroad" (New York *Times,* June 8, 1981). Senator Church's concerns were uncompromisingly jingoistic. They lay not with the detrimental effects of bribery and corruption on the citizens of foreign states, but with the possibility that bribery might rebound on U.S. interests.

The precarious state of the world banking system dramatically illustrates what can result from accounting myopia regarding externalities. In January 1983, a gargantuan debt of $706 billion was owed to banks, governments, and international financial institutions around the world by a group of developing and Eastern bloc countries (*Times,* January 10, 1983). Felix Rohatyn, senior partner of the Lazard Freres investment bank, has estimated that some $500 billion of the amount owed is unlikely to be repaid and is being recycled at increasingly higher interest rates (New York *Review of Books,* November, 1982; *Progressive,* February, 1983, p. 23).

Rohatyn's prediction of financial chaos was emphasized by a series of unexpected shocks to the world financial system. Poland defaulted in March 1981 with a debt of $21 billion; in August 1982, Mexico announced that it could not meet interest payments on its debt of $81 billion; Brazil followed soon after with a declaration that it could not make any further payments toward its $40 billion loans. Argentina has also defaulted on payments toward its $40 billion loans and is currently haggling with the International Monetary Fund (IMF) in an attempt to secure terms for a loan that will not provoke riots in the streets and bring about the collapse of its newfound democracy. The IMF reported that in 1981, 32 countries were in arrears with their debts, compared with 15 countries in 1975 (*Time,* January 10, 1983, p. 42).

The gravity of the situation is underscored by the relationship between doubtful loans and the shareholders' equity. The equity, plus the loss-loan reserves, can be thought of as what a bank would have remaining if it paid off its depositors and creditors. Chemical Bank, for instance, has loans outstanding to Mexico and Argentina of $1.15 billion, representing 92 percent of shareholders' equity. Equivalent ratios for Chase Manhattan and Citicorp are 77 percent and 95 percent, respectively. In the aggregate, the nine largest U.S. banks have loaned out about 130 percent of their equity to Mexico, Brazil, and Argentina (*Time,* January 10, 1983).

Many critics are now asking why banks failed to anticipate this situation and why accounting reports failed to disclose the doubtful value of the banks' loan assets. The nine largest banks have set aside a total of $3.6 billion in loss-loan reserves, only 12 percent of the total indebtedness of Mexico, Argentina, and Brazil. The tendency of the banks to "throw good money after bad" has been attributed to their fear of precipitating a collapse: it is easier to lend more money to a borrower in difficulty, hoping that the situation will improve, than to run the risk of panicking the world financial system into a collapse.

Accounting practice has helped cover up the deteriorating financial position of U.S. banks, and in doing so, has encouraged financial irresponsibility and mismanagement among both borrowers and lenders. Many observers fear that the final "cost" will not fall on the banking corporations or the borrowers. Judging from the way Poland and Argentina were assisted, it would seem that the U.S. government is willing to go to great lengths to keep U.S. banks afloat. The recent FDIC salvage operation of the Continental Illinois Bank confirms this proposition.

The cost of this solution will not be assumed by the banks. Through inflationary pressures—another form of appropriation in real terms—bank losses will eventually be imposed on U.S. citizens, culminating in a transfer of U.S. wealth into the hands of foreign dollar holders.

Felix Rohatyn's estimates that if $500 billion—amounting to $2,500 per capita for U.S. citizens—is never repaid, then this is a measure of the diminution of the quality of life and of greater alienation for the individual. This is but one way in which the debt crisis might rebound on U.S. interests.

With hungry Brazilian mobs looting supermarkets, over 50 people dead after food riots in the Dominican Republic, and the central banker of Argentina in jail, major social instability, throughout the Latin American continent is considered a real possibility (*Fortune,* November 7, 1984; New York *Times,* May 11, 1984). This scenario has led to speculation as to the effect on the U.S. economy of a mass default—leading to increases in inflation, loss of jobs, and a decline in exports (*Business Week,* November 7, 1983). It has been estimated that the value of U.S. exports to the 30 most troubled debtor nations fell by $10 billion in 1982, costing 300,000 U.S. jobs and resulting in a $1 billion loss of profits to U.S. exporters.

Accounting policy issues are deeply entangled in this delicate financial situation. Early on in the crisis, U.S. banks used accounting time limits as to when a loan had to be declared nonperforming, as a way of pressuring countries into an agreement. (Debtor nations were told that if they were declared in default, they would have difficulty raising further loans.) In October 1983, Argentina called the banks' bluff by suspending payment of all interest on its $45 billion debt, causing the banks to reduce their quarterly earnings. By mid-1984, U.S. bank stocks were in major decline (*Wall Street Journal*, June 8, 1984). At about that time, federal bank regulators—not the accounting profession's rule-making bodies—instructed the banks to adopt more stringent procedures for treating interest on nonperforming loans (*Wall Street Journal*, June 19, 1984).

The new requirements were modest under the circumstances: banks were debarred from treating interest that was more than 90 days overdue as profit. This doesn't prevent banks' taking to income, interest on loans that a debtor can only repay out of further borrowing. In such circumstances, the bank is really paying itself in order to declare a profit!

Nor do the new regulations deal with the much larger problem of requiring banks to write off billions of dollars of overseas loans as unrecoverable. Such draconian measures seem unavoidable in the near future, as the present refinancing agreements have merely deferred, not resolved, the problem. In 1985, the obligations of several debtor countries will "balloon" under existing agreements, and there is little expectation that they will be able to honor their commitments (*Wall Street Journal*, June 22, 1984).

There is, however, an even more subtle interpretation of this most serious debasement of accounting principles and standards. As long as loan principals remain at their face value as assets on the balance sheets of banks, it remains undecided who, ultimately, will assume the all-but-undeclared loss. And if the financial arrangements for Poland and Argentina are anything to go by, then it is the U.S. government—with taxpayers' money—that the banks are hoping will play the tooth fairy.

The accounting profession is a major accomplice to this—perhaps biggest of all—appropriation from the community. By failing to challenge the values placed on the loan-assets shown in the financial statements of banks, auditors and accountants are keeping alive the prospect of the biggest bail-out in corporate history.

Limitations of Social Accounting

What has been pedantically termed "social constituency accounting" in this work strongly resembles what other accounting scholars have called "social accounting." For both Estes (1976) and Ramanathan (1976), the vital aspect of any social accounting system is that externalities are recognized and reported on. What is instructive about the social constituency view discussed previously is that we are able to highlight the deficiencies, not just of this approach, but also of more orthodox social accounting proposals.

The primary drawback of the social constituency view (as well as of orthodox social accounting suggestions) is that its concept of an externality—and therefore its notion of alienation—is ambiguous. The ambiguity originates in the notion of an externality that, because of its marginalist derivations, is a subjective and arbitrary concept. For instance, in the asbestos-related claims against Manville Corporation, if the courts recognize claims of the employees against the company, then an externality exists, and the legal damages reflect the measure of the alienation involved. Suppose, however, that the employees were completely unsuccessful. Would we have to conclude that no alienation exists? The situation would become even more ambiguous if socially concerned accountants insisted that some provision for a possible liability be made, thereby adding to the legitimacy of legal claims—and the possible success of the prosecution.

The source of the ambiguity lies in deciding and valuing what is sacrificed or given up. An externality might be thought to exist if asbestos production had a deleterious effect on some members of the community. But what if proper safety precautions were so prohibitively expensive as to have drastic repercussions on the material well-being of all parties concerned. Might we conclude that no externality is involved, and that living with asbestos is far more desirable than living without it?

From the above it seems that whenever an externality is said to exist, this implies that a superior state of affairs is foregone, and this is the benchmark against which to measure the externality. If a river is polluted, fishermen are said to suffer externalities because an unpolluted river is implicitly assumed to be the sacrificed alternative. When Lockheed bribed the prime minister of Japan, an externality was said to exist because it was implicitly assumed that business without bribes was being sacrificed.

Unfortunately, there is no discussion in marginalist theory as to how to systematically determine which possibilities are foregone, or how to value them (i.e., the opportunity cost). Alternatives are either "pregiven" or "subjectively determined" by economic agents; they are not enumerated by the theory itself.

This theoretical lacuna permits certain biases to affect the contemplated set of alternatives and, therefore, the assessment of whether an externality exists. For instance, on what grounds did we conclude that the only options availabile to Manville employees were to live with asbestos or to live without it?

The subsequent discussion of emancipatory accounting and capitalist alienation explores these issues. It defines alienation "objectively" in terms of the "alternatives" admitted under capitalism, and it argues that the existence and magnitude of alienating externalities depends not on a "pregiven" or arbitrarily assumed set of foregone opportunities, but on "objective" social conditions that are inherently alienating because they preclude a more egalitarian social order.

Emancipatory Accounting and Capitalist Alienation

Capitalism is defined, as a social system, by its class structure and the forms assumed by conflict under it. Capitalists and laborers are the two primary social categories under capitalism in that each citizen obtains the means of subsistence either by working or through the ownership of property, or through some combination of the two. The subsistence received by labor is essential for reproducing the worker and, therefore, the continuance of production. Profits, in contrast, do not help reproduce the productive process because capitalists—qua capitalists—make no personal contribution to production. In this very specific sense, capitalists appropriate from the production process without giving anything in return; their property income is not a material relation in that it is superfluous to social production; it is an expropriative social relation specific to capitalism.

Capitalist alienation is expressed in the appropriation of value created by labor, which is consumed by property owners, and in the very structure of the division of labor itself. These two sources of alienation are sometimes identified as social alienation and subjective alienation, respectively. While appropriation through unequal exchange (social alienation) is an important part of human alienation, it does not account for the way the division of labor itself assumes a distorted and "unproductive" form because it serves as a vehicle for expropriation. In particular, the task of securing a profit return gives a special character to the division of labor. The police and the military help support property entitlements; the courts assist in the preservation of property rights; managers and management accountants strive to reproduce property relations through a multiplicity of management control techniques; and ideological support is provided by religions, education, media, and other institutions.

Emancipatory accounting includes information systems capable of recognizing the alienating effects of capitalism and therefore is more effective in detecting capitalist alienation than any of the other accountability systems discussed previously. The need for the critical potential of emancipatory accounting is illustrated by those occasions on which private and public interests are at variance. For instance, the market imperative makes it irrational for Hooker Chemical, or any other producer of toxic waste, to do anything other than minimize costs of disposal (including any litigation costs). Similarly, why should firms like J. David, Slater Walker, National Student Marketing, and S-J Minerals, forego profits to avoid depleting public confidence in savings and investment? The market imperative drives institutions to make profits and adopt any political, social, or accounting device to realize that aim. This behavior is the logical consequence of an economy organized according to the priorities, rights, duties, and obligations of property relations and wage labor.

Because of their marginalist underpinnings, accounting measures of profit and wealth are indexes of expropriation and social alienation. In the light of this, accountants may want to reassess their own work and the way that the subject is presently constructed. The certification requirements imposed by the Securities Acts in the United States and by the Companies Acts in the United Kingdom established a public responsibility for auditors that rivals any "private" relationship between auditor and client. While some may feel that the profession has failed in its public charge, the responsibility is still treated by many with the utmost seriousness.

Implications of the Analysis

Contemporary accounting has been contrasted with three alternative accounting systems: marginalist entity accounting, social constituency accounting, and emancipatory accounting. Compared with contemporary accounting, these three hypothetical perspectives have provided insights into problems of alienation emanating from the unequal exchanges in which corporations engage.

Figure 14.1 suggests ways to reduce the alienating effects of accounting theory and practice. The notion of a corporate entity was exposed as a fiction and this "entity" was shown to be afflicted by numerous social antagonisms and antinomies. The discussion of externalized alienation showed how corporations may appropriate social wealth from beyond their legal boundaries. Capitalist alienation was shown to point to the unstable foundations of capitalism itself that are the root of much of the rapacious and exploitative behavior expressed at the other levels of alienation.

The above considerations are not merely academic or abstract; they have immense practical importance for the day-to-day practice, teaching, and researching of accounting. Harold Tyler, the judge who sentenced the two auditors of NSM, concluded that too many people in the accounting profession exhibited "some sort of myopia as to what is really the public responsibility of someone who performs services as a public servant" (*Wall Street Journal,* December 30, 1974). Tyler's comment asserts the existence of a public interest separate from private interests, and the responsibility of public accountants to both discern and satisfy the public interest. What this book has attempted to do is to explore what that public interest might consist of.

General Implications for Public Policy

It is traditional in works such as this for the author to be granted a certain license in the concluding sections to move beyond the safety of careful argument and evidence and to speculate about approaches to solving pressing dilemmas and difficulties. This license is used in full measure here.

At the time of writing this final chapter—July 1984—there is growing public disquiet in the United States about the efficacy of public accounting and its congressionally established watchdog, the Securities and Exchange Commission. Several congressional investigations are planned for 1985. The detailed complaints are numerous and include many of the controversies discussed in this work. What is of interest here is whether the previous analysis has anything to contribute to the debate that is bound to ensue.

We may begin by showing how Congress's newfound interest in the accounting profession accords with the perspective discussed previously. The recent upsurge of criticism of accounting is borne not out of a new liberal idealism seeking to establish greater democratic accountability of corporations, but from pressures from large and powerful institutions that have suffered as a result of accounting practice and malpractice. Notice that practice as well as malpractice is included here because distributional conflicts, aimed at changing generally accepted accounting practice, are as much responsible for the recent politicization of accounting issues as socially relative notions of malpractice or wrongdoing.

The point is well made by examples cited in the financial press. Bank failures, overcharging by major defense contractors, profit manipulation by management on a widespread scale, the proliferation of debt defeasance and other off–balance sheet financing techniques, and failure to resolve on-going controversies over accounting for pensions, taxes, and inflation are all blamed—in varying degrees—on accountants (*Wall Street Journal,* January 31, 1984; *Fortune,* June 25, 1984; *Wall Street Journal,* April 30, 1984; New York *Times,* May 13, 1984). The verity and plausibility of the accusations are not at issue here; rather, what is significant is that the very terrain of conflict over wealth redistribution has changed: the conflicts in which accounting is embroiled are no longer conducted under the ostensibly disinterested guise of the market, but have shifted from the economic to the political arena.

If accounting is presently in a state of crisis, then the previous analysis gives us a way of understanding what the nature of that crisis is. In Marxist theory, social crises emanate from the antagonisms, conflicts, and anti-nomies that underlie a social system; they reflect the inherently unstable and contradictory nature of such systems and are manifest in the dialectical movements of the system through time (Mandel, 1962; Ollman, 1976). Crises, therefore, signify threats to a prevailing social order that could lead to its overthrow or to a radical transformation in its character—such as a major redistribution of wealth between various social constituencies. Surely this is the predicament facing accounting: the current politicization of accounting portends adverse distributional consequences, both for the profession and for its various clients.

A successful response to the crisis requires, at a minimum, that the profession have the motivation, the ability, and the opportunity to change its ways. It is questionable whether any of these conditions hold at present. The motivational dilemmas of the profession arise from its contradictory allegiances to, on one hand, vested interests envehicled by Congress and the Securities and Exchange Commission, and on the other hand, private corporate clients, who may hire and fire their auditors and offer them lucrative contracts for tax and management advisory services. Serving the public interest has obvious economic benefits to the profession: the Companies Acts in the United Kingdom, and the Securities Acts in the United States have given the profession a legal monopoly over auditing and require corporations to purchase audit services. Despite the economic benefits of audit and attestation work, revenue from management advisory services now rivals that from auditing for some of the Big Eight firms, thereby weakening the motivational basis to resolve social conflicts in the favor of public interests, rather than corporate client interests.

In addition to doubts about the profession's motivational commitment to change, there are serious questions about its *ability* to instigate change. "Ability" includes not merely a narrow ability to implement established policies, but also the imaginative capacity to reconceptualize a subject's problems and content in a useful and productive way. Previous chapters offer a glimpse of what an exciting, stimulating, and intellectually challenging enterprise the study of accounting could be. In an all-too-brief literature review, we have reconceptualized accounting by enriching it with work from economics, anthropology, sociology, philosophy, and other disciplines. This reconceptualization, which could form an entirely new basis for accounting studies, has enabled us to see accounting not as mere bookkeeping and record keeping, but as capitalism's prime adjudicator in social conflict.

Regrettably, intellectual eclecticism is not the norm in accounting. Few auditors or accountants are able—or motivated—to undertake the kind of sociohistorical analysis that has been explored here, whether as an analysis of the profession as a whole or of an individual client firm. The conflicts at work in the individual firm, the social genesis of those antagonisms, their contemporary direction and momentum, and the socially creative potential of accounting in such processes are not serious agenda items for the profession, either in practice, in education, or in research. In fact, an ethos that is completely antithetical to this kind of social creativity currently prevails in accounting. Educators do not offer a systematic study of social change and of the part that accounting has been—and could be—playing in initiating change. Instead, a form of rote learning dominates most levels of education: students parrot Financial Accounting Standards Board rules and procedures without acquiring the epistemological faculties needed to critically scrutinize this catechism. The profession offers no objection to this kind of undergraduate "education" because it produces the sort of malleable, compliant cannon fodder it needs for its junior levels.

Matters are little better at more senior levels of scholarship. As the brief theoretical review in previous chapters shows, most accounting academics accept as ultimate truth a primitive form of neoclassical economics and then proceed to inflict this on their doctoral students and colleagues. Research has become a quest for the irrelevant and the arcane: the study of refined statistical procedures used to annihilate trivial problems and the contemplation of obtuse economic models that promise answers to real problems, but only in the always distant long run. These exercises in scholastic irrelevancy are generously supported by a profession that is relieved to have its academics running aimlessly through the woods.

Reasons for the disarray in academia are not hard to find. With the relatively recent fiscal crisis of the state, universities have been forced to reconsider their social allegiances. As a result, they have grossly extended their dependence on the business sector. In some universities, the business school constitutes over 40 percent of the student body. This expansion has not been without a price: academic priorities are dictated more by corporate interests than by the broader community interests that many academic institutions once served. On today's business school campus we find a strain of rabid antiintellectualism that translates into a hostility toward everything that is "unprofitable." In terms of the analysis of this book, this attitude represents a major ideological shift that has clear distributional consequences.

Professors—especially those in accounting—have responded with gusto to the challenges of the new business environment. Staffing pressures have forced many departments to hire adjunct professors from the firms "downtown," many of whom have little sympathy with developing an accounting to serve anyone other than their immediate clients. Those who do take full-time positions with universities do so, increasingly, on a strictly part-time basis. Expert witness work, often undertaken initially as an occasional activity, quickly becomes a professor's major source of income from, and dependency on, professional firms and their clients. So much concern was there about problems of "independence" among academics, that in 1982 the American Accounting Association commissioned its own inquiry into the matter.

The mainstream of accounting academia is in a poor position to offer any kind of leadership to the profession. Even the subject's so-called thinkers tend to scoff at what they see as the subject's essentially technical and procedural core. The irony here is the lack of self-reflection by these scholars: by denouncing the subject in this fashion, these academics are denouncing themselves. Accounting does not wait to be found or discovered, like an atomic particle or a pulsar; subjects like accounting must be invented or created, and thus the pitiful intellectual state of a discipline is due to a failure on the part of the inventors, not the object of study.

Symbolically, the most important debasement of academic accounting by corporate interests is what is termed the "conceptual framework" project. Now widely regarded as "dead in the water," the project is a leftover from an early skirmish with congressional critics in which, as a defense, the profession promised to sponsor an investigation that would solve the basic intellectual problems of the subject in about two years flat. Understandably, the promise never materialized. However, the price paid for using academic respectability to fend off criticism in this way was to seriously depreciate the academic currency.

This might present a bleak outlook for anyone seeking changes that might dramatically improve the quality of accounting practice. Yet this dismal picture does contain some suggestions for beginning to address the situation. The analysis indicates that the root problems are systemic and institutional: they center on a misalignment between the profession and the various social constituencies it arbitrates among. There are various mechanisms available for restoring evenhandedness and impartiality to the profession's affairs, especially by restructuring the financial ties through which professional firms are co-opted and pressured. A more fundamental question remains, however, regarding the future of a profit-making profession that serves as one of society's main adjudicators in conflicts over the distribution of wealth. No one would seriously consider putting federal judges on an incentive bonus system, whereby defendants determine the bonuses awarded. Although this analogy might initially appear a little far-fetched, if you are persuaded by the primary thesis of this book, as to the crucial arbitration role of accounting in social conflict, then the analogy is relevant to arrangements for paying for auditing in the United States and in the United Kingdom.

If the problems facing accounting could be resolved with a "quick-fix," then there would be little point in writing a book such as this. For this author, it is academics and scholars who are guilty of the most serious derelictions, because they have installed an intellectual regime—founded on marginalist ideology—that is worse than mediocre and irrelevant: it is rapacious in affect, and condemns its advocates as pitiably ignorant of how they are being used.

There are educational and scholarly alternatives. The previous chapters suggest an alternative theoretical basis for the subject, one that systematically acknowledges accounting's heritage in arbitrating in social conflict. Radical history, sociology, politics, anthropology, philosophy, etc., have all been shown to have a place in this new curriculum for accounting. Ironically, however, the unifying force for these studies has existed all along in accounting's methodology and language: it is the concept of "value." Value is probably the most frequently used term in the accounting vocabulary; curiously, it is rarely defined, and few accountants have discovered the rich configurations of meaning it provides in other disciplines. Yet, in exploring new approaches to accounting, it is the much neglected concept of value that has offered one of the most promising theoretical vantage points for this study.

Bibliography

Abercrombie, N., *Class Structure and Knowledge,* London: Basil Blackwell, 1980.

Adorno, T. et al., *The Positivist Dispute in German Sociology,* London: Heinemann, 1976.

Aglietta, Michael, *A Theory of Capitalist Regulation—The US Experience,* London: New Left Books, 1979.

Alexander, Sidney, "Income Measurement in a Dynamic Economy" in *Five Monographs on Business Income,* New York: American Institute of Accountants, 1950, pp. 1–95.

Allen, Victor, *Social Analysis: A Marxist Critique and Alternative,* Harlow: Longmans, 1975.

American Accounting Association, "Report to the Financial Accounting Standards Board from Subcommittee on Conceptual Framework for Financial Accounting and Reporting: Elements of Financial Statements and their Measurement, of the Committee on Financial Reporting," June 1977.

Amin, Samir, *The Law of Value and Historical Materialism,* New York: Monthly Review Press, 1978.

Arrow, K. et al., "Capital-labor Substitution and Economic Efficiency," *Review of Economics and Statistics,* 43 (1961) pp. 225–34, 246–48.

Arthur, C.J., "Dialectic of the Value-Form" in *Value: The Representation of Labour in Capitalism,* edited by Diane Elson, London: CSE Books, 1979.

Ashby, Ross, *An Introduction to Cybernetics,* London: Methuen, 1956.

Axthelm, Peter, "This Gun for Hire," *Newsweek,* March 1, 1976.

Babanael, Josh, "US Agrees to a Loan to State for Purchase of Love Canal House," New York *Times,* August 1, 1980.

Bailey, Samuel, *A Critical Dissertation of the Nature Measure and Causes of Value: Chiefly in Reference to the Writings of Mr. Ricardo and His Followers,* London: R. Hunter, 1825.

Bandyopadhyay, Pradeep, "Critique of Wright: 2. In Defense of a Post-Sraffian Approach" in *The Value Controversy,* by Ian Steedman, Paul Sweezy, et al. London: Verso, 1981.

Baran, Paul A., *The Political Economy of Growth,* New York: Monthly Review Press, 1957.

Baran, Paul A. and Paul M. Sweezy, *Monopoly Capital,* New York: Monthly Review Press, 1966.

Barbon, Nicholas, *A Discourse On Trade,* London: J.H. Hollander, Reprint.

Baritz, Loren, *The Servants of Power: A History of the Use of Social Science in American Industry,* New York: John Wiley and Sons, 1960.

Beaver, William, *Financial Reporting: An Accounting Revolution,* Englewood Cliffs: Prentice Hall, 1981.

Beauvoir, de, Simone, *The Second Sex,* New York: Bantam Books, 1952.

Bedburn, Tom, "Phone Refunds Ordered by PUC," Los Angeles *Times,* February 14, 1980, pp. 1, 17.

Bell, Daniel, *The End of Ideology,* New York: Glencoe, 1960.

Benston, George J., "Analysis of the Role of Accounting Standards for Enhancing Corporate Governance and Social Responsibility," *Journal of Accounting and Public Policy,* 1 (Fall 1982) pp. 5–17.

_____, "The Market for Public Accounting Services, Demand, Supply and Regulation," *The Accounting Journal* 11 (winter 1979–80), pp. 4–46.

Berle, A.A. and G.C. Means, *The Modern Corporation and Private Property,* New York: The Macmillan Company, 1934.

Bertalanffy, von, Ludwig, *General Systems Theory,* Harmondsworth, Middlesex: Penguin Books, 1971.

Blackburn, Robin, *Ideology in Social Science: Readings in Critical Social Theory,* London: Fontana, 1972.

Blang, Mark, *The Methodology of Economics On How Economists Explain,* Cambridge: Cambridge University Press, 1980.

Bloor, D., "Wittgenstein and Mannheim on the Sociology of Mathematics" in *Studies in the History of the Philosophy of Science,* Vol. 4, 1973.

Boeke, J.H., *Indische Economie,* Haarlem: Tjeenk, Willink & Zoom, 1940.

Böhm-Bawerk, E., *Karl Marx and the Close of his System,* London: Merlin Press, 1975.

_____, *Capital and Interest,* translated by George D. Huncke and Hans F. Sennholz, South Holland, Ill.: Libertarian Press, 1969.

Botein, Bernard, *The Trial of the Future,* New York: Simon and Schuster, 1963.

Boulding, K., "Economics as a Moral Science," *American Economic Review* LIX (1969), pp. 1–2.

Braverman, Harry, *Labor and Monopoly Capitalism: The Degradation of Work in the Twentieth Century,* New York: Monthly Review Press, 1974.

Briloff, Abraham J., *Unaccountable Accounting,* New York: Harper & Row, 1972.

Brown, Michael, *Laying Waste: The Poisoning of America by Toxic Chemicals,* New York: Pantheon Books, 1980.

Bukharin, Nikolai, *Economic Theory of the Leisure Class,* New York: Monthly Review Press, 1972.

Burchell, Stuart et al., "The Roles of Accounting in Organizations and Society," *Accounting Organizations and Society,* 1980, Vol. 5, No. 1, pp. 5–27.

Burrell, G. and G. Morgan, *Sociological Paradigms and Organizational Analysis,* London: Heinemann, 1979.

Business Week, Accounting, "Utilities Fight to Escape the Tax-Credit Trap," December 5, 1977.

Business Week, Communication, "The Attack on Bell's Millions," April 17, 1978.

Business Week, "A Dark Future for Utilities," May 28, 1979, pp. 108–11.

Canning, John, *The Economics of Accountancy,* New York: Ronald Press, 1929.

Cantillon, Richard, "Essai sur la Nature du Commerce en Général," London (Royal Economic Society ed.), 1730.

Cary, John, "An Essay Towards Regulating the Trade and Employing the Poor in this Kingdom," 2d ed., London, 1719.

Caws, Peter, *The Philosophy of Science: A Systematic Account,* Princeton: Van Nostrand, 1965.

Chambers, R.J., "Income and Capital: Fisher's Legacy," *Journal of Accounting Research,* 9 (spring 1971), pp. 137–49.

Chisholm, Roderick M., *Theory of Knowledge,* Englewood Cliffs: Prentice Hall, 1966.

Christenson, Charles, "The Methodology of Positive Accounting," *Accounting Review* (January 1983), pp. 1–23.

Clark, J.B., "Distribution as Determined by Rent," *Quarterly Journal of Economics* 5 (1906), pp. 289–318.

_____ , *The Distribution of Wealth,* New York: The Macmillan Company, 1899.

Cornforth, M., *Communism and Philosophy: Contemporary Dogmas and Revisions of Marxism,* London: Lawrence and Wishart, 1980.

_____, *The Theory of Knowledge,* New York: International Publishers, 1971.

Couchman, Charles, *The Balance Sheet,* Journal of Accountancy Publishing Co., 1929.

Cunningham, W., *The Growth of English Industry and Commerce,* 5th ed., Vol. 21, Cambridge: Cambridge University Press, 1927.

Daly, Mary, *Beyond God the Father,* Boston: Beacon Press, 1973.

Danto, Arthur C., *What Philosophy Is,* Harmondsworth, Middlesex: Pelican Books, 1971.

Davis, Lance, *American Economic Growth: An Economist's History of the United States,* New York: Harper & Row, 1972.

Dobb, Maurice, *Theories of Value and Income Distribution Since Adam Smith: Ideology and Economic Theory,* Cambridge: Cambridge University Press, 1973.

_____, *Studies in the Development of Capitalism,* New York: International Publishers, 1946.

_____, *Political Economy and Capitalism: Some Essays in Economic Tradition,* London and Henley: Routledge & Kegan Paul, 1937.

Domhoff, William, *Who Rules America,* Englewood Cliffs: Prentice Hall, 1967.

Dopuch, Nicholas, "Empirical Vs. Non-Empirical Contributions To Accounting Theory Development," University of Alabama: University of Alabama Doctoral Consortium, 1980.

Dopuch, Nicholas, and Shyam Sunder, "FASB's Statements on Objectives and Elements of Financial Accounting: A Review," *Accounting Review* LV (January 1980), pp. 1–21.

Dorfman, Joseph, "New Light on Veblen," in *Thorstein Veblen: Essays, Reviews and Reports,* edited by Joseph Dorfman, Clifton: Augustus M. Kelley, 1973.

Dyckman, Thomas R.; David H. Downes, and Robert P. Magee, *Efficient Capital Markets and Accounting: A Critical Analysis,* Englewood Cliffs: Prentice Hall, 1975.

Easton, Steward, *The Heritage of the Past,* New York: Holt, Rinehart & Winston, 1966.

Edwards, R.S., *Contested Terrain: The Transformation of the Workplace in the Twentieth Century,* New York: Basic Books, 1979.

Edwards, R.S., "The Nature and Measurement of Income" in *Studies in Accounting Theory,* edited by W.T. Baxter and S. Davidson, London: Sweet and Maxwell, 1962.

Edwards, R.S., and P. Bell, *The Theory and Measurement of Business Income,* Berkeley and Los Angeles: University of California Press, 1961.

Elson, Diane, "The Value Theory of Labour" in *Value: The Representation of Labour in Capitalism,* edited by Diane Elson, London: CSE Books, 1979.

Embree, J., *Sauye Mura: A Japanese Village,* London and Henley: Routledge & Kegan Paul, 1946.

Espinas, George, *Les Origines du Capitalisme,* Vol. 1, Paris-Lille: Librairie Emile Raoust, 1933–49.

Estes, Ralph, *Corporate Social Accounting,* New York: Wiley, 1976.

Fama, E.F., "Agency Problems and the Theory of the Firm," *Journal of Political Economy* 88 (1980), pp. 288–307.

Fama, E.F., and M.H. Miller, *Theory of Finance,* New York: Holt, Rinehart & Winston, 1972.

Farr, William, "Felons Change of Leniency Greater in L.A. Courts, Rand Survey Shows," Los Angeles *Times,* April 25, 1973, Part 2, p. 3.

Firestone, J.M., and R.W. Chadwick, "A New Procedure for Constructing Measurement Models of Ratio Scale Concepts," *International Journal of General Systems* 2 (1975), pp. 35–53.

Firestone, Shulamith, *The Dialectic of Sex,* New York: Bantam Books, 1970.

Fisher, Irving, *The Nature of Capital and Income,* New York: Macmillan, 1906.

Fogel, Robert, "The New Economic History: Its Findings and Methods," *Economic History Review* 19 (December 1966), pp. 642–56.

Friedman, Milton, *Capitalism and Freedom,* Chicago: University of Chicago Press, 1962.

_____, *Essays in Positive Economics,* Chicago: University of Chicago Press, 1953.

Fromm, Eric, *Marx's Concept of Man,* New York: Frederick Ungar Publishing, 1961.

Gair, Harry A., quoted in Marshall, *Law and Psychology in Conflict,* Garden City: Doubleday, 1969.

Galbraith, John Kenneth, *The New Industrial Estate, A Mentor Book,* Boston: Houghton Mifflin, 1967.

_____, *The Affluent Society,* Boston: Houghton Mifflin, 1958.

_____, *The Great Crash,* Boston: Houghton Mifflin, 1954.

Garegnani, P., "Heterogeneous Capital, the Production Function and the Theory of Distribution," *Review of Economic Studies* VII (July 1970).

Gintus, Herbert, "Power and Alienation" in *Readings in Political Economy,* edited by James Weaver, Rockleigh: Allyn & Bacon, 1972.

Goddard, Davis, "Anthropology: The Limits of Functionalism" in *Ideology in Social Science: Readings in Critical Social Theory,* edited by R. Blackburn, London: Fontana, 1972.

Goltz, G., *Ancient Greece at Work,* London, 1926.

Gonedes, N.J., and M. Dopuch, "Capital Market Equilibrium, Information Production, and Selecting Accounting Techniques: Theoretical Framework and Review of Empirical Work," in supplement to *Journal of Accounting Research, Studies On Financial Accounting Objectives,* 1974, pp. 48–129.

Gordon, Lawrence, *Accounting and Corporate Social Responsibility,* Lawrence: University of Kansas Press, 1978.

Gouldner, Alvin, *For Sociology: Renewal and Critique in Sociology Today,* New York: Basic Books, 1973.

Graaf, De, J.V., *Theoretical Welfare Economics,* Cambridge: Cambridge University Press, 1975.

Guardian, Editorial, "The Fall of the House of Slater," October 28, 1975, p. 12.

Habermas, Jurgen, *Knowledge and Human Interests,* translated by J. Shapiro, London: Heinemann, 1971.

Hakansson, Nils, "Empirical Research in Accounting 1960–70: An Appraisal" in *Accounting Research 1960–70: A Critical Evaluation,* edited by N. Dopuch and L. Revsine, Urbana: University of Illinois Press, 1973.

_____, "Normative Accounting Research and the Theory of Decision," *International Journal of Accounting Education and Research* (spring 1969).

Halevy, Elie, *The Growth of Philosophic Radicalism,* translated by Mary Morris, London, 1928.

Harcourt, G.C., *Some Cambridge Controversies in the Theory of Capital,* Cambridge: Cambridge University Press, 1972.

Harcourt, G.C., and N.F. Laing, *Penguin Modern Economic Readings: Capital and Growth,* Hammondsworth, Middlesex: Penguin Books, 1972.

Harre, R., *The Philosophies of Science: An Introductory Survey,* Oxford: Oxford University Press, 1972.

Harris, Joseph, "An Essay Upon Money and Coins," London, 1757.

Harris, Richard J., *A Primer in Multivariate Statistics,* London: Academic Press, 1975.

Hatfield, Henry Rand, *Modern Accounting: Its Principles and Some of its Problems,* New York: D. Appleton & Co., 1909.

Held, David, *Introduction of Critical Theory: Horkheimer to Habermas,* London: Hutchinson University Library, 1980.

Henderson, Paul, "Class Structure and the Concept of Intelligence," in *Schooling and Society: A Sociological Reader,* edited by R. Dale, Georg Esland, and Madeleine MacDonald, London and Henley: Routledge & Kegan Paul, 1976, pp. 142–51.

Hendrickson, E.A., *Accounting Theory,* Homewood: Richard D. Irwin, 1970.

Hicks, John, *Capital and Growth,* Oxford: Oxford University Press, 1965.

Hill, Christian G., "California Pyramids: Modern Wonders of the Western World," *Wall Street Journal,* May 29, 1980, pp. 1, 28.

Hirshleifer, J., *Investment Interest and Capital,* Englewood Cliffs: Prentice Hall, 1970.

_____, "On the Theory of Optimal Investment Decision," *Journal of Political Economy* 66, (1958), pp. 329–72.

Hofstradter, Richard, *Social Darwinism and American Thought,* Boston: Beacon Press, 1955.

Holt, Donald D., "The Tax Break that Turned into a Nightmare," *Fortune,* September 10, 1979, pp. 110–16.

Hoogvelt, Ankie, *The Sociology of Developing Societies,* London: Macmillan Press, 1975.

Hoogvelt, Ankie, and A.M. Tinker, "The Role of the Colonial and Post Colonial State in Imperialism," *Journal of African Studies* 16 (1978), pp. 1–13.

_____, "The Sierra Leone Development Company: A Case Study in Imperialism," monograph, University of Sheffield, 1977, pp. 1–55.

_____, "The Sierra Leone Development Company: A Case Study in Imperialism," *Critique of Anthropology* (June 1977a).

Huart, Clement, and Louis Delaporte, *Iran Antique,* Paris: Michel, 1952.

Hunt, E.K., "The Categories of Productive and Unproductive Labor in Marxist Economic Theory," *Science and Society* XLIII (fall 1979) pp. 303–25.

Jevons, W.S., *Theory of Political Economy,* 2d ed., London, 1879.

_____, *Theory of Political Economy,* 1st ed., London, 1871.

Jones, Gareth Stedman, "History: The Poverty of Empiricism" in *Ideology in Social Science: Readings in Critical Social Theory,* edited by Robin Blackburn, London: Fontana/Collins, 1972.

Johnson, David, "3 Utilities Urge Income Tax Exemption," Los Angeles *Times,* March 12, 1978.

Kalecki, Michal, *Studies in the Theory of Business Cycles,* translated by Ada Kalecka, New York: A.M. Kelley: 1966.

Katouzian, H., *Ideology and Method in Economics,* London: Macmillan Press, 1980.

Kaulla, Rudolf, *Theory of the Just Price,* translated by Robert D. Hogg, London: G. Allen and Unwin, Ltd., 1940.

Kay, Geoffrey, "Why Labour is the Starting Point in Capital" in *Value: The Representation of Labour in Capitalism,* edited by Diane Elson, London: CSE Books, 1979.

Kester, Roy B., *Accounting Theory and Practice,* New York: Ronald Press, 1918.

Keynes, J.M., *The General Theory of Employment, Interest and Money,* London: Macmillan Press, 1936.

_____, "National Self-Sufficiency," *Yale Law Review* 22 (1933) pp. 755–63.

Kidron, D.E. and J.J. Weygandt, *Intermediate Accounting,* 3rd ed., New York: Wiley, 1980.

Kindleberger, Charles R., *The Terms of Trade,* New York: Wiley, 1956.

Klir, George, *An Approach to General Systems Theory,* New York: Van Nostrand, 1969.

Koestler, Arthur, and J.R. Smythies, *Beyond Reductionism: New Perspectives in the Life Sciences,* London: Hutchinson, 1969.

Kornai, Jones, *Anti-Equilibrium: On Economic Systems Theory and the Task of Research,* New York: North Holland, 1971.

Kregel, J.A., *Theory of Capital,* Macmillan Studies in Economics, London: Macmillan Press, 1976.

_____, *The Reconstruction of Political Economy: To Post-Keynesian Economics,* 2d ed., London: Macmillan Press, 1976.

Kroncholz, June, "Rich Deposit: How One Tax Shelter Set Out to Dig Coal Owned by Government," *Wall Street Journal,* February 5, 1979, pp. 1, 33.

Kuhn, Thomas, *The Structure of Scientific Revolutions,* 2d ed., Chicago: University of Chicago, 1970.

Lange, Oskar, *Political Economy,* translated by A.H. Walker, Oxford: Pergamon Press, 1963.

Lee, C.H., *The Quantitative Approach to Economic History,* New York: St. Martins Press, 1977.

Lee, T.A., "The Contribution of Fisher to Enterprise Income Theory: A Comment," *Journal of Business, Finance and Accounting* (autumn 1975) pp. 373–76.

_____, "A Note on the Nature and Determination of Income," *Journal of Business Finance and Accounting* (spring 1974) pp. 145–47.

Lekachman, Robert, *A History of Economic Ideas,* New York: McGraw-Hill, 1976.

Levi-Strauss, Claude, *Les Structures Elementaires de la Parent,* 2d ed., Paris: Mouton, 1967.

_____, *Structural Anthropology,* New York: Basic Books, 1963.

Littleton, A.C., "Values and Price in Accounting," *Accounting Review* 4 (September 1929) pp. 147–54.

_____, "What is Profit?" *Accounting Review* 3 (September 1928) pp. 278–88.

Lowe, E.A., and A.M. Tinker, "Sighting the Accounting Problematic: Towards an Intellectual Emancipation of Accounting," *Journal of Business Finance and Accounting* 4 (1977), pp. 263–76.

Lukacs, Georg, *History and Class Consciousness,* translated by Rodney Livingstone, Cambridge, Mass.: The MIT Press, 1971.

Lundberg, Ferdinand, *The Rich and the Super-Rich,* New York: Bantam Books, 1968.

McBride, William Leon, *The Philosophy of Marx,* London: Hutchinson, 1977.

McClintic, David, "Rich Investors Losses in New 'Ponzi Scheme' Could Hit $100 Million," *Wall Street Journal,* June 26, 1974, pp. 1, 16.

McClurdy, Charles W., "The Knight Sugar Decision of 1895 and the Modernization of American Corporate Law 1869–1903," *Business History Review* 53 (autumn 1979) pp. 304–42.

McConnell, Grant, *Private Power and American Democracy,* New York: Alfred A. Knopf, 1966.

McLellan, David, *Marx,* London: Fontana, 1975.

MacNeal, Kenneth, *Truth in Accounting,* Philadelphia: University of Pennsylvania Press, 1939.

Macpherson, C.B., *The Political Theory of Possessive Individualism: Hobbes to Locke,* Oxford: Oxford University Press, 1962.

Mandel, Ernst, *Late Capitalism,* London: New Left Books, 1975.

_____, "From the Economic Philosophic Manuscripts to the Grundrisse: From an Anthropological to a Historical Conception of Alienation" in *The Formation of the Economic Thought of Karl Marx,* New York: Monthly Review Press, 1971.

_____, *Introduction to Marxist Economic Theory,* New York: Pathfinder Press, 1970.

_____, *Marxist Economic Theory,* New York: Monthly Review Press, 1968.

_____, *Treatise on Marxist Economics,* London: Merlin Press, 1962.

Marcuse, Herbert, *One-Dimensional Man: Studies in the Ideology of Advanced Society,* Boston: Beacon Press, 1964.

Marshall, A., *Principles of Economics,* London: Macmillan Press, 1920.

Marx, K., *The Poverty of Philosophy,* Moscow: Progress Publishers, 1955.

_____, *Theories of Surplus Value: A Selection,* translated by G.A. Bonner and Emile Burns, London, 1951.

May, R.G., and G.L. Sundem, "Research for Accounting Policy Decisions: An Overview," *Accounting Review* (October 1976), pp. 747–63.

May, R.G.; G. Mueller; and T. Williams, *A New Introduction to Financial Accounting,* Englewood Cliffs: Prentice Hall, 1975.

Mead, Margaret, *Sex and Temperament in Three Primitive Societies,* London and Henley: Routledge & Kegan Paul, 1952.

_____, *Cooperation and Competition among Primitive Peoples,* New York: McGraw-Hill, 1937.

Meek, Ronald L., *Smith, Marx and After,* London: Chapman and Hall, 1977.

_____, *Studies in the Labor Theory of Value,* New York: Monthly Review Press, 1975.

_____, *Economics and Ideology and other Essays: Studies in the Development of Economic Thought,* London: Chapman & Hall, 1967.

Michels, Robert, *Political Parties: Sociological Studies of the Oligarchic Tendencies of Modern Democracy,* Glencoe: The Free Press, 1949.

Miller, Arthur S., "Corporate Gigantism and Technological Imperative" in *Program of Policy Studies,* Reprint No. 6, Washington: George Washington University Press, 1969.

Miller, Judith, "S.E.C. Says Occidental Hid Potential Liabilities," New York *Times,* Business Day, July 3, 1980, pp. D1, D6.

Minard, Lawrence, "The Return of the Minus Millionaire," *Forbes,* September 15, 1980, pp. 121–22.

Monies, R.J., "Class and Class Consciousness in the Industrial Revolution: 1780–1850," in *Studies in Economic and Social History,* London: Macmillan Press, 1979.

Morton, A.L., *A People's History of England,* London: Lawrence & Wishort, 1945.

Munson, Richard, "The Electric Companies' Tax Bonanza," *Business and Society Review, (summer 1977), pp. 75–76.*

Nairn, Tom, "The Anatomy of the Labour Party," *New Left Review* 27 (September-October 1964), pp. 38–65.

Nell, Edward J., "The Fall of the House of Efficiency," *Annals of the American Academy of Political and Social Science,* 409 (September 1973), pp. 102–11.

_____, "Economics: the Revival of Political Economy" in *Ideology in Social Science: Readings in Critical Social Theory,* edited by Robin Blackburn, London: Fontana, 1972.

Nelson, Carl L., "A Priori Research in Accounting" in *Accounting Research 1960–70: A Critical Evaluation,* edited by Nicholas Dopuch and L. Revsine, Urbana: University of Illinois Press, 1973.

Newsweek, Cities, "How Equal is Justice?" October 30, 1972.

Newsweek, Medicine, "Fleeing the Love Canal," June 2, 1980, pp. 56–57.

New York *Times,* Editorial, "Those Disastrous Studies at Love Canal," October 17, 1980.

New York *Times,* "10 Love Canal Families in Motels Learn State Will Help No Longer," August 7, 1980.

Ney, Richard, *The Wall Street Gang,* New York: Praeger, 1974.

Nicholaus, Martin, "The Professional Organization of Sociology: A View from Below," in *Ideology in Social Science: Readings in Critical Social Theory,* edited by Robin Blackburn, London: Fontana, 1972.

Nisbet, Robert, *Sociology as an Art Form,* London: Heinemann, 1976.

Novack, George, ed., *Existentialism versus Marxism,* New York: Dell Publishing, 1966.

Ollman, Bertell, *Alienation: Marx's Conception of Man in Capitalist Society,* 2d ed., Cambridge: Cambridge University Press, 1976.

Parker, R.H., and G.C. Harcourt, *Readings in the Concept and Measurement of Income,* Cambridge: Cambridge University Press, 1969.

Parsons, T., *The Social System,* New York: Free Press of Glencoe, 1951.

Pasinetti, L.L., "Switches of Technique and the Rate of Return in Capital Theory," *Economic Journal* 79 (September 1969), pp. 508–31.

Paton, William, and Russell Stevenson, *Principles of Accounting,* New York: Macmillan, 1918.

_____, *Accounting Theory,* New York: Ronald Press, 1922.

Paton, William, and A.C. Littleton, *An Introduction to Corporate Accounting Standards,* Chicago: American Accounting Association, 1940.

Petty, William, *Economic Writings,* Vol. 1, Hull ed., Cambridge, 1899.

Pirsig, Robert M., *Zen and the Art of Motorcycle Maintenance: An Inquiry into Values,* New York: Bantam Books, 1974.

Pollard, Sidney, *The Genesis of Modern Management,* London: Edward Arnold, 1965.

Popper, Karl, *The Logic of Scientific Discovery,* London: Hutchinson, 1959.

Ramanathan, K., "Towards a Theory of Corporate Social Responsibility," *Accounting Review* (July 1976), pp. 516–28.

Ravenstone, Piercy, *A Few Doubts as to the Correctness of Some Opinions Generally Entertained on the Subjects of Population and Political Economy,* London, 1821.

Ravetz, J.R., *Scientific Knowledge and its Social Problems,* Harmondsworth, Middlesex: Penguin University Books, 1973.

Raw, Charles, *A Financial Phenomenon: An Investigation of the Rise and Fall of the Slater Walker Empire,* New York: Harper & Row, 1977.

Rayman, R.A., "Investment Criteria, Accounting Information and Resource Allocation," *Journal of Business Finance and Accounting* 4 (summer 1972) pp. 15–26.

Read, Samuel, *An Inquiry Into the Natural Grounds of Right to Vendible Property of Wealth,* Edinburgh, 1829, p. XXIX.

Reddin, Richard, "Slater Walker: Share Price Falls in Heavy Trading," *Guardian,* October 30, 1975, p. 15.

_____, "No Backlash in Singapore for UK Companies," *Guardian,* October 27, 1975, p. 13.

Ricardo, David, *The Principles of Political Economy and Taxation,* Cambridge: Cambridge University Press, 1952.

Robbins, L., *The Theory of Economic Policy in English Classical Political Economy,* London: Macmillan, 1952.

Robertson, D.H., "Wage Grumbles," *Economic Fragments,* London, 1930.

Robinson, Joan, *Further Contributions to Modern Economics,* London: Basil Blackwell, 1980.

_____, "The Production Function and the Theory of Capital," *Review of Economic Studies* 21 (1953–54) pp. 81–106.

Rorem, C. Rufus, *Accounting Method,* Chicago: University of Chicago Press, 1928.

Samuelson, Paul A., "A Summing Up" in "Paradoxes in Capital Theory: A Symposium," *Quarterly Journal of Economics,* LXXX (November 1966).

Sartre, Jean-Paul, *Search for a Method* translated by Hazel Barnes, New York: Vintage Press, 1968.

_____, *Existentialism and Human Emotions,* Secaucus, NJ: Citadel Press, 1957.

Savay, Norbert, *The Art of the Trail,* New York: Conway, Bogardus, 1929.

Schechter, F., "The Law and Morals of Primitive Trade" in M.J. Herskovits, *The Economic Life of Primitive Peoples,* London: Alfred A. Knopf, 1973.

Schumacher, E.F., *Small is Beautiful: A Study of Economics As If People Mattered,* London: ABACUS, 1974.

Schumpeter, J., *History of Economic Analysis,* New York: Free Press, 1954.

Scitovsky, Tibor, *The Joyless Economy: An Inquiry into Human Satisfaction and Consumer Dissatisfaction,* Oxford: Oxford University Press, 1975.

Scott, D.R., *The Cultural Significance of Accounts,* Lawrence, Kan.: Scholars Book Club, 1933, 1976 reprint edition.

_____, *Theory of Accounts,* New York: Henry Holt & Co., 1925.

Scrope, Poulett, *Political Economy for Plain People,* London, 1833.

Shaikh, Anwar, "The Poverty of Algebra" in *The Value Controversy,* by Ian Steedman, Paul Sweezy et al. London: Verso Editions and NLB, 1981.

_____, "The Transformation from Marx to Sraffa (Prelude to a Critique of the Neo-Ricardians)", Working Paper, New School for Social Research, New York, March 1980.

_____, "Marx's Theory of Value and the 'Transformation Problem'" in *The Subtle Anatomy of Capitalism,* edited by Jesse Schwartz, Santa Monica: Goodyear, 1977.

Shapin, Steven, and Barry Barnes, "Science, Nature and Control: Interpreting Mechanics' Institutes" in *Schooling and Society: A Sociological Reader,* edited by Roger Dale, Georg Esland, and Madeleine MacDonald, London and Henley: Routledge & Kegan Paul, 1976.

Shaw, M., *Marxism and Social Science: The Roots of Social Knowledge,* London: Pluto Press, 1975.

Silverman, David, *The Theory of Organizations: A Sociological Framework,* Heinemann Studies in Sociology, London: Heinemann, 1970.

Smith, Adam, *Wealth of Nations,* edited by E. Cannan, London, 1904.

Smith, Dennis, "The Urban Genesis of School Bureaucracy: A Transatlantic Comparison" in *Schooling and Society: A Sociological Reader,* edited by Roger Dale, Georg Esland, and Madeleine MacDonald, London and Henley: Routledge & Kegan Paul, 1976.

Smith, K.B., *Geschichte der Kultur,* Zurich: Fussli, 1946.

Sprague, Charles E., *The Philosophy of Accounts,* published by the author, 1908.

Sraffa, P., *The Production of Commodities by Means of Commodities,* Cambridge: Cambridge University Press, 1960.

———, editor, *Works and Correspondences of David Ricardo,* Cambridge: Cambridge University Press, 1951.

Steedman, Ian, "Ricardo, Marx and Sraffa" in *The Value Controversy,* by Ian Steedman, Paul Sweezy, et al., London: Verso Editions and NLB, 1981.

Steedman, Ian, Paul Sweezy, et al., *The Value Controversy,* London: Verso Editions and NLB, 1981.

Sterling, R.R., *Theory of the Measurement of Enterprise Income,* Lawrence: University of Kansas Press, 1970.

Stevens, Mark, *The Big Eight,* New York: Macmillan, 1981.

Stigler, G.J., *Production and Distribution Theories,* New York, 1946.

Strick, Anne, *Injustice for All,* Harmondsworth, Middlesex: Penguin Books, 1978.

Sunder, Shyam, "Why is the FASB Making Too Many Accounting Rules?" Managers Journal: *Wall Street Journal,* April 27, 1981, p. 30.

The *Sunday Times,* Insight, "How Jim Slater 'Gave the Boys a Little Bit More,'" October 26, 1975, pp. 17–23.

Sweeney, Henry W., "Maintenance of Capital," *Accounting Review* (December 1930), pp. 277–87.

Sweezy, Paul M., *The Theory of Capitalist Development,* New York: Monthly Review Press, 1942.

———, "Marxian Value Theory and Crisis" in *The Value Controversy,* edited by Ian Steedman and Paul Sweezy, London: Verso Editions and NLB, 1981.

Tawney, R.H., *Religion and the Rise of Capitalism,* London: Penguin, 1937.

Taylor, Ian, Paul Walton, and Hock Young, "Fabian Criminology" in *Critical Criminology,* London and Henley: Routledge & Kegan Paul, 1974, pp. 9–14.

Taylor, P.J., "The Nature and Determinants of Income: Some Further Comments," *Journal of Business Finance and Accounting* (summer 1975), pp. 233–37.

Temple, William, "A Vindication of Commerce and the Arts," (pamphlet) London, 1758.

Thompson, L., *Culture in Crisis: A Study of the Hopi Indians,* New York: Harper & Row, 1950.

Tinker, Anthony M., "Towards a Political Economy of Accounting: An Empirical Illustration of the Cambridge Controversies," *Accounting, Organizations and Society* 5 (1980), pp. 147–60.

Tinker, Anthony M., B.D. Merino, and M.D. Neimark, "The Normative Origins of Positive Theories: Ideology and Accounting Thought" *Accounting, Organizations and Society* 7 (1982), pp. 167–200.

Tobias, Andrew, *The Funny Money Game,* New York: Playboy Press, 1971.

_____, "The $3,754,103 Footnote," in *Great Business Disasters,* edited by Isadora Barmash, New York: Ballantine Books, 1972.

Vatter, William, *The Fund Theory of Accounting and its Implications for Financial Reporting,* Chicago: University of Chicago Press, 1947.

Veblen, Thorstein, *Absentee Ownership and Business Enterprise in Recent Times,* New York: B.W. Huebsch, 1923.

_____, "The Limitations of Marginal Utility," *Journal of Political Economy* 17 (November 1909).

_____, "Professor Clark's Economics," *Quarterly Journal of Economics* 22 (1908), pp. 147–95.

_____, *The Theory of Business Enterprise,* New York: C. Scribner's Sons, 1904.

Walras, L., *Elements of Pure Economics,* translated by W. Jaffe, London: G. Allen and Unwin, Ltd., 1954.

Watts, Ross L., and Jerold L. Zimmerman, "The Demand for and Supply of Accounting Theories: The Market for Excuses," *Accounting Review* LIV (April 1979) pp. 273–306.

_____, "Towards a Positive Theory of Determination of Accounting Standards," *Accounting Review* LIII (January 1978) pp. 112–34.

Whitley, Richard, "Components of Scientific Activities, their Characteristics and Institutionalisation in Specialities and Research Areas: A Framework for the Comparative Analysis of Scientific Developments," Working Paper, Manchester Business School (undated).

Wiener, N., *The Human Use of Human Beings,* New York: Macmillan, 1931.

Williams, Raymond, "Base and Superstructure in Marxist Cultural Theory," *New Left Review* 82 (December 1972) pp. 3–16.

Wittgenstein, Ludwig, *Remarks on the Foundations of Mathematics,* London: Basil Blackwell, 1967.

Woodman, Harold, "Economic History and Economic Theory: The New Economic History in America," *Journal of Interdisciplinary History* 3 (autumn 1972).

Wormester, Rene, *The Story of Law,* New York: Simon and Schuster, 1962.

Wyse, Thomas, "Education Reform; or, the Necessity of a National System of Education," London, 1836.

Yaffe, David, "Value and Price in Marx's *Capital,*" *Revolutionary Communist,* no. 1, January 1975.

Yankelovich, Daniel, "Who Gets Ahead in America?" *Psychology Today,* July 1979.

Young, Michael F.D., "Curriculum Change: Limits and Possibilities," *Educational Studies* 1 (June 1975), pp. 129–38.

Zaretsky, Eli, *Capitalism, the Family and Personal Life,* London: Pluto Press, 1976.

Zerzan, John, and Paula Zerzan, *Industrialism and Domestication,* Seattle: The Black Eye Press, 1979.

Zimmerman, Jerold L., "Positive Research in Accounting," Working Paper Series No. MERC 80-70, June 1980.

Zukav, Gary, *The Dancing Wu Li Masters: An Overview of the New Physics,* New York: Morrow, 1979.

Index

About the Author

TONY TINKER was born and educated in London, England. He has held accounting positions with several organizations, including the National Health Service, Shell-Mex and B.P., Unilever, and the London Playboy Club. He studied for the examinations of the Association of Certified and Corporate Accountants at South West London College and was admitted to associate membership of the association in 1970 after attaining a national placing in the finals examination. He became a fellow of the association in 1975.

Dr. Tinker obtained his master's degree from Bradford University in 1970 and his doctorate from the University of Manchester in 1975. He spent five years as a lecturer in economic studies at the University of Sheffield and then joined the University of Washington in Seattle (1977–78), University of California, Los Angeles (1978–80), and New York University (1980–84). He is currently a faculty member at Baruch College, City University of New York.

Dr. Tinker is presently chairman of the Public Interest Section, and a council member, of the American Accounting Association. He is on the editorial boards of, and serves as referee for, a range of business and social science journals and has published in leading journals of several disciplines including sociology, cybernetics, business finance, organization theory, accounting, management science, and systems theory.